The American Cancer Society's

Healthy Eating Cookbook

3rd Edition

The American Cancer Society's

Healthy Eating Cookbook

3rd Edition

©2001 Liz Steger, New York

A celebration of
food, friends,
and healthy living

Published by
The American Cancer Society
1599 Clifton Road NE
Atlanta, Georgia 30329 USA

5 4 3   16 17 18 19 20

Library of Congress Cataloging-in-Publication Data

The American Cancer Society's healthy eating cookbook : a celebration
    of food, friends, and healthy living. — 3rd ed.
        p. cm.
    Includes index.
    ISBN 0-944235-57-3
        1. Cancer—Diet therapy—Recipes.   2. Cancer—Prevention.
    I. American Cancer Society.   II. Title: Healthy eating cookbook.
    RC271.D52A44 2005
    641.5'631—dc22

                                                                    2005016749

Designed by Shock Design, Inc., Atlanta, GA
Cover design by Jill Dible, Atlanta, GA
Cover photograph ©2001 Liz Steger, New York

Printed in the United States of America

On the cover: *Microwave Fish Fillets* (page 102).
For an enticing presentation, broil the microwaved fillet for a few minutes
until the topping begins to brown. Rest the fish on a colorful bed of
grilled vegetables such as eggplant, asparagus, and red pepper, and
surround with grilled polenta for additional flavor and texture. Fresh
herbs add an appealing final touch.

ISBN 0-944235-57-3

Represented in more than 3,400 communities throughout the country and Puerto Rico, the American Cancer Society is a nonprofit health organization dedicated to eliminating cancer as a major health problem.

The American Cancer Society is the largest private source of cancer research dollars in the United States. Founded in 1913 by 10 physicians and 5 concerned members of the community, the organization now has over 2 million volunteers. Most offer their time free of charge to the American Cancer Society to work to conquer cancer and improve the lives of those affected by it.

The American Cancer Society's Healthy Eating Cookbook, Third Edition, is just one example of the many ways the Society seeks to fulfill its mission of saving lives and diminishing suffering from cancer. The regularly updated *American Cancer Society Guidelines on Nutrition and Physical Activity for Cancer Prevention* are another. We invite you to contact the American Cancer Society (800-ACS-2345 or http://www.cancer.org) for more information about healthy eating, being active, and preventing cancer, and to learn more about what we can do for you.

Other cookbooks published by the American Cancer Society

Celebrate! Healthy Entertaining for Any Occasion

Kids' First Cookbook: Delicious-Nutritious Treats to Make Yourself!

Also published by the American Cancer Society

A Breast Cancer Journey: Your Personal Guidebook, Second Edition

American Cancer Society Consumers Guide to Cancer Drugs, Second Edition, Wilkes and Ades

American Cancer Society's Complementary and Alternative Cancer Methods Handbook

American Cancer Society's Complete Guide to Prostate Cancer, Bostwick et al.

American Cancer Society's Guide to Pain Control: Understanding and Managing Cancer Pain, Revised Edition

Angels & Monsters: A child's eye view of cancer, Murray and Howard

Because...Someone I Love Has Cancer: Kids' Activity Book

Cancer in the Family: Helping Children Cope with a Parent's Illness, Heiney et al.

Cancer: What Causes It, What Doesn't

Caregiving: A Step-By-Step Resource for Caring for the Person with Cancer at Home, Revised Edition, Houts and Bucher

Coming to Terms with Cancer: A Glossary of Cancer-Related Terms, Laughlin

Couples Confronting Cancer: Keeping Your Relationship Strong, Fincannon and Bruss

Crossing Divides: A Couple's Story of Cancer, Hope, and Hiking Montana's Continental Divide, Bischke

Eating Well, Staying Well During and After Cancer, Bloch et al.

Good for You! Reducing Your Risk of Developing Cancer

Healthy Me: A Read-along Coloring & Activity Book, Hawthorne (illustrated by Blyth)

Informed Decisions: The Complete Book of Cancer Diagnosis, Treatment, and Recovery, Second Edition, Eyre, Lange, and Morris

Kicking Butts: Quit Smoking and Take Charge of Your Health

Our Mom Has Cancer, Ackermann and Ackermann

When the Focus Is on Care: Palliative Care and Cancer, Foley et al.

Contents

Acknowledgments

The American Cancer Society would like to acknowledge the many people who helped create this third edition of *The American Cancer Society's Healthy Eating Cookbook*. We also thank the individuals who helped prepare earlier editions of this book, including Margaret Anthony, Theo Von Hoffman, Shayla Simpson, Susan Islam, Alice Parrott Miller, Emily Shell Parrott, Jennifer Miller, Betty Frizzell, Diana Priest, Jodie Worrell, and countless others.

Content Review
Colleen Doyle, MS, RD
Ted Gansler, MD

Editor
Amy Brittain

Managing Editor
Gianna Marsella, MA

Book Publishing Manager
Candace Magee

Senior Lead, Content
Chuck Westbrook

Eating Well, Living Well

Eating Well, Living Well

Eating well—it's just one step on the path to better health. And the American Cancer Society is here to help you along the way, pointing you in the right direction when it comes to healthier eating. Even small changes in the way you prepare foods can have a real impact on your health!

There are lots of simple, daily steps you can take to help reduce your risk of cancer (as well as heart disease and diabetes). The good news is that these healthy choices will also help you feel better, look better, and give your body plenty of energy for your busy life.

It's deliciously easy to start eating well and living well. Why not start today on that path to better health? Let's get cooking!

About the New Edition

Throughout this book you'll find helpful ideas for incorporating these guidelines into your cooking and eating habits. The third edition of *The American Cancer Society's Healthy Eating Cookbook* reflects the most up-to-date recommendations for reducing your cancer risk through healthy eating, but you'll still find all of your favorite recipes—including many celebrities' personal recipes for delicious, healthy dishes.

We've also included healthy substitutions, and added *Simple Tips in the Kitchen*, quick ways to judge portion sizes, and smart grocery shopping tips to help you eat and cook for better health.

Eat Your Way to Better Health

The *American Cancer Society Guidelines on Nutrition and Physical Activity for Cancer Prevention* are a good place to start on your path to healthy living. Following these guidelines—for example, eating plenty of vegetables, fruits, and whole grains and limiting foods high in saturated fat, sugar, and calories—can help you eat your way to better health.

The American Cancer Society's Guidelines on Nutrition and Physical Activity for Cancer Prevention

1. **Eat a variety of healthy foods, with an emphasis on plant sources.**
   - Eat five or more servings of a variety of vegetables and fruits each day.
   - Choose whole grains over processed (refined) grains and sugars.
   - Limit your consumption of red meats, especially processed meats and those high in fat.
   - Choose foods that help you maintain a healthy weight.

2. **Adopt a physically active lifestyle.**
   - Adults: Be active for at least 30 minutes on five or more days per week. The more active you can be, the better!
   - Children and adolescents: Be active for at least 60 minutes on five or more days per week.

3. **Maintain a healthy weight throughout life.**
   - Lose weight if you are currently overweight by eating fewer calories and being more active.

4. **If you drink alcoholic beverages, limit your consumption.**

Pass the Produce, Please

Eating more vegetables and fruits as part of a healthy diet can help your heart and reduce your cancer risk. Vegetables and fruits are packed with vitamins, minerals, fiber, and antioxidants (compounds that block damage to healthy cells), and they are generally low in fat and calories. Try to eat at least five servings of vegetables and fruits each day. (Sound like a lot? Serving sizes are fairly small, so it might not be as tough as it seems.) Focus on colorful vegetables and fruits (for example, broccoli, tomatoes, carrots, red peppers, oranges, strawberries, and kiwi), which offer nutrient-packed, cancer-fighting compounds.

Think you can get the same health benefits by taking a vitamin or mineral supplement? Not so—there's lots of evidence that eating a diet rich in vegetables and fruits can reduce cancer risk, but no evidence at this time that supplements can.

Simple Tips in the Kitchen

Here are a few ways to up your intake of fruits and vegetables:
- Add fresh or dried fruits to leafy green salads. Try chopped apples, raisins, kiwi, or orange sections.

- Top your cereal with fresh fruit, like banana slices or berries.
- Add chopped carrots, broccoli, or a mix of your favorite vegetables to soups, salads, and casseroles.
- Boost your fiber intake by adding your favorite canned or dried beans to soups, stews, and salads.

WHAT COUNTS AS A SERVING?

Fruits
- 1 medium piece of fruit
- ½ cup chopped, cooked canned or frozen fruit
- ¾ cup 100% fruit juice

Vegetables
- 1 cup raw leafy vegetables
- ½ cup chopped, cooked canned or frozen vegetables
- ½ cup cooked dry beans
- ¾ cup 100% vegetable juice

Great Grains

Confused about carbohydrates? Grain products like breads, rice, cereals, and pasta are still an important part of a healthy diet. Try to eat whole grains for at least half of your daily grain servings. When you look at ingredient labels, look for whole wheat, pumpernickel, rye, oatmeal, or other whole grain as the first ingredient. This is a sign that the product is a reliable source of good-for-you fiber.

The type of carbohydrates to limit are *refined* grains (white bread and white rice, for example) and foods high in sugar like cakes, cookies, and pastries. Replacing these carbohydrates with healthier whole grains will add more nutrients to your diet and help you cut back on calories too.

Simple Tips in the Kitchen
Here are some ideas to help you incorporate more healthy grains into your diet:
- Substitute whole-wheat flour for half (or more) of the white flour called for in a recipe.
- Add one-quarter cup bran or oatmeal to meat loaf and other casseroles.
- Make muffins using oatmeal, bran, or whole-wheat flour.
- Use whole cornmeal when making cornbread.
- Try whole-wheat pasta for a healthy fiber boost.

The Skinny on Fat

For years you've heard that lowfat diets are the way to go to improve your health. But it may be more important to consider the *type* of fat in your diet rather than the total *amount* of fat. We now know that you can do your heath a favor by limiting how much *saturated* and *trans* fat you eat and incorporating more *monounsaturated* and *polyunsaturated* fat in your diet.

Eating a diet high in saturated fat increases your risk of heart disease and some forms of cancer. This is the type of fat found primarily in red meats and dairy products, so cutting back on beef, lamb, and pork will help reduce the amount of saturated fat in your diet. Choosing lower-fat dairy products like skim milk, fat-free yogurt, and reduced-fat cheeses will help too, and will still provide you with the important calcium and protein you need.

Trans fats are another type of fat to avoid because they are bad for your heart. These fats are found in margarines, crackers, cookies, snack foods, fried foods, and other foods made with partially hydrogenated vegetable oils (check the label on packaged food before you buy to see if partially hydrogenated vegetable oils are listed as an ingredient).

Monounsaturated and polyunsaturated fats are heart-healthier fats and do not increase cancer risk. Monounsaturated fats are found mainly in canola and olive oils, and avocados. Polyunsaturated fats are found in other vegetable oils, soft (tub) margarine, tofu, and nuts. To further reduce your intake of saturated fat, substitute healthier oils for butter or lard.

Omega-3 fatty acids, another type of polyunsaturated fat, are found in high-fat fish like salmon, mackerel, and albacore tuna. Eating fish a few times a week in place of red meat is a great way to boost your health.

Bottom line: the type of fat you eat is most important to consider, but keep in mind that high-fat foods tend to be high in calories, so watch your portion sizes!

Simple Tips in the Kitchen

Here are some quick tips for reducing the saturated fat in your meals:
- Use evaporated skim milk instead of whole milk or cream in baked goods, sauces, and soups.
- Use reduced-fat yogurt to replace all or part of the sour cream or mayonnaise in a recipe.
- Substitute fat-free cottage cheese for ricotta cheese in casseroles.
- Choose lean meats—look for "loin" or "round" in the name of the cut.
- Trim fat from meat before you cook it. Cook poultry with the skin on to keep it moist, but remove the skin before eating.

LOSE THE FAT, NOT THE FLAVOR

Not sure which spices will add the right zip to meals? Try spicing up your favorite low-fat dishes with these fresh herbs and spices for a punch of flavor.

Basil: tomato dishes, soups, salads
Chili powder: beans, poultry, soups, stews
Cilantro: tomato dishes, beans, salads, corn
Cinnamon: winter squash, sweet potatoes, cooked fruit, baked goods
Cloves: cooked fruits, carrots, squash, poultry
Dill: fish, rice dishes, salad dressings, potatoes
Ginger: cooked fruits, seafood, vegetable stir-fry, breads
Marjoram: fruit juice, potatoes, poultry, meat
Nutmeg: beans, apple dishes, seafood, meat
Oregano: tomato dishes, broccoli, poultry, seafood
Sage: soups, stews, stuffing, vegetables
Thyme: beans, tomato dishes, poultry

Calories Still Count

"Eat this!" "Don't eat that!" With so much information and advice available about what we should or shouldn't eat to improve our health, we may forget that watching calories is essential for controlling our weight. Maintaining a healthy weight is important in reducing cancer risk, and when it comes to keeping down your weight, calories count! Substituting vegetables, fruits, and other low-calorie foods for foods high in calories, fat, and added sugar can help you cut back on calories. Another key? Watching your portion sizes, especially of foods high in fat and added sugar.

What a Standard Portion Size Looks Like

Do you know what a half cup of pasta looks like on your plate? How high one cup of milk fills your glass? How many ounces of cereal you typically pour into your bowl? If not, get out the measuring cups, spoons, and scale. Measure your meals for a week or so to see what a standard portion looks like in your own plates, bowls, and glasses. Here's a handy set of shortcuts that may help you judge how much you're eating:

- A half-cup serving of vegetables or fruit is about the size of your fist.
- A medium apple is the size of a baseball.
- A three-ounce portion of meat, fish, or poultry is about the size of a deck of cards.
- A single-serving bagel is the size of a hockey puck.
- One and a half ounces of low-fat or fat-free cheese is the size of a pair of dice.
- One tablespoon of peanut butter is about the size of the tip of your thumb.

Try these other tips at home to help keep calories under control:

- Serve appropriate portion sizes and store the rest for leftovers.
- Rather than placing serving dishes on the table (tempting you to eat more during the meal), serve in the kitchen.
- Trade in your dinner plate for your salad plate. Serving your meals on a smaller plate will give the illusion that you are eating larger portions.
- Avoid eating directly out of a bag or carton; consider buying foods packaged in individual serving sizes to help you control portions.

Your Start to Living Smart

Congratulations! You've taken the first step to a healthier lifestyle. Just a few simple changes in your everyday diet can add up to better health—without

Most of your favorite recipes can easily be changed to include more vegetables, fruits, and fiber and cut down the fat and calories. Try the following steps when altering recipes.

Step 1: Increase the vegetables, fruits, and fiber.
• Add chopped or precut vegetables.
• Add chopped fresh or dried fruits.
• Use whole grains for all of part of the recipe.
• When possible, leave skins on fruits and vegetables.

Step 2: Lower the amount of fat and calories.
• Ask yourself: "Can I reduce or replace oil? Can I use low-fat milk instead of cream?" You can also reduce fat by trying the methods below.
• You can usually cut fats like oil, butter, or margarines by one-third to one-half in recipes. Try a small cutback at first, then cut back little by little when you make the recipe again.
• To replace some moisture and flavor loss when reducing fat, make up the difference with broth, nonfat milk, fruit juice, and extra herbs, spices, and vegetables.
• For a moist baked product when reducing fat, add dried fruits or applesauce.
• Remember to use measuring spoons and cups to avoid guessing how much oil to use. An extra teaspoon of oil is 45 calories and five grams of fat.
• Use only small amounts of high-fat foods like avocado, coconut, cheese, and nuts.

Step 3: Cut back on high-fat meats.
• Replace red meat with leaner cuts or meats that are lower in fat. For example, if a recipe calls for ground beef, use extra-lean ground beef, ground sirloin, or ground turkey breast mixed with lean ground beef.
• Watch your portion size. Aim for three ounces (the size of a deck of cards).

sacrificing flavor or time. Let the more than 300 delicious recipes in the pages that follow keep you on track. *The American Cancer Society's Healthy Eating Cookbook* can make it fun to eat right!

Keep in mind that healthy eating is only part of the recipe for a healthy lifestyle. Try to be physically active for at least 30 minutes on five or more days per week—walking, swimming, gardening, even dancing counts. The important thing is to find something you enjoy doing—and have fun!

For more information on living a healthier life, contact the American Cancer Society at 800-ACS-2345 or visit us at www.cancer.org.

With these smart steps, you can look forward to a healthier future!

SHOPPING LIST: BASIC INGREDIENTS FOR A HEALTHY KITCHEN

The first step to cooking healthy is to stock your kitchen with a variety of foods that you can throw together for healthy meals in a hurry. Keep these foods on hand for fast meals on busy nights.

In the Cupboard

❑ Whole-grain cereals, oatmeal

❑ Beans: black, pinto, kidney, chickpeas, lentils, refried

❑ Rice: brown, long-grain, rice mixes

❑ Pasta: whole-wheat spaghetti, fettucini, penne, bowtie

❑ Other grains: couscous, orzo, cornmeal, whole-wheat bread and crackers, bread crumbs

❑ Onions, garlic

❑ Canned tomatoes: diced, whole, seasoned, sun-dried, sauce, paste

❑ Canned vegetables, mixed vegetables, green beans, mushrooms, other favorites

❑ Canned and dried fruits: applesauce, cranberries, other favorites

❑ Sauces: pasta, pizza, salsa

❑ Soups: low-fat and low-sodium canned soups, broth, bouillon, and dried soup mixes

❑ Meats: canned tuna, salmon, minced clams, chicken

❑ Peanut butter

❑ Evaporated milk

❑ Your favorite herbs and spices

❑ Oils: olive, canola, peanut, and nonfat cooking spray

SHOPPING LIST: BASIC INGREDIENTS FOR A HEALTHY KITCHEN

In the Refrigerator
- ❑ Vegetables and fruits

- ❑ 100 % vegetable and fruit juices

- ❑ Low-fat milk and yogurt (low in added sugar)

- ❑ Cheeses (reduced fat, when possible): cheddar, mozzarella, Swiss, Monterey Jack, cottage, Parmesan

- ❑ Whole-wheat and corn tortillas

- ❑ Eggs

- ❑ Minced garlic

- ❑ Sauces: Worcestershire, soy, teriyaki, and chili

- ❑ Ketchup and mustard (spicy and dijon)

- ❑ Salad dressings made with olive oil or that are reduced fat

- ❑ Reduced-fat sour cream, mayonnaise, cream cheese

- ❑ Vinegars: cider, red and white wine, balsamic

- ❑ Fresh herbs

In the Freezer
- ❑ Frozen vegetables, fruits and 100 % juices

- ❑ Frozen chopped onions and chopped green peppers

- ❑ Breads: whole-grain breads, dinner rolls, English muffins, bagels

- ❑ Meats: chicken breast, ground turkey breast, extra lean hamburger

- ❑ Seafood: red snapper, salmon, orange roughy, cod, flounder, sole, shrimp, scallops

The American Cancer Society's

Healthy Eating Cookbook

3rd Edition

Appetizers

Appetizers

Healthy Spinach Dip

1 10-ounce package frozen chopped
    spinach, thawed
1 cup low-fat plain yogurt
1/2 cup low-fat cottage cheese
1 to 2 tablespoons 1% low-fat milk
1/2 cup fresh parsley, chopped
1/2 cup green onions, chopped
3 tablespoons low-fat mayonnaise
1/2 teaspoon (or more) fresh dill,
    minced or 1/4 teaspoon dried
    dill weed
1/2 teaspoon seasoned salt (optional)
Freshly ground pepper to taste

Drain spinach and mix with yogurt in a medium bowl. In a blender, purée cottage cheese with enough milk to make the consistency of sour cream. Add parsley, green onions, mayonnaise, dill, seasoned salt, and pepper to spinach mixture and mix well. Cover and refrigerate for 5 hours to overnight. Makes 14 (1/4 cup) servings.

➤ Approx. per serving: 70 calories; 1 gram of fat

Easy Spinach Dip

1 10-ounce package frozen chopped
    spinach, or 1 pound fresh spinach,
    chopped
1 cup low-fat sour cream or low-fat
    small curd cottage cheese
1/2 cup low-fat yogurt
1/2 cup fresh parsley, finely chopped
1/4 cup scallions (including tops),
    finely chopped
1 teaspoon salt
Freshly ground pepper

If using fresh spinach, wash and trim stems. Boil in a large saucepan or steam spinach until wilted, then drain thoroughly and chop. If using frozen spinach, squeeze by hand to remove all moisture or wrap in paper towels and squeeze. In a bowl, combine spinach, sour cream or cottage cheese, yogurt, parsley, scallions, salt, and pepper to taste and mix well. Cover and refrigerate for at least 4 hours or overnight to blend flavors. Makes 2 cups.

➤ Approx. per serving: 60 calories; 4 grams of fat

Appetizers

Hummus

1/4 cup tahini (sesame paste)
1 teaspoon cumin or more to taste
1/2 teaspoon salt
2 large cloves garlic, finely chopped
3 tablespoons lemon juice
3 tablespoons hot water
1 19-ounce can garbanzo beans,
    drained
Chopped fresh parsley

Combine tahini, cumin, salt, and garlic in a small bowl. While mixing, slowly pour in lemon juice, then hot water. Purée garbanzo beans in a blender or a food processor, or pass through a food mill. Add tahini mixture to purée and process or mix well. Season to taste. Sprinkle with chopped parsley and serve with fresh vegetables or toasted pita bread. Makes 1 1/2 cups.

➤ Approx. per serving: 104 calories; 4 grams of fat

Guacamole

2 ripe avocados, skinned and mashed
1/2 lemon, juiced
2 tablespoons onion, finely chopped
1 tablespoon olive oil
Salt and pepper to taste

Mash the avocado well and stir together with lemon juice, onions, and olive oil. Add salt and pepper to taste. Cover and refrigerate for one hour before serving. Makes 10 servings.

➤ Approx. per serving: 80 calories; 8 grams of fat

Fresh Vegetables with Dill Cucumber Dip

1 12-ounce container plain firm low-fat
    yogurt
1 cup cucumber (no seeds or skin),
    cut in small pieces
1 teaspoon dried dillweed
1/4 cup lemon juice
Salt and pepper to taste
A variety of fresh vegetables – cut in
    strips. You can use any of the
    following:
asparagus tips
heads of broccoli
carrot sticks
celery sticks
cucumber sticks
green beans
parsnip sticks
snow peas
green, yellow, or red pepper

Combine yogurt, cucumber, dillweed, and lemon juice in a blender or food processor and blend until smooth. Add salt and pepper to taste and chill until ready to serve. Arrange vegetable strips in a circle on a large platter and place the dip in a small bowl in the middle.

➤ Approx. per serving: 12 calories; 1 gram of fat

Black Bean Dip

1 15-ounce can black beans, drained
1/2 cup fat-free mayonnaise
1/2 cup fat-free sour cream
1 clove garlic, mashed
1 4-ounce can chopped green chili
    peppers
1 teaspoon chili powder
1 tablespoon salt

Mash the black beans in a bowl well with a fork. Add mayonnaise, sour cream, garlic, chilies, chili powder, and salt. Stir well. Cover and refrigerate for one hour before serving. Makes 8 servings.

➤ Approx. per serving: 70 calories; 0 grams of fat

Appetizers

Tasty Tuna Dip

1 cup low-fat cottage cheese
1 7-ounce can water-packed tuna
Fresh lemon juice to taste
1/4 teaspoon fresh dill, crushed or
    1/8 teaspoon dried dillweed
2 green onions, sliced
Paprika

Place cottage cheese into a food processor and process until creamy. Add tuna, lemon juice, and dill and process until smooth. Stir in green onions. Spoon tuna dip into a serving bowl and refrigerate for 1 hour or longer. Garnish with paprika. Serve with low-fat crackers or crudités. Makes 6 (1/4 cup) servings.

➤ Approx. per serving: 70 calories; 1 gram of fat

Salmon Slices with Lime Juice and Basil

1 pound salmon fillets with skin
1/2 cup fresh lime juice
2 tablespoons fresh basil or dill, finely
    chopped
1 teaspoon granulated sugar
Salt and freshly ground white pepper
    to taste
Fresh basil leaves

Place fillets skin side down on a cutting board and slice thinly with a very sharp knife. Discard skin and arrange salmon slices in a shallow dish. Combine lime juice, chopped basil, sugar, salt, and white pepper in a small bowl and mix well. Pour mixture over salmon, cover, and marinate in refrigerator for 5 hours. Drain, reserving marinade. Arrange salmon slices on a serving platter and drizzle a small amount of reserved marinade over salmon. Garnish with fresh basil leaves. Serve with thin slices of pumpernickel bread. Makes 8 servings.

➤ Approx. per serving: 86 calories; 3 grams of fat

Scallop Ceviche

2 pounds fresh scallops
3 tomatoes, seeded and chopped
1 cup fresh lime juice
1 cup fresh cilantro (coriander),
   chopped
1 medium onion, chopped
1 small red bell pepper, chopped
2 fresh jalapeño peppers, seeded and
   minced
2 cloves garlic, minced
4 limes, cut into thin wedges
Parsley, chopped

Place scallops in a colander, rinse with cold water and drain. Combine scallops, tomatoes, lime juice, cilantro, onion, red and jalapeño peppers, and garlic in a glass bowl. Toss gently until scallops are coated with lime juice, then cover. Marinate in refrigerator for 5 hours, stirring several times. Spoon scallop mixture into individual serving bowls. Garnish with lime wedges and parsley. Makes 8 first-course servings.

➤ Approx. per serving: 126 calories; 2 grams of fat

Oriental Shrimp

4 cups water
2 stalks celery with leaves
1 thick slice onion
1 clove garlic, halved
1 bay leaf
1 pound large fresh shrimp in shells
1/4 pound fresh snow peas

Combine 4 cups of water, celery, onion, garlic, and bay leaf in a large saucepan. Bring to a boil, reduce heat, and simmer for 5 minutes. Add shrimp and simmer for 3 to 5 minutes or until shrimp turn pink. Place shrimp in a colander, drain and rinse with cold running water. Shell and devein shrimp. Bring several cups water to a boil in a large saucepan and add trimmed snow peas. Blanch for 2 minutes or just until pliable, then drain. Place snow peas into a bowl of ice water to halt cooking, then drain. Wrap a snow pea around each shrimp, securing with a toothpick. Arrange shrimp on a serving platter on a bed of lettuce. Cover and refrigerate until serving time. Makes 4 servings.

➤ Approx. per serving: 100 calories; 0.9 grams of fat

Tuna Cheese Soufflés

1 7-ounce can water-packed white
    tuna or albacore, drained
1/4 cup fresh parsley, chopped
1/4 cup onion, chopped
2 tablespoons low-fat mayonnaise
6 green olives, chopped
1 tablespoon fresh lemon juice
1/4 teaspoon pepper
3 egg whites
9 slices whole-wheat bread
3 tablespoons Parmesan cheese,
    freshly grated
3 tablespoons dry bread crumbs
Paprika

Preheat oven to 250°. Combine tuna, parsley, onion, mayonnaise, olives, lemon juice, and pepper in a blender or food processor and mix until smooth. Beat egg whites in a small mixer bowl until stiff. Fold gently into tuna mixture. Cut bread slices into quarters and arrange on a baking sheet. Bake for 30 minutes or until dry. Spoon tuna mixture onto toast squares. Mix Parmesan cheese and bread crumbs in a small bowl and sprinkle over tuna mixture. Sprinkle with paprika. Broil for 5 minutes or until light brown and bubbly. Serve immediately. Makes 36 appetizers.

➤ Approx. per appetizer: 32 calories; 0.9 grams of fat

Crab-Stuffed Cherry Tomatoes

1 pint cherry tomatoes
1 6-ounce can crab meat
2 green onions, finely chopped
2 tablespoons dry bread crumbs
1 teaspoon fresh parsley, finely minced
1 teaspoon white wine vinegar
1/2 teaspoon fresh dill, finely minced or
    1/4 teaspoon dried dillweed
Paprika

Slice stem end from tomatoes and scoop out pulp. Invert tomatoes and place on a paper towel to drain. Combine crab meat, green onions, bread crumbs, parsley, vinegar, and dillweed in a small bowl and mix well. Spoon mixture into tomatoes. Line a microwave-safe plate with a paper towel and arrange tomatoes. Microwave on high for 2 to 4 minutes or until heated through, turning plate several times. Sprinkle with paprika. Makes 5 servings.

➤ Approx. per serving: 53 calories; 1 gram of fat

Appetizers

Oysters Rockefeller

Rock salt
36 fresh oysters on the half shell
4 medium onions, chopped
8 ounces cooked spinach
2 stalks celery, chopped
3 sprigs of parsley
1/4 cup cream
1/4 teaspoon cayenne pepper
Salt and pepper to taste

Preheat oven to 450°. Spread a bed of rock salt into 2 shallow baking dishes and arrange oysters in shells on the bed. Place onions, spinach, celery, parsley, cream, salt, and black and cayenne peppers into a blender and process until puréed. Spoon purée over oysters. Bake for 4 minutes. Serve oysters on the bed of rock salt to retain heat. Makes 36 servings.

➤ Approx. per oyster: 25 calories; 0.9 grams of fat

Polynesian Crab

1 6-ounce package frozen snow crab, thawed, drained and flaked
2 green onions with tops, chopped
1/4 cup coconut, flaked
1/4 cup light mayonnaise
1/4 teaspoon curry powder
Salt and freshly ground pepper to taste

Combine snow crab, green onions, coconut, mayonnaise, curry powder, salt, and pepper in a medium bowl and mix well. Refrigerate for 1 to 2 hours to blend flavors. Serve with oriental rice crackers and fresh pineapple pieces. Makes 1 cup.

➤ Approx. per serving: 26 calories; 2 grams of fat

Crab-Cucumber Slices

1 medium (9-inch) cucumber
1 6-ounce can crab meat, drained
2 tablespoons low-fat plain yogurt
2 tablespoons chives or green onion,
     chopped
Salt and freshly ground pepper to taste
Paprika

Score cucumber lengthwise to make decorative edge, then slice 1/4-inch thick. Combine crab meat, yogurt, chives, salt, and pepper in a small bowl. Place a small spoonful of crab mixture onto each cucumber slice and sprinkle lightly with paprika. Arrange cucumber slices on a serving plate and cover with plastic wrap. Chill in refrigerator for up to 4 hours before serving. Makes 36 appetizers.

➤ Approx. per appetizer: 25 calories; 0.5 grams of fat

Dilled Salmon Mousse

1/2 cup water or clam juice
1 envelope unflavored gelatin
1/2 cup low-fat cottage cheese
1 to 2 tablespoons 1% low-fat milk
3/4 cup low-fat plain yogurt
1/2 cup celery, finely chopped
2 tablespoons fresh dill, minced or
     1 tablespoon dried dillweed
1 tablespoon onion, grated
1 tablespoon fresh lemon juice
1 teaspoon salt (optional)
Dash of hot pepper sauce
2 7-1/2-ounce cans sockeye salmon,
     drained

Place cold water or clam juice in a small saucepan. Sprinkle gelatin over liquid and let stand for 5 minutes. Dissolve gelatin over medium heat. Cool to room temperature. Combine cottage cheese and enough milk for desired consistency in a blender and process until smooth. Stir yogurt, celery, dill, onion, lemon juice, salt, hot pepper sauce, and blended cottage cheese into gelatin mixture. In a bowl, mash salmon with a fork or blend in a food processor until finely flaked. Fold salmon into gelatin mixture and pour into a 4-cup mold. Cover and chill for 3 hours or until firm. Unmold mousse onto a serving plate. Arrange crackers or chopped, fresh vegetables around mold before serving. Makes 16 (1/4 cup) servings.

➤ Approx. per serving: 54 calories; 2 grams of fat

Ginger Steak Rumaki

*3/4 pound (1/2-inch thick) lean sirloin,
   round or flank steak*
1/4 cup light soy sauce
1 teaspoon Worcestershire sauce
1 teaspoon onion, minced
1 teaspoon granulated sugar
1 clove garlic, minced
1/2 teaspoon ginger
1 10-ounce can water chestnuts

Freeze steak for 30 minutes for easier slicing. Trim off fat, then slice cross grain into about 25 1/8 x 3-inch strips. Combine soy sauce, Worcestershire sauce, onion, sugar, garlic, and ginger in a large bowl. Add steak and stir until coated with sauce. Marinate at room temperature for 30 minutes or in refrigerator overnight, stirring occasionally. Drain and wrap steak strip around each water chestnut, securing with a toothpick. Arrange rumaki on an ungreased baking sheet and broil for 3 to 4 minutes or until medium-rare. Arrange on a serving platter and serve immediately, while hot. Makes 5 servings.

➤ Approx. per serving: 195 calories; 7 grams of fat

Baked Chicken Fingers

4 boneless, skinless chicken breasts
2 tablespoons cornstarch
1 egg
1 cup buttermilk
1 teaspoon salt
1 teaspoon black pepper
1 teaspoon garlic powder
1 teaspoon onion powder
1 cup all-purpose flour
1 cup bread crumbs
Nonfat cooking spray

Preheat oven to 350°. Cut chicken breast into 1/2-inch strips. Mix together in a bowl with the cornstarch, covering each strip evenly. In another bowl combine the egg, buttermilk, salt, pepper, garlic powder, and onion powder. In a separate bowl combine flour and bread crumbs. Cover the bottom of a nonstick baking pan with cooking spray. Dip each piece of chicken in egg mixture and then in flour mixture. Place each strip on baking pan. Bake for approx. 40 minutes, turning once, until chicken is cooked throughout and browned. Makes 8 servings.

➤ Approx. per serving: 270 calories; 3 grams of fat

Appetizers

Chicken Puffs

1/2 cup cooked boneless, skinless
    chicken, finely minced
1-1/2 tablespoons low-fat mayonnaise
1 tablespoon dry bread crumbs
2 teaspoons scallions, minced
1/4 teaspoon salt (optional)
1/4 teaspoon dry mustard
1/4 teaspoon curry powder
1/4 teaspoon Worcestershire sauce
6 slices whole-wheat bread
1 egg white
Paprika

Combine chicken, mayonnaise, crumbs, scallions, salt, mustard, curry powder, and Worcestershire sauce in a small bowl. Mix well and chill in refrigerator for several hours, if desired. Preheat oven to 250°. Cut each bread slice into 4 squares and arrange on a baking sheet. Bake for 30 minutes. Beat egg white in a small mixing bowl until soft peaks form. Preheat oven to 500°. Fold egg white into chicken mixture gently and sprinkle with paprika. Bake for 5 minutes. Serve immediately. Makes 24 appetizers.

➤ Approx. per appetizer: 26 calories; 0.7 grams of fat

Stuffed Mushroom Caps

24 thin slices bread, crusts trimmed
24 medium fresh mushrooms
1 cup fine whole-wheat bread crumbs
1/4 cup fresh parsley, finely chopped
1 clove garlic, minced
Salt and freshly ground pepper to taste
4 teaspoons corn oil margarine
2/3 cup part-skim mozzarella cheese,
    shredded

Preheat oven to 300°. Flatten bread with a rolling pin and cut 24 rounds with a 1 1/2-inch cookie cutter. Press bread rounds into miniature muffin cups and bake for 20 to 25 minutes or until light brown. Remove from pan and let cool. Wash mushrooms and pat dry with paper towels. Remove stems completely and discard. Combine bread crumbs, parsley, garlic, salt, and pepper in a food processor and mix well. Add margarine and continue to process until mixed. Spoon a small amount of crumb mixture into each mushroom cap. Sprinkle with cheese. Place 1 stuffed mushroom into each baked bread cup and arrange on a baking sheet. Preheat oven to 400°. Bake for 10 minutes or broil for 1 minute if desired. Serve hot. Makes 24 appetizers (4 appetizers per serving).

➤ Approx. per serving: 167 calories; 5 grams of fat

Mozzarella-Vegetable Canapés

1/2 cup carrots, finely chopped
1/2 cup radishes, finely chopped
1/4 cup onion, finely chopped
2 tablespoons green bell pepper,
    finely chopped
2 tablespoons low-fat mayonnaise
1 tablespoon low-fat plain yogurt
1 clove garlic, minced
1/2 teaspoon salt (optional)
1/4 teaspoon pepper
48 small rye crackers or melba rounds
4 ounces part-skim mozzarella cheese,
    cut into 48 small slices
Paprika

Preheat oven to 500°. Combine carrots, radishes, onion, green pepper, mayonnaise, yogurt, garlic, salt, and pepper in a small bowl and mix well. Spread 1/2 tablespoon of mixture on each cracker. Top with a mozzarella slice and sprinkle with paprika. Place canapés onto a baking sheet and bake for 5 minutes. Serve immediately. Makes 48 appetizers.

➤ Approx. per appetizer: 20 calories; 0.6 grams of fat

Hot Fruit Kabobs

1 cup grapefruit juice
1/2 cup honey
2 tablespoons kirsch (optional)
1 tablespoon fresh mint, finely chopped
3 peaches, peeled, pitted, and cut into
    bite-sized pieces
4 bananas, peeled and cut into bite-
    sized pieces
2 apples, cut into wedges
1 fresh pineapple, peeled, cored and
    cut into bite-sized pieces
2 grapefruit, sectioned
Bamboo skewers

Combine grapefruit juice, honey, kirsch, and mint in a small bowl and mix well. Arrange fruit in a shallow bowl and pour grapefruit juice mixture over fruit. Marinate for 1 hour. In a shallow dish, soak bamboo skewers in water for 10 minutes. Preheat broiler. Drain fruit, reserving marinade. Thread fruit onto skewers and place skewers into a broiler pan. Broil for 5 minutes, brushing frequently with marinade. Makes 6 servings.

➤ Approx. per serving: 370 calories; 0.9 grams of fat

Soups

Chilled Fresh Tomato Soup

4 pounds fresh tomatoes
2 cups chicken broth, either home-
    made or canned
2 tablespoons onion, chopped
2 teaspoons granulated sugar
1/2 teaspoon fresh basil, chopped or
    1/4 teaspoon dried basil
1/2 teaspoon salt (optional)
1/4 teaspoon pepper

Dip tomatoes into a large saucepan of boiling water for 30 seconds. Remove and immediately place tomatoes into a large bowl of cold water. Let stand until cool enough to handle. Peel tomatoes with a knife, allowing skin to slip off easily. Cut each tomato in half crosswise and squeeze gently to remove seed. Then cut core from tomato and cut into quarters. Place 1/4 of the tomatoes at a time in a blender and process until puréed. Combine tomatoes, chicken broth, onion, sugar, basil, salt, and pepper in a large bowl. Refrigerate for several hours to blend flavors. Serve chilled. Makes 6 servings.

➤ Approx. per serving: 92 calories; 1 gram of fat

Tomato-Zucchini Soup

1 tablespoon corn oil margarine
1/2 cup celery, chopped
3 shallots, chopped
2 large cloves garlic, minced
4 cups chicken broth, either home-
    made or canned
3 tomatoes, chopped
1 zucchini, thinly sliced
1 tablespoon tomato paste
1 teaspoon fresh parsley, chopped or
    1/2 teaspoon dried parsley
1/2 teaspoon fresh cilantro, chopped
    (coriander)
1 bay leaf
4 to 6 tablespoons low-fat plain yogurt

Melt margarine in a soup pot over low heat. Add celery, shallots, and garlic and sauté until tender. Add chicken broth, tomatoes, zucchini, tomato paste, parsley, cilantro, and bay leaf. Simmer for 2 hours. Discard bay leaf. Ladle soup into soup bowls. Garnish with yogurt. Makes 4 to 6 servings.

➤ Approx. per serving: 115 calories; 4 grams of fat

Soups

Vegetable Soup with Pasta

1 tablespoon olive oil
2 cups onions, chopped
1 pound fresh carrots, sliced
1 large green or red bell pepper,
   chopped
2 cloves garlic, minced
10 cups chicken broth, either homemade or canned
2 cups unpeeled potatoes, cut into
   bite-sized pieces
2 cups turnips, chopped
2 pounds fresh green beans, cut in
   2-inch pieces
2 cups tri-colored small pasta shells,
   cooked
1/2 teaspoon salt (optional)
1/4 teaspoon pepper
1-1/2 cups fresh parsley, chopped

Heat olive oil in a soup pot over medium heat. Add onions and sauté until tender. Add carrots, bell pepper, and garlic and cook for 5 minutes. Add chicken broth, potatoes, and turnips. Bring to a boil, reduce heat, and cover partially. Cook for 10 minutes or until potatoes are almost tender. Add green beans and simmer for 5 minutes. Add pasta, salt, and pepper. Simmer for 10 minutes longer. Ladle soup into soup bowls. Garnish each with 2 tablespoons of parsley. Makes 12 servings.

➤ Approx. per serving: 152 calories; 3 grams of fat

Oriental Spinach Soup

1 10-ounce package frozen chopped
   spinach
1 tablespoon cornstarch
1-1/2 cups water, divided
2 10-1/2-ounce cans chicken broth,
   either homemade or canned
1/2 cup celery, diagonally sliced
1/2 cup fresh carrots, thinly sliced
2 tablespoons green onions, sliced
2 teaspoons light soy sauce

Cook spinach according to package directions, omitting salt, and drain well. In a saucepan, dissolve cornstarch in 1/4 cup of water. Stir in remaining 1-1/4 cups of water and chicken broth. Add spinach, celery, carrots, green onions, and soy sauce. Bring to a boil over medium-high heat, stirring constantly. Cook until clear and thickened and continue to stir. Reduce heat and simmer for 5 minutes. Makes 8 cups (1-1/3 cups per serving).

➤ Approx. per serving: 31 calories; 0.5 grams of fat

Hearty Minestrone

3 tablespoons olive oil
1 large onion, chopped
6 large fresh mushrooms, sliced
3 cloves garlic, chopped
1 tablespoon fresh basil, chopped or
     1-1/2 teaspoons dried basil
1 teaspoon fresh oregano, chopped or
     1/2 teaspoon dried oregano
1 teaspoon fresh parsley, chopped
5 cups water
1 20-ounce can mixed vegetable juice
     cocktail
4 carrots, thinly sliced
2 zucchini, sliced
1/2 small head cabbage, shredded
1/2 cup elbow macaroni

Heat olive oil in a 6-quart saucepan over medium heat. Add onion, mushrooms, garlic, basil, oregano, and parsley and sauté for several minutes. Add water and vegetable juice cocktail, then bring to a boil over medium-high heat. Add carrots, zucchini, cabbage, and macaroni. Cook just until vegetables and macaroni are tender. Makes 8 servings.

➤ Approx. per serving: 98 calories; 2 grams of fat

Split Pea and Barley Soup

6 cups chicken broth, either home-
     made or canned
1-1/2 cups dried split peas
1/2 medium onion, coarsely chopped
1 medium carrot, coarsely chopped
1 stalk celery, coarsely chopped
1 clove garlic, minced
1/2 cup pearl barley
Salt and freshly ground white pepper
     to taste

Place broth, split peas, onion, carrot, celery, and garlic into a 3-quart soup pot. Bring to a boil over medium-high heat, reduce heat, and simmer, uncovered, for 1 hour. Mix soup, using small amount at a time, in a food processor or blender. Combine puréed soup and barley in a soup pot. Bring to a boil, reduce heat, and simmer for 30 to 40 minutes or until barley is tender. Add salt and white pepper. Makes 6 servings.

➤ Approx. per serving: 265 calories; 2 grams of fat

Soups

Split Pea Soup

1 ham bone from cooked ham
1-1/4 cup (12 ounces) split green peas
8 cups water
4 onions, sliced
Salt and pepper to taste

Trim any fat from ham bone, but leave meat. Combine all ingredients except salt and pepper in a stockpot. Bring to a boil and skim fat. Lower heat to keep from sticking. Simmer, partially covered, for 1-1/2 to 2 hours or until peas are soft, stirring occasionally. Makes 10 servings.

➤ Approx. per serving: 93 calories; 0.3 grams of fat

French Onion Soup

2 tablespoons corn oil margarine
1-1/2 pounds onions, quartered and
    thinly sliced
2 cups fresh carrots, peeled and
    grated
1 tablespoon light brown sugar
3 tablespoons all-purpose flour
1 teaspoon paprika
6 cups beef broth, either homemade
    or canned
1 teaspoon fresh thyme or
    1/2 teaspoon dried thyme
1/4 teaspoon salt (omit if using
    canned broth)
1/4 teaspoon pepper
6 slices (1 to 1-1/2 ounces each)
    whole-wheat or white French bread
1/3 cup part-skim mozzarella cheese,
    grated

Melt margarine in a large soup pot over low heat. Add onions and carrots. Cover and cook over very low heat for 20 minutes. Add brown sugar and cook until onions are brown, stirring constantly. Add flour and paprika, stirring until onions are coated. Add broth, thyme, salt, and pepper and mix well. Bring to a boil over medium-high heat, stirring constantly. Reduce heat and simmer, uncovered, for 30 minutes. Preheat oven to 250°. Place bread onto a baking sheet and dry bread slices in an oven for 30 minutes to make croutons. Ladle soup into ovenproof soup bowls, then place bowls onto a baking sheet. Put 1 crouton into each bowl and sprinkle with cheese. Place baking sheet with bowls 4 inches below broiler and broil 3 to 4 minutes or until cheese is lightly browned and bubbly. If your soup bowls are not ovenproof, place cheese-topped croutons onto baking sheet and broil until bubbly. Ladle piping hot soup into soup bowls and top with croutons. Makes 6 servings.

➤ Approx. per serving: 233 calories; 6 grams of fat

Chilled Melon Bisque

1 ripe cantaloupe
1 cup low-fat plain yogurt
3 tablespoons fresh lemon juice
1/2 teaspoon fresh ginger root, peeled
and grated or 1/4 teaspoon dried
ginger
2 tablespoons fresh mint leaves,
chopped

Slice cantaloupe in half and remove seeds. Scoop cantaloupe pulp into a food processor or blender and process until puréed. Should make about 1-1/2 cups. Add yogurt, lemon juice, and ginger. Process until blended. Refrigerate until serving time. Pour cantaloupe mixture into small bowls. Garnish with fresh mint. Makes 4 servings.

➤ Approx. per serving: 96 calories; 1 gram of fat

Potato and Leek Soup

6 medium leeks
8 cups chicken broth, either homemade or canned
4 medium potatoes, peeled and
chopped
1 clove garlic, minced
1 cup 1% low-fat milk
Salt and freshly ground pepper to taste
3 tablespoons fresh parsley or chives,
minced

Trim leeks, leaving about 2 inches of green portion. Cut lengthwise halfway through white portion. Spread leeks apart and rinse well under cold running water. Slice leeks thinly by hand. Combine leeks, chicken broth, potatoes and garlic in a large saucepan and bring to a boil over medium-high heat. Reduce heat, cover partially, and simmer for 30 minutes or until vegetables are tender. Purée vegetable mixture in a blender or food processor. Heat over low heat and stir in milk, and salt and pepper to taste. Ladle soup into soup bowls and garnish with parsley. Makes 12 cups.

➤ Approx. per serving: 94 calories; 1 gram of fat

New England Seafood Chowder

4 slices whole-wheat bread
2 tablespoons corn oil margarine
4 cups onions, sliced
2 tablespoons all-purpose flour
2 cups clam juice
2 cups water
5 cups potatoes, sliced
2 teaspoons fresh thyme or
   1 teaspoon dried thyme
3/4 teaspoon salt (optional)
1/2 teaspoon pepper
2 pounds boneless fish fillets, cut into
   bite-sized pieces
2 cups 1% low-fat milk
1/2 cup fresh parsley, chopped

Preheat oven to 250°. Cut bread into cubes and spread in a single layer on a baking sheet. Bake for 30 minutes or until dry. Croutons should measure about 1-1/2 cups. Melt margarine in a large soup pot over low heat. Add onions and sauté for 10 minutes. Stir in flour and cook for 2 minutes, stirring constantly. Add clam juice and water. Bring to a boil over medium-high heat, stirring constantly. Add potatoes, thyme, salt, and pepper. Reduce heat and simmer for 10 minutes. Add fish and milk. Continue to simmer for 5 minutes or just until fish is opaque. Do not overcook. Ladle into soup bowls. Sprinkle with parsley and croutons. Makes 12 first-course or 8 main-dish servings.

➤ Approx. per serving: 198 calories; 5 grams of fat

Winter Soup

2 tablespoons vegetable oil
1 medium onion, chopped
2 14-1/2-ounce cans fat-free chicken
   broth, either homemade or canned
1/3 cup tomato sauce
1/2 cup macaroni, uncooked
1 15-ounce can white beans (cannelloni
   or Great Northern beans), drained
Pepper to taste

Heat oil in a large soup pot over medium-low heat. Add onion and cook for 3 minutes. Add broth and tomato sauce, bring to a boil, then stir in macaroni. Reduce heat, cover, and simmer for 10 minutes. Add pepper to taste, then stir in white beans. Heat mixture thoroughly. Serve in soup bowls with croutons, cornbread or crackers, or a sprinkle of Parmesan cheese. Makes 4 to 6 servings.

➤ Approx. per serving: 295 calories; 8 grams of fat

Curried Winter Squash Soup

1-1/2 cups onions, finely chopped
1 tablespoon margarine
4 to 5 teaspoons curry powder
2 medium butternut squash
3 cups low-sodium chicken broth,
    either homemade or canned
1 medium apple, peeled, cored,
    and chopped
1 cup apple juice
Salt and freshly ground pepper
    to taste

Melt margarine in a large saucepan over low heat. Add onions and curry powder. Cover and simmer for 8 minutes or until onions are soft. Peel, seed, and chop squash and add with broth and apple to saucepan. Bring to a boil over medium-high heat, reduce heat, and cover partially. Simmer for 25 minutes or until squash and apple are very tender. Strain, reserving liquid and solids. Process solids until smooth in a food processor with a steel blade or in a blender. Add 1 cup reserved liquid and continue to process until smooth. Return puréed soup to saucepan. Add enough remaining reserved soup liquid and apple juice to make desired consistency. Add salt and pepper. Heat to serving temperature and serve immediately. May substitute pumpkin or other winter squash for butternut. May substitute 1% low-fat milk for apple juice for a less sweet taste. Makes 8 servings.

➤ Approx. per serving: 100 calories; 3 grams of fat

Chinese Chicken-Noodle Soup

8 cups chicken broth, either home-
    made or canned
1/2 pound chicken or turkey breast,
    skinned, boned, and cut into
    small pieces
4 scallions, sliced
3 carrots, sliced
2 tablespoons light soy sauce
1 teaspoon sugar
1 tablespoon sherry
1/2 teaspoon fresh ginger root,
    finely minced
4 ounces whole-wheat vermicelli,
    broken into 1-inch pieces

Place chicken broth into a large soup pot and bring to a boil over medium-high heat. Add chicken, scallions, carrots, soy sauce, sugar, sherry, and ginger. Reduce heat, cover, and simmer for 20 minutes. Bring to a boil, then add vermicelli. Cook over medium-high heat for 15 minutes. Ladle into soup bowls. Makes 8 servings.

➤ Approx. per serving: 136 calories; 2 grams of fat

Soups

Gazpacho

6 large ripe tomatoes, seeded and
    chopped or 1-1/2 cups canned
    imported plum tomatoes, drained
2 red bell peppers, cored, seeded, and
    coarsely chopped
2 large cucumbers, peeled, seeded,
    and coarsely chopped
1 medium yellow onion, coarsely
    chopped
1 clove garlic
1-1/2 cups canned tomato juice
1/4 cup red wine vinegar
1 tablespoon olive oil
Pinch of cayenne pepper or dash hot
    pepper sauce
Salt and freshly ground pepper to taste
1/2 cup fresh parsley, chopped

In a food processor fitted with a metal blade or in a blender, place tomatoes, red peppers, cucumbers, onion, and garlic a small amount at a time, adding enough tomato juice to each batch to keep blades from clogging. Process until well mixed but do not purée completely. Combine processed vegetable mixture, vinegar, olive oil, cayenne pepper, salt, and pepper in a large bowl and cover. Refrigerate for 4 hours or longer, adjusting seasonings if necessary. Ladle soup into soup bowls. Garnish with parsley. Makes 8 servings.

➤ Approx. per serving: 64 calories; 2 grams of fat

Asparagus and Pea Soup

1-1/4 pounds asparagus, trimmed and
    cut into 1/4-inch pieces
1 10-ounce package frozen peas,
    thawed
5 cups chicken broth, either home-
    made or canned
1 cup water
1 tablespoon fresh tarragon, chopped
    or one teaspoon dried tarragon,
    crumbled
Salt and pepper to taste
Tarragon sprigs

Combine asparagus, peas, broth, tarragon, and water in a large saucepan over medium-high heat. Bring to a boil and simmer, uncovered, for 10 minutes until asparagus is tender. In a blender or food processor, purée mixture in batches until smooth. Pour into saucepan, season with salt and pepper to taste, and heat. Ladle soup into soup bowls. Garnish with fresh tarragon sprigs. Makes 4 servings.

➤ Approx. per serving: 149 calories; 2 grams of fat

Jesse Barfield

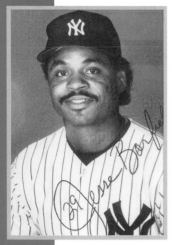

As a player and coach, Jesse Barfield has made his mark both on and off the baseball diamond. His 12 years with the Toronto Blue Jays included five years with the club's minor league teams and seven years in the majors. In 1985 he was the American League home run leader with 40. Jesse also spent four years with the New York Yankees and a year with the Tokyo Giants before turning his energies to the front office as community affairs director for the Houston Astros. Jesse has also served as batting coach for the Seattle Mariners.

Market Day Soup

1/4 cup each black beans, navy beans, red beans, Garbanzo beans, Pinto beans, split peas, lentils, barley, black-eyed peas, and baby lima beans
1 ham hock
bay leaf
1/8 teaspoon thyme
1 quart tomatoes or 6 fresh peeled and cut up
2 medium chopped onions
6 stalks celery
2 cloves garlic
Salt and pepper to taste
1 pound boneless, skinless chicken breast, cut in pieces
1/2 pound smoked sausage, cut in pieces
2 tablespoons chopped fresh parsley

Soak beans overnight with 1 tablespoon of salt. Drain beans and add 3 quarts of water, ham hock, bay leaf, and thyme. Cover and simmer about 3 hours. Add tomatoes, onions, celery, garlic, salt, and pepper. Simmer 1-1/2 hours uncovered. Add chicken and sausage; simmer until chicken is tender. Ten minutes before serving add parsley.

➤ Approx. per serving: 268 calories; 7 grams of fat

Soups

Chicken-Cabbage Soup

3 cups chicken broth, either homemade or canned
3 cups water
2 cups fresh tomatoes, chopped
1 potato, peeled and chopped
1/2 cup carrot, shredded
1/2 cup celery, chopped
1/2 cup onion, chopped
4 peppercorns
1 bay leaf
3 cups cabbage, shredded
1 cup cooked boneless skinless
   chicken, chopped
1/4 cup fresh lemon juice
1 tablespoon granulated sugar

Combine broth, water, tomatoes, potato, carrot, celery, and onion in a large saucepan. Add peppercorns and bay leaf and simmer for 1 hour, stirring occasionally. Add cabbage and continue to simmer for 10 minutes. Add cooked chicken, lemon juice, and sugar. Heat to serving temperature. Remove bay leaf. Ladle soup into soup bowls. Makes 6 to 8 servings.

➤ Approx. per serving: 113 calories; 2 grams of fat

Curried Carrot Soup

1 tablespoon corn oil margarine
4 cups carrots, chopped
1 cup onion, chopped
1/2 teaspoon curry powder
1/2 teaspoon cumin
1/2 teaspoon coriander
5 cups water
1/2 teaspoon salt (optional)
1/4 teaspoon white pepper
1 cup low-fat cottage cheese
1 cup 1% low-fat milk
1 teaspoon fresh lemon juice
1/2 cup green bell pepper, chopped
1/2 cup fresh parsley, chopped

Melt margarine in a large soup pot over low heat. Add carrots and onion. Sauté for 5 minutes, adding curry powder, cumin, and coriander. Add water, salt, and white pepper. Bring to a boil over medium-high heat, reduce heat, and cover partially. Simmer for 15 minutes. Pour carrot mixture into a blender and process until puréed. Return mixture to soup pot. Place cottage cheese, milk, and lemon juice into blender and process until smooth. Pour into carrot mixture. Heat to serving temperature over low heat. Ladle into soup bowls. Garnish with green pepper and parsley. Soup may be served chilled. Makes 6 servings.

➤ Approx. per serving: 111 calories; 4 grams of fat

White Bean and Spinach Soup

1 pound dried white beans
8 cups water, divided
8 cups beef broth, either homemade
    or canned
2 cups fresh carrots, grated
1-1/2 cups onion, chopped
4 cloves garlic, minced
1 teaspoon fresh thyme or
    1/2 teaspoon dried thyme
3 bay leaves
1/4 teaspoon pepper
1/8 teaspoon cayenne pepper
6 cups fresh spinach, torn
2 16-ounce cans tomatoes, coarsely
    chopped
1/2 teaspoon granulated sugar
1/2 teaspoon salt (omit if using
    canned broth)

Soak beans in 4 cups of water overnight in a large saucepan. Drain soaking water and add beef broth and 4 cups of fresh water. Bring to a boil over medium-high heat, then reduce heat. Add carrots, onions, garlic, thyme, bay leaves, and black and cayenne peppers. Bring to a boil, reduce heat, then cover and simmer for 1 hour or until beans are tender. Add spinach, tomatoes with liquid, sugar, and salt. Bring to a boil, reduce heat, and simmer for 5 minutes. Discard bay leaves. Ladle into soup bowls. Makes 8 servings.

➤ Approx. per serving: 240 calories; 2 grams of fat

Turnip, Turkey, and Pea Soup

1 pound green split peas
1 large onion, chopped
1 large turnip, peeled and diced into
    1/2-inch cubes
2 carrots, diced into 1/2-inch cubes
2 10-ounce packages frozen green
    peas, thawed
1/4 teaspoon dried thyme, crumbled
8 cups water
2 cups chicken broth, either home-
    made or canned
Salt and pepper to taste
3 tablespoons olive oil
2 turkey breasts, cooked and chopped
3 slices day old rye bread, crusts
    discarded, cut into 1/2-inch cubes

Combine split peas, onion, turnip, carrots, green peas, thyme, and water in a large kettle or stockpot over medium-high heat. Bring to a boil, and simmer, uncovered, for 1-1/2 hours, stirring occasionally. Stir in broth, salt and pepper to taste and simmer, uncovered, for 5 minutes. Heat oil in a skillet over high heat and sauté turkey for 2 minutes, then set aside. Sauté bread cubes in skillet until crisp. Ladle into soup bowls and top each serving with turkey and croutons. Makes 6 to 8 servings.

➤ Approx. per serving: 398 calories; 9 grams of fat

Soups

Chilled Spinach Borscht

1 pound fresh spinach or 1 10-ounce
    package frozen spinach, thawed
1 large cucumber, peeled and
    chopped
1/2 medium yellow onion, chopped
1 cup fat-free buttermilk, divided
4 cups chicken broth, either homemade
    or canned
1 teaspoon vinegar
1/2 teaspoon fresh dill, chopped or
    1/4 teaspoon dried dillweed
Salt and pepper to taste
Chopped cucumber for garnish

Rinse spinach well and place into a saucepan with a small amount of salted water. Cook over medium heat until tender. Drain and chop spinach. Place cucumber and onion into a blender and process until puréed. Place purée into a large bowl and stir in half of the buttermilk. Add chicken broth and vinegar, blending well. Stir in spinach, remaining buttermilk, dill, salt, and pepper. Chill until serving time. Ladle into soup bowls. Garnish with chopped cucumber. Makes 8 servings.

➤ Approx. per serving: 53 calories; 1 gram of fat

Moscow Borscht

4 cups beef or chicken broth, either
    homemade or canned
2 large fresh beets, peeled and
    chopped
1 large potato, peeled and chopped
1 onion, chopped
1 medium carrot, sliced
1/4 small head cabbage, shredded
1 tomato, chopped
2 tablespoons fresh parsley, chopped
    or 1 tablespoon dried parsley
1 teaspoon fresh dill, chopped or
    1/2 teaspoon dried dillweed
1 teaspoon fresh lemon juice
1 teaspoon salt (optional)
Freshly ground pepper to taste
3 tablespoons low-fat plain yogurt or
    Mock Sour Cream (see recipe on
    the next page)

Combine broth, beets, potato, onion, and carrot in a saucepan. Bring to a boil over medium-high heat. Reduce heat, cover, and simmer for 30 minutes. Skim if necessary. Add cabbage, tomato, parsley, and dill. Cover and simmer for 30 minutes longer or until vegetables are tender. Add lemon juice, salt, and pepper. Ladle soup into soup bowls. Garnish each serving with 1 rounded teaspoon yogurt or Mock Sour Cream. Makes 8 servings.

➤ Approx. per serving: 65 calories; 1 gram of fat

Mock Sour Cream

1 cup low-fat cottage cheese
1/4 cup fat-free buttermilk
1/2 teaspoon (or more) fresh
    lemon juice

Combine cottage cheese and buttermilk in a blender. Process until smooth. Stir in lemon juice to taste. Makes 1 cup. (4 to 8 servings)

➤ Approx. per serving: 10 calories; 0.2 grams of fat

Black Bean Soup

1 pound dried black beans, rinsed
8 cups water
1 tablespoon corn oil or safflower oil
2 medium onions, chopped
1 green bell pepper, chopped
1 carrot, peeled and shredded
4 cloves garlic, minced
2 teaspoons fresh oregano or
    1 teaspoon dried oregano
1/2 teaspoon cumin seed, crushed
1 teaspoon salt (optional)
1/2 teaspoon pepper
2 tablespoons fresh lemon juice
2 cups brown rice, cooked
1 cup low-fat plain yogurt
Chopped green onions

Place beans and water in a large saucepan and boil for 2 minutes over medium-high heat. Remove from heat, cover, and let stand for 1 hour. Heat oil in a skillet over medium heat. Add onions, green pepper, carrot, garlic, oregano, and cumin. Sauté until vegetables are soft, then stir into beans, adding salt and pepper. Bring to a boil, reduce heat and cover. Simmer for 1-1/2 to 2 hours or until beans are very tender, stirring occasionally. Stir in lemon juice. Spoon rice into soup bowls and ladle bean soup over rice. Top with yogurt and green onions. Makes 8 servings.

➤ Approx. per serving: 314 calories; 6 grams of fat

Soups

Bean and Basil Soup

3 quarts water
2 cups onions, chopped
2 cups carrots, peeled and diced
1 cup potato, peeled and diced
1 teaspoon salt (optional)
2 cups fresh green beans, chopped
     or 2 10-ounce packages frozen
     green beans
1 cup macaroni, uncooked
1/4 cup tomato paste
1/4 cup Parmesan cheese, freshly
     grated
2 tablespoons fresh basil or
     2 teaspoons dried basil
3 cloves garlic, mashed
1 16-ounce can white beans, drained

Combine water, onions, carrots, potato, and salt in a stockpot and cook over medium heat until vegetables are almost tender. Add green beans and macaroni. Cook until vegetables and macaroni are tender. Combine tomato paste, cheese, basil, and garlic in a small bowl and mix well. Vigorously stir 2 cups of hot soup into cheese mixture then stir cheese mixture into hot soup. Add beans and cook until heated through. Ladle soup into soup bowls. Makes 6 servings.

➤ Approx. per serving: 306 calories; 5 grams of fat

Cream of Broccoli Soup

3 cups broccoli florets and peeled
     stems, finely chopped
1-1/2 cups water
1 tablespoon corn oil margarine
1/2 cup onion, chopped
1 tablespoon all-purpose flour
3 cups 1% low-fat milk
1/2 teaspoon salt (optional)
1/2 teaspoon pepper
1/4 teaspoon paprika
1/4 teaspoon celery seed
1/8 teaspoon cayenne pepper

Combine broccoli and water in a 3-quart saucepan and bring to a boil. Lower heat, cover and simmer for 10 minutes. Drain, saving liquid. Melt margarine in a larger saucepan over low heat and add onion and sauté until soft. Add flour and continue to cook for several seconds, stirring constantly. Stir in reserved liquid and cook until thickened. Add milk, broccoli, salt, black pepper, paprika, celery seed, and cayenne pepper, mixing well. Heat to serving temperature over low heat. Makes 6 servings.

➤ Approx. per serving: 101 calories; 3 grams of fat

Fresh Spring Vegetable Soup

8 small new red potatoes, cut in half

1 small bag baby carrots, ends removed

2 bunches radishes, stems removed

1 cup asparagus tips

1 cup tender green beans, cut in half

1 bunch green onions, washed, peeled, and chopped

3 pounds fresh tomatoes, chopped

4 cloves garlic, chopped

2 tablespoons butter

1/4 cup chopped fresh dill

1 teaspoon salt

1 teaspoon pepper

4 cups vegetable broth, either home-made or canned

Heat butter in large pan and add garlic, green onions, and dill. Cook until tender and add tomatoes, vegetable broth, salt, and pepper and simmer for 30 minutes. While ingredients are simmering, boil new potatoes in water for 10 minutes, remove and set aside. Add carrots to boiling water and cook 7 minutes. Remove carrots from water and set aside. Add radishes and boil for one minute and drain. Stir asparagus tips, green beans, and cooked vegetables into broth mixture and cook for an additional 10 minutes. Serve immediately. Makes 8 to 10 servings.

➤ Approx. per serving: 169 calories; 4.5 grams of fat

Salads

Lemon-Broccoli Salad

2 pounds fresh broccoli
3 tablespoons vegetable or chicken
  broth, either homemade or canned
3 tablespoons fresh lemon juice
1 tablespoon olive oil
1/2 teaspoon salt (optional)
1/4 teaspoon pepper

Separate broccoli into florets, peel stems, and slice crosswise. In a covered saucepan over medium heat, steam broccoli in a small amount of water for 5 minutes or until tender-crisp. Drain, reserving liquid for soup. Plunge broccoli into a bowl of ice water immediately to stop cooking process, then drain. Combine broth, lemon juice, olive oil, salt, and pepper in a blender and process until mixed. Place broccoli into a salad bowl, add dressing, and toss to coat. Marinate in refrigerator for several hours. Makes 6 servings.

➤ Approx. per serving: 65 calories; 3 grams of fat

Traditional Broccoli Salad

2 medium heads of broccoli
Non-fat cooking spray
6 slices turkey bacon
2 tablespoons red-wine vinegar
3/4 cup reduced-fat mayonnaise
1/4 cup sugar
1/8 teaspoon celery seed
1/2 small red onion, chopped

Chop the broccoli heads into bite-size pieces. In a covered saucepan over medium heat, steam broccoli in a small amount of water for 8 minutes or until just tender. Plunge broccoli into a bowl of ice water immediately to stop cooking process, then drain. Set aside. Spray the bottom of a skillet with cooking spray. Cook bacon until crisp. Blot bacon in paper towels to remove grease and crumble into small bits. In a medium bowl combine vinegar, mayonnaise, sugar, and celery seed. Add onion and bacon and mix well. Add broccoli and toss lightly to cover. Makes 8 servings.

➤ Approx. per serving: 130 calories; 10 grams of fat

Salads

Broccoli-Vegetable Salad

1 medium head broccoli
1 medium cucumber, peeled, grated, and drained
2 carrots, peeled and grated

Dressing
3/4 cup low-fat plain yogurt
1/4 cup scallions, chopped
1/4 cup green bell pepper, chopped
1 tablespoon fresh lemon juice
1 teaspoon fresh dill or 1/2 teaspoon dried dillweed
1/4 teaspoon salt (optional)

Break broccoli into florets. Peel and thinly slice stems. Place broccoli florets and stems into a saucepan with boiling water. Boil for 5 minutes, then drain. Combine broccoli, cucumber, and carrots in a salad bowl. Dressing: Combine yogurt, scallions, green pepper, lemon juice, dill, and salt in a small bowl and mix well. Add dressing and toss gently. Serve at room temperature or chilled. Makes 6 servings.

➤ Approx. per serving: 47 calories; 0.8 grams of fat

Broccoli Pasta Salad

1 large bunch broccoli
2 cups cooked whole-wheat fusilli or shell pasta, drained
1 large red bell pepper, seeded and sliced
2 stalks celery, chopped
1 medium yellow squash, chopped
1/2 cup scallions, chopped
1/2 cup cherry tomatoes, halved

Dressing
1/3 cup white wine vinegar
2 tablespoons olive oil
2 tablespoons fresh lemon juice
2 tablespoons fresh parsley, minced
1 tablespoon fresh basil, chopped or 1/2 teaspoon dried basil
1 teaspoon dry mustard
1 clove garlic, pressed

Divide broccoli into florets, then peel and slice stems. Combine pasta, broccoli, red pepper, celery, squash, scallions, and cherry tomatoes in a large bowl. Dressing: Combine ingredients in a small bowl. Whisk until blended. Add dressing and toss until mixed. Chill salad slightly before serving. Makes 6 to 8 servings.

➤ Approx. per serving: 137 calories; 5 grams of fat

Salads

Cherry Tomatoes with Parsley and Garlic

2 pints cherry tomatoes (about 40),
    cut into halves
4 teaspoons fresh lemon juice
1 tablespoon olive oil
2 cloves garlic, minced
1/2 teaspoon salt (optional)
2/3 cup fresh parsley, coarsely
    chopped

Preheat oven to 350°. Combine tomatoes, lemon juice, olive oil, garlic, and salt in a medium baking dish and toss lightly. Bake for 5 minutes or until heated through. Stir in parsley just before serving. Makes 8 servings.

➤ Approx. per serving: 30 calories; 2 grams of fat

Julienne Vegetable Salad with Lemon Dressing

1 cup carrots, cut into julienne strips
1 cup zucchini, cut into julienne strips
1 cup green beans, cut into 1-1/2-inch
    pieces
1 cup celery, cut into julienne strips
Salt and freshly ground pepper to taste

Combine carrots, zucchini, green beans, and celery in a medium bowl. Mix, then add Lemon Dressing (below) and continue tossing to mix. Add salt and pepper. Cover and refrigerate until serving time. Makes 6 (2/3 cup) servings.

Lemon Dressing
1/4 cup fresh lemon juice
2 tablespoons fresh parsley, chopped
    or 1 tablespoon dried parsley
2 tablespoons green onion tops or
    fresh chives, chopped
1 tablespoon olive oil
1 clove garlic, minced

Combine lemon juice, parsley, green onion tops, olive oil, and garlic in a small bowl and mix well with whisk.

➤ Approx. per serving: 45 calories; 2.5 grams of fat

Salads

Spinach and Grapefruit Salad

2 large bunches fresh spinach
3 medium red grapefruit
1 tablespoon sesame seed
2 tablespoons vegetable or chicken
   broth, either homemade or canned
1 tablespoon corn oil or safflower oil
1 tablespoon white wine vinegar
1 tablespoon fresh lemon juice
1 tablespoon honey
1/4 teaspoon salt (optional)
1/4 teaspoon pepper

Wash spinach, pat dry, and discard stems. Peel and section grapefruit and cut into bite-sized pieces. Toast sesame seeds in an ungreased skillet over medium heat until golden brown, tossing frequently. Combine broth, oil, vinegar, lemon juice, honey, salt, and pepper in a blender and process until mixed. Combine spinach and grapefruit in a salad bowl. Add dressing, toss to mix, and sprinkle with sesame seed. Makes 8 servings.

➤ Approx. per serving: 80 calories; 3 grams of fat

Spinach-Mushroom Salad

1 pound fresh spinach leaves, washed,
   dried and torn into bite-sized pieces
1/2 pound fresh mushrooms, sliced
1/3 cup red wine vinegar
1 tablespoon Worcestershire sauce
2 teaspoons corn oil or safflower oil
1 clove garlic, crushed
1/4 teaspoon freshly ground pepper
1 hard-boiled egg, chopped

Combine spinach and mushrooms in a large salad bowl, then set aside. Combine vinegar, Worcestershire sauce, oil, garlic, and pepper in a small saucepan and bring to a boil over medium-high heat. Remove from heat and allow to cool. Pour dressing over spinach and mushrooms and toss to mix. Garnish with egg. Serve immediately. Makes 6 servings.

➤ Approx. per serving: 54 calories; 3 grams of fat

Sally Kellerman

Sally Kellerman's career goes deep, with stage, screen, recording, and television credits. She's been nominated for several awards, including an Academy Award and Golden Globe Award for her roll as "Hot Lips" Houlihan in the motion picture **M*A*S*H.** Sally was also nominated for best actress at the Monte Carlo Film Festival for her performance in the title role of PBS' **The Big Blonde** by Dorothy Parker. As a singer, she has been recording and performing live for more than 25 years.

Spinach Salad Supreme

2 medium red potatoes
1 large or 2 medium bunches
    fresh spinach
1 hard-boiled egg, chopped
2 tablespoons sunflower seeds,
    shelled
1 scallion, sliced
2 carrots, grated

Dressing
1/2 cup low-fat plain yogurt
1 tablespoon red wine vinegar
1 tablespoon scallion, finely chopped
1/2 teaspoon fresh tarragon or
    1/4 teaspoon dried tarragon
1/2 teaspoon granulated sugar
1/2 teaspoon fresh basil or
    1/4 teaspoon dried basil
Salt and pepper to taste

In a small saucepan over medium heat, steam potatoes in a small amount of water until tender. Allow potatoes to cool, then chop. Wash and dry spinach. Place spinach into a plastic bag and chill in refrigerator until crisp. Then place spinach onto a serving platter and arrange potatoes, egg, sunflower seed, scallion, and carrots in a circular pattern over spinach. Dressing: Combine yogurt, vinegar, scallion, tarragon, sugar, basil, salt, and pepper in a blender. Process until blended. Drizzle dressing over salad. Serve immediately. Makes 6 servings.

➤ Approx. per serving: 117 calories; 3 grams of fat

Salads

Low-Fat Waldorf Salad

3 medium tart apples, peeled, cored
    and cut in 1/2-inch cubes
1 tablespoon lemon juice
1 cup seedless red or green grapes
2 medium stalks celery, chopped
2 medium green onions, finely
    chopped
2 tablespoons reduced-calorie
    mayonnaise
2 tablespoons plain low-fat yogurt
2 tablespoons apple juice
1/4 teaspoon celery seeds
1 large bunch watercress, stems
    removed
2 tablespoons chopped walnuts

In a large bowl toss the apples with the lemon juice. Add grapes, celery, and green onion and toss again. In a small bowl combine mayonnaise, yogurt, apple juice, and celery seeds and mix well. Spoon over the fruit mixture and toss gently. Wash the watercress, pat dry on paper towels, and arrange on four individual salad plates. Mount the fruit mixture on top and sprinkle with walnuts. Makes 4 servings.

➤ Approx. per serving: 149 calories; 5 grams of fat

Coleslaw Dijon

6 cups cabbage, grated
4 cups fresh or frozen corn, cooked
    and drained
2 carrots, grated
2 stalks celery, sliced
1/4 cup vegetable or chicken broth,
    either homemade or canned
2 tablespoons corn oil or safflower oil
2 tablespoons white wine vinegar
2 teaspoons Dijon mustard
1/2 teaspoon salt (optional)
1/2 teaspoon celery seed
2 scallions, sliced

Combine cabbage, corn, carrots, and celery in a large bowl. In a separate small bowl, combine broth, oil, vinegar, mustard, salt, and celery seed, mixing well. Stir in scallions. Add to cabbage mixture and toss gently to mix. Chill for several hours to allow flavors to develop. Makes 12 servings.

➤ Approx. per serving: 30 calories; 3 grams of fat

Yogurt Tomato Salad

1 medium cucumber, peeled
1 teaspoon salt (optional)
2 medium tomatoes, cored, cut into
    1/2-inch cubes and drained
1 tablespoon onion, finely chopped
1 cup low-fat plain yogurt
1/4 cup fresh parsley, chopped
2 tablespoons fresh cilantro
    (coriander), chopped
1 teaspoon cumin

Halve cucumber lengthwise, remove seeds, then slice thinly. Place cucumber into a bowl, sprinkle with salt, and let stand for half an hour. Drain, squeezing cucumber slightly to remove excess moisture. Add tomatoes and onion. Mix yogurt, parsley, cilantro, and cumin in a separate bowl. Pour over vegetables and gently toss. Cover and chill until serving time. Makes 4 (3/4 cup) servings.

➤ Approx. per serving: 61 calories; 1 gram of fat

Napa Oriental Slaw

1 medium head Napa (Chinese)
    cabbage
2 tablespoons salt
2 or 3 carrots, peeled and shredded
2 tablespoons corn oil or safflower oil
2 tablespoons water
1/2 cup green onions, chopped
1 teaspoon fresh ginger root, minced
1/4 cup granulated sugar
1/4 cup red wine vinegar
1 teaspoon dried red pepper, crushed

Cut core from cabbage, then rinse and drain leaves. Cut leaves into shreds and place into a large bowl. Sprinkle with salt, add enough water to cover cabbage, and let stand for 1 hour. Drain, rinse cabbage, and squeeze dry. Place shredded cabbage onto a platter and sprinkle with carrots. Heat oil and water in a saucepan over medium heat and add green onions and ginger root. Cook for 2 minutes. Mix sugar and vinegar in a small bowl, then add with red pepper to green onion mixture. Pour mixture over cabbage and carrots, tossing lightly. Makes 4 to 6 servings.

➤ Approx. per serving: 158 calories; 5 grams of fat

Salads

Dilled Carrot Salad

1-1/2 pounds carrots, sliced
1/4 cup fresh parsley, chopped
3 tablespoons vegetable or chicken
    broth, either homemade or canned
2 tablespoons white wine vinegar
1 tablespoon olive oil
2 teaspoons granulated sugar
2 teaspoons fresh dill, chopped or
    1 teaspoon dried dillweed
1/2 teaspoon salt (optional)
1/4 teaspoon pepper

Steam carrots in a saucepan over medium heat until tender-crisp. Drain and place carrots into a large bowl. Combine parsley, broth, vinegar, olive oil, sugar, dill, salt, and pepper in a small bowl and mix well. Pour mixture over warm carrots. Marinate in refrigerator for several hours. Makes 6 servings.

➤ Approx. per serving: 67 calories; 3 grams of fat

Cucumber Salad

2 cucumbers
1 tablespoon salt
1 red onion, sliced
3/4 cup vinegar
1/4 cup granulated sugar
Salt and freshly ground pepper to taste
Fresh dill, chopped

Thinly slice unpeeled cucumbers. Place cucumber slices into a bowl and sprinkle with 1 tablespoon of salt. Let stand for 1 hour. Drain, pat cucumber slices dry, then place into a bowl with red onion slices. Combine vinegar and sugar in a small saucepan and cook over low heat, stirring constantly; or in a microwave-safe dish, heat in microwave until sugar is dissolved. Allow to cool and pour mixture over cucumbers. Let stand for 30 to 60 minutes. Drain and place cucumber slices into a salad bowl. Season with salt and pepper. Garnish with dill. Makes 6 to 8 servings.

➤ Approx. per serving: 53 calories; 0.2 grams of fat

Salads

Orange Salad

2 cups carrots, shredded
1 orange, peeled and chopped
1/4 cup orange juice
2 tablespoons low-fat plain yogurt
2 tablespoons raisins
Dash of freshly grated nutmeg
Spinach or lettuce leaves

Combine carrots and orange in a medium bowl. In a separate small bowl, combine orange juice and yogurt, mixing well. Pour over carrot and orange mixture. Add raisins and nutmeg. Toss to mix and chill in refrigerator. Arrange spinach leaves on serving plates and spoon salad over leaves. Makes 4 (1/2 to 3/4 cup) servings.

➤ Approx. per serving: 65 calories; 0.3 grams of fat

Carrot and Orange Salad

4 carrots, grated
2 oranges, sectioned and cut into
    bite-sized pieces
2 cups watercress, chopped
3 tablespoons red wine vinegar
3 tablespoons orange juice
1 tablespoon olive oil
1 tablespoon honey
1-1/2 teaspoons Dijon mustard
1/4 teaspoon salt (optional)

Place carrots into a bowl. Add boiling water to cover carrots, then let stand for 5 minutes. Drain and squeeze carrots dry. Allow carrots to cool, then combine with oranges in a bowl. Rinse watercress and pat dry. Discard stems, chop watercress, and mix with carrots and oranges. Combine vinegar, orange juice, olive oil, honey, mustard, and salt in a small bowl, mixing well. Pour over carrot mixture and continue to mix. Marinate for 2 hours or longer. Makes 6 servings.

➤ Approx. per serving: 74 calories; 2 grams of fat

Vivica Fox

Vivica Fox was discovered while having lunch at the Sunset Boulevard restaurant and the rest is Hollywood history. Her film debut was in **Born on the Fourth of July**. And her performance in **Independence Day** earned her rave reviews. Other film credits include **Set It Off**, **Booty Call**, **Batman & Robin**, **Soul Food**, and **Double Take**. She also has a successful television career, starring in the shows **Getting Personal** and **City of Angels** as well as many notable guest appearances.

Perfect Caesar Salad

1/2 cup fat-free mayonnaise
1/4 cup skim milk
1/4 cup grated Parmesan cheese
2 teaspoons Dijon mustard
2 teaspoons lemon juice
1 anchovy filet, mashed
1 garlic clove, crushed
1 teaspoon fresh parsley
1/4 teaspoon pepper
1 bunch Romaine lettuce
1 cup toasted croutons
Lemon slices for garnish

Combine mayonnaise, milk, Parmesan cheese, mustard, lemon juice, anchovy filet, garlic, parsley, and pepper in a small bowl and mix well. Cover and refrigerate before serving. Wash the lettuce and shred into a bowl. Add the dressing and croutons and toss well. Sprinkle with freshly ground pepper and decorate with lemon slices before serving immediately.

➤ Approx. per serving: 207 calories; 7 grams of fat

Salads

New Potato Salad

6 medium-large red skin potatoes
1/2 cup low-fat cottage cheese
1/2 cup low-fat plain yogurt
1/4 cup fresh chives or green onions,
  finely chopped
1 teaspoon salt (optional)
Freshly ground pepper to taste

Scrub unpeeled potatoes and cut into halves or quarters. Place potatoes into a large saucepan with water to cover and cook over medium heat until tender. Drain and pat dry then cut into 1/2-inch cubes and allow to cool. In a blender combine cottage cheese and yogurt and process until creamy. Combine all ingredients in a large bowl and chill until serving time. Makes 10 (1/2 cup) servings.

➤ Approx. per serving: 89 calories; 0.5 grams of fat

Black Bean, Rice, and Chicken Salad

2 teaspoons olive oil
1/4 cup lime juice
1/2 cup cilantro, chopped
1/4 cup Italian parsley
1/4 cup red wine vinegar
1/2 teaspoon granulated sugar
2 tablespoons cumin
1/2 teaspoon red pepper flakes
12 ounces boneless, skinless
  chicken breast
1 cup fat-free chicken broth, either
  homemade or canned
1 cup rice, cooked
1 16-ounce can black beans, rinsed
  and drained
1/2 cup green onions, chopped
1 cup red bell pepper, chopped
1/2 avocado, chopped

Combine oil and next 7 ingredients in a small bowl and set aside. In a large pan over low heat, simmer chicken breasts in broth until cooked, then cut into 1/2-inch pieces. Remove chicken and combine with rice, black beans, green onions, and red pepper in a large bowl. Pour dressing over chicken mixture and refrigerate for at least 2 hours. Stir chopped avocado into salad just before serving. Makes 6 servings.

➤ Approx. per serving: 267 calories; 6 grams of fat

Salads

Black-Eyed Peas Vinaigrette

1 pound dried black-eyed peas
1/4 cup vegetable or skimmed chicken
    broth, either homemade or canned
1/4 cup red wine vinegar
1 tablespoon olive oil
2 tablespoons fresh oregano, chopped
    or 1 tablespoon dried oregano
1-1/2 teaspoons Dijon mustard
2 cloves garlic, minced
1 teaspoon salt (optional)
1/2 teaspoon pepper
1 cup fresh carrots, grated
1 cup onion, chopped
1 cup fresh parsley, chopped

Cook black-eyed peas according to package directions. Combine broth, vinegar, olive oil, oregano, mustard, garlic, salt, and pepper in a small bowl, mixing well. Let stand while peas cook. Drain peas and combine with carrots, onion, and parsley, tossing to mix. Add dressing and continue to toss until coated. Cover and marinate in refrigerator for several hours to overnight. Makes 12 servings.

➤ Approx. per serving: 79 calories; 2 grams of fat

Colorful Pasta Salad

1-1/3 cups whole-wheat corkscrew pasta
1-1/3 cups tricolored corkscrew pasta
1 teaspoon crushed red pepper, seeded
1 medium red pepper, cut into thin strips
1 medium yellow squash or zucchini,
    halved lengthwise and sliced
1 10-ounce package frozen peas,
    thawed or 1-1/2 cups cooked fresh
    peas, cooled
1 3-ounce can pitted olives, drained
1/4 cup Parmesan cheese, shredded
1/4 cup almonds, chopped
1/2 cup green onion, sliced
2 tablespoons fresh tarragon, oregano,
    basil, or dill, snipped
1 8-ounce bottle fat-free Italian dressing
1 cup celery, chopped

Boil water with crushed red pepper in a medium saucepan and cook pasta al dente according to package directions. Rinse pasta with cool water, drain thoroughly, and cool to room temperature. In a large mixing bowl, combine pasta, pepper, yellow squash or zucchini, peas, olives, Parmesan cheese, almonds, green onion, and herbs. Add dressing to pasta mixture and toss gently to mix. Cover and chill for 2 hours. Makes 8 to 10 servings.

➤ Approx. per serving: 230 calories; 5 grams of fat

Marinated Beef and Pasta Salad

1 pound mostaccioli, ziti, or other
    medium pasta shape, uncooked
2 tablespoons vegetable oil
3 tablespoons lemon juice
2 tablespoons red wine vinegar
1/2 cup fresh parsley, chopped
1 tablespoon dried oregano or fresh
    oregano, chopped
1 tablespoon dried thyme or fresh
    thyme, chopped
2 tablespoons Dijon mustard
10 large mushrooms, cleaned and
    sliced
2 cups cooked flank steak or roast
    beef, cut into julienne strips
2 cups snow peas, chopped in half
1 red bell pepper, seeded and cut into
    julienne strips
1 yellow bell pepper, seeded and cut
    into julienne strips
Salt and freshly ground pepper to taste

Boil 4 cups of water in a large saucepan, add pasta, and cook until al dente according to package directions, then drain. Combine vegetable oil, lemon juice, vinegar, parsley, oregano, thyme, mustard, mushrooms, and beef in a large bowl and mix well. Add snow peas and peppers, mixing thoroughly. Add pasta and toss to mix. Serve immediately or refrigerate for 1 hour and serve cold. Makes 10 to 12 servings.

➤ Approx. per serving: 290 calories; 6 grams of fat

White Bean, Red Onion, and Tomato Salad

1 16-ounce can white beans
1 tablespoon olive oil
Salt and freshly ground pepper to taste
2 large ripe tomatoes, seeded and
    diced
1/4 cup red onion, finely diced
2 tablespoons fresh oregano or
    2 teaspoons dried oregano

Place beans into a small bowl. Add olive oil, salt, and pepper, mixing gently. Add tomatoes, onion, and oregano and toss to mix. Makes 4 servings.

➤ Approx. per serving: 174 calories; 6 grams of fat

Salad Niçoise

1 large head Romaine lettuce
3 medium new potatoes (red preferred)
1/2 pound fresh green beans
1/4 cup red wine vinegar
5 tablespoons vegetable or chicken
    broth, either homemade or canned
1-1/2 scallions, sliced
2 tablespoons olive oil
1-1/2 teaspoons Dijon mustard
1/2 teaspoon salt (optional)
1/4 teaspoon pepper
Lettuce leaves
2 7-ounce cans water-packed tuna
    (albacore preferred), drained
3 medium tomatoes, quartered
1 hard-boiled egg, chopped
1 tablespoon capers, drained
12 radishes, washed and sliced
Parsley sprigs for garnish

Rinse lettuce, drain, and refrigerate until crisp. Cook potatoes in a saucepan or steamer over medium heat until tender. Drain, cut into bite-sized pieces, and place into a bowl. Steam green beans until tender-crisp in a saucepan or steamer. Drain, cut into bite-sized pieces, and place into a separate bowl. Combine vinegar, broth, scallions, olive oil, mustard, salt, and pepper in a small bowl and mix well. Pour half the dressing over potatoes and remaining half over green beans. Marinate for 1 hour or longer. Drain potatoes and green beans, reserving dressing. Arrange and cover a serving platter with lettuce leaves. Mound potatoes in center, arrange green beans in circle around potatoes, and tuna in circle around beans. Place tomato quarters, egg, capers, radishes, and parsley around edge according to your visual taste and shape of platter. Drizzle reserved dressing over salad. Serve immediately. Makes 10 servings.

➤ Approx. per serving: 187 calories; 6 grams of fat

Minestrone Salad

12 ounces whole-wheat elbow pasta
1 tablespoon fresh lemon juice
1 16-ounce can Great Northern beans,
    drained and rinsed
1-1/2 cups no-oil Italian salad dressing
2 cups fresh broccoli florets
1 cup zucchini, cut into rounds and
    sliced into strips
1 cup fresh carrots, cut into rounds
1/2 cup green onions with tops,
    chopped
1/2 cup red and/or green bell pepper,
    seeded and chopped
Lettuce leaves
Tomato slices for garnish

Cook pasta according to package directions, adding lemon juice to water, then drain. Mix pasta with beans and salad dressing in a large bowl and refrigerate overnight. In a saucepan or steamer, steam broccoli until tender-crisp. Place broccoli immediately into a bowl of ice water to stop cooking process, then drain well. Add broccoli, zucchini, carrots, green onions, and bell pepper to pasta mixture and mix gently. Let stand for 2 to 3 hours before serving. Arrange lettuce on salad plates and spoon salad onto lettuce. Garnish with tomato slices. Makes 8 servings.

➤ Approx. per serving: 326 calories; 6 grams of fat

Marinated Black Bean Salad

1 pound dried black beans
3 cups brown rice, cooked
1 cup onion, chopped
1 cup green bell pepper, seeded and
    chopped
1/4 cup fresh cilantro (coriander) or
    parsley, chopped
2 tablespoons olive oil
3 tablespoons red wine vinegar
3 tablespoons vegetable or chicken
    broth, either homemade or canned
2 teaspoons fresh thyme or
    1 teaspoon dried thyme
2 cloves garlic, minced
1/2 teaspoon pepper

Cook beans according to package directions and drain well. Place beans, rice, onion, and green pepper into a large bowl. In a separate small bowl, place cilantro, oil, vinegar, broth, thyme, garlic, and pepper and mix well. Add to bean mixture, toss gently, and marinate in refrigerator for several hours. Makes 12 servings.

➤ Approx. per serving: 153 calories; 4 grams of fat

Salads

Garbanzo Bean Salad

1/2 pound dried garbanzo beans
1/2 cup celery, chopped
1/2 cup green bell pepper, seeded
   and chopped
1/2 cup green onions, sliced
1/4 cup fresh parsley, chopped
1 2-ounce jar diced pimento, drained
2/3 cup reduced-calorie Italian salad
   dressing
1/4 teaspoon black pepper, freshly
   ground
Lettuce leaves

Sort and wash beans, then place into a large heavy saucepan. Add enough water to cover by 2 inches and let stand overnight. Drain, add fresh water to cover and bring to a boil over medium-high heat. Reduce heat, cover, and simmer for 1 hour or until beans are tender. Drain and allow beans to cool. Combine beans, celery, green pepper, green onions, parsley, and pimento in a large bowl. Add salad dressing and pepper, mixing well. Cover and chill for several hours to overnight, stirring occasionally. Arrange lettuce leaves on salad plate and spoon salad over lettuce leaves using slotted spoon. Makes 8 servings.

➤ Approx. per serving: 137 calories; 4 grams of fat

Almond Chicken Salad

4 cups cooked skinless boneless
   chicken breast, chopped
1 cup celery, chopped
1 cup seedless green grapes, halved
1 teaspoon salt (optional)
1/4 teaspoon pepper
1/2 cup fat-free mayonnaise
1/2 cup low-fat plain yogurt
1/4 cup almonds, chopped and
   toasted
Lettuce

Combine chicken, celery, grapes, salt, and pepper in a large bowl. In a small bowl, blend mayonnaise and yogurt, then add to chicken mixture and toss to mix. Chill for several hours. Add almonds just before serving and toss lightly. Arrange lettuce on salad plates and spoon salad onto lettuce. Makes 8 to 10 servings.

➤ Approx. per serving: 101 calories; 3 grams of fat

Salads

Springtime Chicken Salad

2 tablespoons lemon juice
1/2 cup reduced-fat mayonnaise
2 tablespoons parsley
1/4 cup slivered almonds, toasted
1 cup celery, chopped
3 cups chicken breast, cooked
  and chopped
1 cup apple, chopped or
  1 cup grapes, sliced
Salt and pepper to taste
Romaine or red leaf lettuce

Combine lemon juice, mayonnaise, almonds, celery, chicken, apple or grapes, salt, and pepper in a large bowl and mix well. Place lettuce onto 4 plates and place chicken mixture on top. Sprinkle with parsley. Makes 4 servings.

➤ Approx. per serving: 329 calories; 11 grams of fat

Chicken Salad with Melon

1 small honeydew or cantaloupe
6 cups cooked skinless chicken,
  cubed
2 cups celery, chopped
2 cups seedless green or red grapes
1 cup water chestnuts, sliced
  (optional)
1/2 cup low-fat cottage cheese
1 to 2 tablespoons 1% low-fat milk
1/2 cup low-fat plain yogurt
1 teaspoon curry powder
Salt and freshly ground pepper
  to taste

Divide melon, discard seed, and scoop out pulp with a melon baller. Combine melon balls, chicken, celery, grapes, and water chestnuts in a large bowl. Place cottage cheese into a blender and process until smooth, adding enough milk to make smooth. Combine blended cottage cheese, yogurt, and curry powder in a small bowl, mixing well. Fold gently into chicken mixture and season with salt and pepper to taste. Makes 10 cups.

➤ Approx. per cup: 146 calories; 2 grams of fat

Salads

Mexican Chicken Salad

1 medium head lettuce
1 15-ounce can kidney beans, drained
1 cup cooked skinless chicken,
    chopped
1/2 cup green bell pepper, seeded
    and chopped
2 scallions, chopped
1/2 cup fresh cilantro (coriander),
    chopped
3 tablespoons chicken broth, either
    homemade or canned
2 tablespoons corn oil or safflower oil
2 tablespoons red wine vinegar
1 tablespoon fresh lime juice
1-1/2 teaspoons granulated sugar
1 clove of garlic, minced
3/4 teaspoon chili powder
1/2 teaspoon salt (optional)

Rinse lettuce, then drain, pat dry, and shred. Place lettuce, beans, chicken, green pepper, and scallions into a salad bowl. Combine cilantro, broth, oil, vinegar, lime juice, sugar, garlic, chili powder, and salt in a blender and process until well mixed. Pour over chicken mixture just before serving and toss lightly. Makes 8 servings.

➤ Approx. per serving: 138 calories; 5 grams of fat

Chicken Salad Supreme

2-1/2 cups skinless chicken, boiled
    and diced
1 cup celery
1 cup white seedless grapes, sliced
1/2 cup slivered almonds, toasted
1/2 cup fat-free mayonnaise
1 cup fat-free plain yogurt
1/2 teaspoon curry powder
1 teaspoon salt
1 teaspoon pepper

Combine chicken, celery, grapes, almonds, curry powder, mayonnaise, yogurt, salt, and pepper in a large bowl and mix well. Cover and chill in refrigerator. Serve over lettuce or in half of a honeydew melon. Makes 4 servings.

➤ Approx. per serving: 228 calories; 8 grams of fat

Salads

Old Fashioned Rice Salad

1 head of lettuce
3 cups cooked rice
2 hard boiled eggs
1/2 cup reduced-fat mayonnaise
1/2 cup chopped sweet pickle
1/2 cup green onions, chopped
1 teaspoon salt
1 teaspoon pepper
1 tablespoon mustard

Wash lettuce and remove stem. Set aside lettuce leaves. Chop eggs into small pieces and combine rice, eggs, mayonnaise, pickle, onions, salt, pepper, and mustard in a medium bowl. Combine well. Serve on a bed of lettuce leaves. Makes 6 servings.

➤ Approx. per serving: 250 calories; 9 grams of fat

Wild Rice and Black-Eyed Pea Salad

5 cups wild rice, cooked
1 16-ounce can black-eyed peas, drained
1/2 cup green bell pepper, seeded and chopped
1/2 cup celery, chopped
1/2 cup cucumber, chopped
1/2 cup water chestnuts, chopped
1/2 cup niblet corn, drained
1 tomato, chopped
1/2 cup low-fat salad dressing of choice

Cook wild rice according to package directions. Combine black-eyed peas, green pepper, celery, cucumber, water chestnuts, corn, and wild rice in a large bowl, mixing well. Fold in tomato and salad dressing and serve. Makes 6 to 8 servings.

➤ Approx. per serving: 141 calories; 0.6 grams of fat

Salads

Middle East Bulgur Salad

2 pounds bulgur wheat
5 cups of warm water
1 teaspoon cayenne pepper
1/4 teaspoon crushed red pepper
1 teaspoon salt
1/4 teaspoon black pepper
1 large onion, chopped
1 bunch green onions, chopped
1/2 pound cucumber, peeled and
    chopped
1 pound tomatoes, chopped
1 bunch fresh parsley
Juice of 2 lemons
1/4 cup olive oil

In a large bowl place bulgur wheat and water. Set aside for at least 2 hours, until the bulgur wheat is soft and the water all soaked up. Add cayenne and red pepper, salt, and black pepper to bowl and mix well. Mix in onions, green onions, cucumber, tomatoes, and parsley. Combine lemon juice and olive oil in a small bowl and stir well. Serve salad on plates and drizzle dressing over top. Makes 8 servings.

➤ Approx. per serving: 640 calories; 12 grams of fat

Tuna Pasta Salad

2 cups fettuccine, curly spinach
    noodles, or vegetable nonegg
    noodles
1 7-ounce can water-packed white
    tuna or albacore, drained
1 7-ounce can water chestnuts, diced
4 green onions, diced
1 stalk celery, diced
1/2 cup low-fat plain yogurt
1/4 cup low-fat mayonnaise
1 tablespoon light soy sauce
1 clove garlic, finely minced
1 teaspoon fresh parsley or
    1/2 teaspoon dried parsley

Cook and drain fettuccine according to package directions. Combine fettuccine, tuna, water chestnuts, green onions, and celery in a large bowl. In a small bowl, combine yogurt, mayonnaise, soy sauce, garlic, and parsley, mixing well. Add to tuna mixture and toss lightly. Chill in refrigerator before serving. Makes 4 servings.

➤ Approx. per serving: 407 calories; 6 grams of fat

Salads

Summertime Shrimp Salad

5 quarts water
1 cup celery leaves
2 tablespoons salt
1/2 cup pickling salt
Juice and rind of 2 lemons
2 small onions, chopped
5 pounds medium shrimp
4 small onions, sliced
14 bay leaves
1/4 cup vegetable oil
1/2 cup red wine vinegar
1 teaspoon salt
1 tablespoon and 2 teaspoons celery
  seed
1 small jar capers, drained
Dash of hot pepper sauce
Red leaf or Romaine lettuce

Combine first 6 ingredients in a large pot, and bring to a boil over medium-high heat. Add shrimp and cook for 5 minutes. Drain well and rinse shrimp in cold water. Peel and devein cooked shrimp. Combine shrimp, sliced onions, and bay leaves in a large shallow dish. In a small bowl, combine vegetable oil, vinegar, salt, celery seed, capers, and hot pepper sauce, mixing well. Pour over shrimp, cover and chill overnight. Remove shrimp from marinade with a slotted spoon, and serve on a bed of lettuce. Makes 8 to 10 servings.

➤ Approx. per serving: 310 calories; 10 grams of fat

Summer Fruit Salad with Mozzarella Cheese

1-1/2 cups honeydew melon, diced
1-1/2 cups cantaloupe, diced
1 cup fresh peaches, sliced
1 cup seedless grapes
1 cup pitted dates, chopped
3/4 cup part-skim mozzarella cheese
1/2 cup almonds, chopped
1/3 cup honey
1/3 cup frozen limeade concentrate,
  thawed
1 tablespoon corn oil or safflower oil
2 medium bananas, chopped
Romaine or other lettuce leaves
Fresh strawberries

Combine melons, peaches, grapes, dates, cheese, and almonds in a large bowl and toss lightly. In a mixer bowl, combine honey, limeade concentrate, and oil and beat until whipped. Add to fruit mixture, fold in bananas, and toss lightly. Arrange lining of Romaine leaves in a salad bowl and spoon salad onto leaves. Garnish with strawberries. Makes 12 servings.

➤ Approx. per serving: 180 calories; 5 grams of fat

Wild Rice Salad

1/2 cup uncooked wild rice
2-1/2 cups water, divided
1/2 cup long-grain white rice
1 slice lemon
1 medium carrot, peeled, trimmed,
    and diced
1/2 green bell pepper, cored, seeded,
    and diced
1/2 red bell pepper, cored, seeded,
    and diced
1/2 cup fresh or frozen green peas
1 stalk celery, washed and thinly sliced
3 green onions, washed, trimmed, and
    thinly sliced
Chopped parsley

Vinaigrette Dressing
1/4 cup cider vinegar
1 teaspoon Dijon mustard
2 tablespoons safflower oil
1 teaspoon fresh thyme or
    1/2 teaspoon dried thyme

Place wild rice into a bowl. Cover with hot water, let stand for 1 hour, then drain. In a saucepan, bring 1-1/2 cups of water to a boil and add wild rice. Cover and cook over medium heat for 20 minutes. Pour wild rice into a colander and rinse under hot running water, shaking occasionally. Drain well. Bring 1 cup of water to a boil in a saucepan and add long-grain rice and lemon slice. Cover and cook over medium heat for 20 minutes. Pour long-grain rice into a colander and rinse under hot running water, shaking occasionally. Drain well. Combine rices in a large bowl. In a saucepan, cook carrot in boiling water for 8 to 10 minutes or until just tender. Drain carrot in a colander and rinse under cold water. Then, one at a time, place peppers into a saucepan of boiling water. Cook each pepper for 1 minute. Drain and rinse with cold water. Add cooked carrot, blanched peppers, peas, celery, and green onions to rice mixture. Dressing: Combine vinegar and mustard in a small bowl. Whisk in oil a couple drops at a time. Stir in thyme. Add dressing to salad mixture and mix well. Let stand for 1 hour or longer. Spoon salad into a bowl. Garnish with chopped parsley. Makes 6 to 8 servings.

➤ Approx. per serving: 135 calories; 5 grams of fat

Poultry

Mandarin Orange Chicken with Broccoli

1/4 cup unbleached flour
1 tablespoon paprika
1/2 teaspoon salt (optional)
1/4 teaspoon pepper
8 chicken breast halves, skinned
    and boned
3 tablespoons corn oil margarine
1/4 cup onion, minced
1 cup chicken broth, either home-
    made or canned
1 cup 1% low-fat milk
1-1/2 pounds broccoli
1 8-ounce can mandarin oranges,
    drained

Combine flour, paprika, salt, and pepper in a plastic bag, then shake to mix. Place chicken breasts into seasoned flour one at a time, shaking to coat well. Melt margarine in a skillet over medium heat. Add onion and sauté over medium-high heat until tender. Add chicken and sauté for 5 minutes on each side, then remove chicken. Add broth and bring to a boil over medium heat. Cook for 5 minutes, stirring frequently. Add milk and simmer for 5 minutes, stirring frequently. Add chicken, baste with sauce, and simmer over low heat for 10 minutes, basting chicken several times. Cut broccoli into florets, then peel and slice stems. In a steamer or saucepan in a small amount of water, steam broccoli until tender. Arrange chicken in middle of each serving plate. Spoon sauce over chicken and broccoli. Garnish with mandarin oranges. Makes 8 servings.

➤ Approx. per serving: 249 calories; 8 grams of fat

Quick Pineapple Chicken

1 (3-pound) chicken, skinned and
    cut up
Salt and pepper to taste
1 microwave-safe roasting bag
1 medium onion, sliced
1/2 medium green bell pepper, cored,
    seeded, and cut into strips
2 8-ounce cans tomato sauce
1 tablespoon cornstarch
2 8-ounce cans crushed pineapple,
    drained
1 tablespoon light brown sugar
2 teaspoons fresh lemon juice
1/2 teaspoon salt (optional)
1/4 teaspoon ginger

Sprinkle chicken with salt and pepper to taste. Place roasting bag into a glass 2-quart baking dish. Arrange chicken, with larger pieces around edges, in roasting bag. Place onion and pepper over chicken. Blend tomato sauce and cornstarch in a small bowl. Stir in pineapple, brown sugar, lemon juice, salt, and ginger, mixing well. Pour mixture over chicken and close bag tightly. (Do not use twist-tie with metal strip.) Make six 1/2-inch slits in top of bag and microwave on high for 28 to 30 minutes or until chicken is tender, turning dish once. Makes 4 servings.

➤ Approx. per serving: 558 calories; 11 grams of fat

Orange Chicken

1 chicken, skinned and cut-up
Salt and pepper to taste
All-purpose flour
2 tablespoons corn oil or safflower oil
1 large onion, sliced
1 can (6 ounce) frozen orange juice
    concentrate
Cooked rice

Preheat oven to 350°. Sprinkle chicken with salt and pepper, then coat with flour. Heat oil in a large skillet over medium heat. Add chicken and cook over medium-high heat until brown. Arrange chicken in a 9 x 13-inch baking dish. In skillet, sauté onion in pan drippings until tender. Arrange onion over chicken. Spread orange juice concentrate over chicken, then bake for 1 hour. Serve over rice. Makes 4 servings.

➤ Approx. per serving: 656 calories; 17 grams of fat

Parmesan-Yogurt Chicken

1 (2-pound) fryer, skinned and cut up
2 tablespoons fresh lemon juice
Salt and pepper to taste
1/2 cup low-fat plain yogurt
1/4 cup low-fat mayonnaise
1/4 cup scallions, sliced
2 tablespoons Dijon mustard
1 tablespoon Worcestershire sauce
1 teaspoon fresh thyme or
    1/2 teaspoon dried thyme
1/4 teaspoon cayenne pepper
1/4 Parmesan cheese, freshly grated

Preheat oven to 350°. In a large glass baking dish, arrange chicken in a single layer. Drizzle with lemon juice, then sprinkle with salt and pepper. Combine yogurt, mayonnaise, scallions, mustard, Worcestershire sauce, thyme, and cayenne pepper in a small bowl and mix well. Spread mixture over chicken and bake for 50 minutes. Drain off juices. Sprinkle chicken with Parmesan cheese. Preheat broiler and broil chicken 4 inches from heat source for about 3 minutes or until cheese melts and browns slightly. Makes 4 to 6 servings.

➤ Approx. per serving: 424 calories; 9 grams of fat

Creole Chicken

4 chicken breasts, skinned and boned
2 tablespoons olive oil
1 green bell pepper, seeded and
    chopped
1 medium onion, sliced
1 cup celery, chopped
1 16-ounce can tomatoes, diced
1/2 teaspoon salt
1/8 teaspoon pepper
1/4 cup steak sauce
Cooked rice

Lightly flour chicken breasts. Heat oil in a skillet over medium-high heat and sauté chicken until lightly browned, then remove. Sauté green pepper, onion, and celery in skillet until tender. Stir in tomatoes. Add steak sauce, salt, and pepper, then add chicken. Spoon sauce over chicken, cover, and simmer for 10–15 minutes or until chicken is tender. Cook rice according to package directions. Serve over rice. Makes 4 servings.

➤ Approx. per serving: 246 calories; 9 grams of fat

Chicken with Mushrooms and Yogurt

6 chicken pieces, skinned
1 tablespoon all-purpose flour
2 teaspoons corn oil margarine
2 medium onions, thinly sliced
1/4 pound fresh mushrooms, sliced
1/2 cup water (or 1/4 cup water and
*   1/4 cup white wine)*
1/2 cup low-fat plain yogurt
Salt and freshly ground pepper to taste

Sprinkle chicken pieces with flour. Melt margarine in a large nonstick skillet over high heat and cook chicken for 5 minutes on each side or until brown. Reduce heat and cook for 10 more minutes on each side or until cooked throughout. Remove chicken and set aside in a warm baking dish. Add onions and mushrooms to skillet. Cook for 5 to 10 minutes or until tender, stirring frequently. Add water and bring to a full boil over high heat, stirring to deglaze the skillet. Remove from heat. Stir in yogurt, salt, and pepper. Arrange chicken pieces in serving dish and spoon sauce over top. Makes 6 servings.

➤ Approx. per serving: 302 calories; 7 grams of fat

Ginger Orange Chicken

1 tablespoon corn oil margarine
1-1/4 pounds chicken breasts, skinned,
*   boned, and cut into 1-inch cubes*
2 large leeks, cleaned, trimmed, and
*   cut into julienne strips*
2 green onions, chopped
1 tomato, peeled, seeded, and
*   chopped*
1/4 cup dry white wine
1 tablespoon fresh ginger root, grated
1/2 cup fresh orange juice
1 tablespoon all-purpose flour
1/2 teaspoon orange rind (zest), grated
1/4 teaspoon granulated sugar
1 cup seedless green grapes
Salt and freshly ground pepper to taste

Melt margarine in a large heavy skillet over medium-high heat. Add chicken and cook over high heat for 2 to 3 minutes or until light brown. Remove chicken and place in a warm baking dish. Add leeks and green onions to skillet and stir-fry until soft and wilted. Add tomato, wine, and ginger root and mix well to deglaze skillet. Combine orange juice, flour, orange rind (zest), and sugar in a small bowl and mix well. Stir into leek mixture and bring to a boil over medium heat, stirring constantly. Add chicken, grapes, salt, and pepper. Heat and serve. Makes 4 servings.

➤ Approx. per serving: 258 calories; 6 grams of fat

Poultry

Chicken Teriyaki

6 8-ounce chicken breasts, halved
    and skinned
1 cup dry white wine
1/2 cup water
1/3 cup light soy sauce
1 clove garlic, finely minced
1/2 teaspoon ginger, ground

Place chicken breasts into a large shallow dish. Combine wine, water, soy sauce, garlic, and ginger in a small bowl and mix well. Pour mixture over chicken, cover, and marinate in refrigerator overnight. Preheat broiler. Spray broiler rack with vegetable cooking spray, then place in broiler pan. Drain chicken, reserving marinade. Arrange chicken breasts on broiler rack and broil 8 to 10 inches from heat source for 10 to 15 minutes on each side, basting occasionally with reserved marinade. Makes 6 servings.

➤ Approx. per serving: 284 calories; 3 grams of fat

Lemon Spiked Chicken

6 chicken breast halves, skinned
    and boned
2 tablespoons plus 1 teaspoon
    corn oil margarine, divided
1-1/2 tablespoons all-purpose flour
1 teaspoon fresh tarragon or
1/2 teaspoon dried tarragon
1/2 teaspoon salt (optional)
1/4 pound fresh mushrooms, thinly
    sliced
1/4 cup hot water
1 teaspoon instant chicken bouillon
1/2 lemon, thinly sliced
3 cups cooked rice

Cut each chicken breast into inch-thin strips. Place 2 tablespoons margarine into a 2-quart glass casserole and microwave on high for 1 minute. Add chicken, then sprinkle with flour, tarragon, and salt. Cover and microwave on high for 4 minutes, stirring at 1-minute intervals. Place remaining 1 teaspoon of margarine into a 1-quart glass casserole and microwave on high for 1 minute. Add mushrooms, tossing to mix. Microwave on high for 1-1/2 minutes, stirring after 1 minute. Add to chicken. Combine hot water and bouillon in a small bowl and stir until dissolved. Pour mixture over chicken and arrange lemon slices on top. Microwave on high for 5 minutes or until chicken is tender. Serve over rice. Makes 6 servings.

➤ Approx. per serving: 314 calories; 6 grams of fat

Joanna Kerns

While best known for her long-running portrayal of Maggie Seaver on the hit series **Growing Pains**, Joanna Kerns' talents also include producing, directing, and writing. As a director, Joanna has worked on the AMC series **Remember WENN**, as well as episodes of **Boston Public**, **Ally McBeal**, **Suddenly Susan,** and **Clueless**. As a writer, she penned an episode of **Growing Pains** that garnered some of the series' highest ratings. As a producer, she has several projects in the works. As an actress, Joanna's lengthy list of credits includes recurring roles in **The Closer** and **Chicago Hope**, as well as a host of successful films and made-for-TV movies.

Patrick's Coq Au Vin

6 skinless chicken breasts
6 cups cooked rice

Marinade:
1 onion, thinly sliced
2 carrots, thinly sliced
1 bottle Cabernet Sauvignon
1 teaspoon cracked black pepper
Bouquet garni

Sauce:
1 tablespoon olive oil
20 pearl onions, peeled
1/4 lb. pancetta, chopped
Salt and pepper to taste
3 tablespoons brandy
1/2 cup fat-free chicken stock
1 pound button mushrooms, sliced
3 cloves garlic
Bouquet garni
1 tablespoon tomato paste
4 sprigs fresh rosemary

Combine marinade with chicken. Marinate for 30 minutes (or longer) in refrigerator. Heat half of the olive oil in a large sauté pan. Cook pearl onions until they caramelize, stirring frequently. Add the pancetta and cook until transparent. Remove onions and pancetta from pan and reserve. Pat chicken dry and brown in the remaining oil in sauté pan. Salt and pepper chicken. Pour brandy over and flame. Add the reserve marinade and stock. Add mushrooms, garlic, bouquet garni, tomato paste, and rosemary. Cover and simmer 30 to 40 minutes until chicken is tender. When chicken is done, remove bouquet garni and skim fat if necessary. If the sauce is too thin, remove chicken from sauce and reduce until it lightly coats the back of a spoon. Put chicken back and add onions and pancetta, then simmer for 2 minutes. Serve over rice. Garnish with chopped herbs. Makes 6 servings.

➤ Approx. per serving: 571 calories; 17 grams of fat

Tarragon Chicken

1 tablespoon corn oil margarine
2 shallots, minced
1/2 pound fresh mushrooms, sliced
1/2 cup all-purpose flour
Salt and pepper to taste
2 chicken breasts, skinned, boned,
    and halved
1/2 cup dry white wine
1/2 cup chicken broth, either
    homemade or canned
2 teaspoons fresh parsley, chopped
1 teaspoon fresh tarragon or
    1/2 teaspoon dried tarragon

Melt margarine in a 10-inch skillet over medium heat. Add shallots and sauté for 3 to 4 minutes. Add mushrooms and sauté for 3 to 4 minutes. Remove vegetables and keep warm. Combine flour, salt, and pepper in a small dish, then coat chicken with flour mixture. In skillet, sauté chicken until brown on both sides. Remove chicken and keep warm. Add wine and chicken broth to skillet, stirring to deglaze. Add parsley and tarragon and cook over high heat until mixture is reduced to sauce consistency. Add sautéed vegetables, mixing well. Arrange chicken on a serving platter. Spoon sauce over chicken. Makes 4 servings.
➤ Approx. per serving: 264 calories; 7 grams of fat

Chicken and Fresh Vegetable Sauté

1 tablespoon corn oil margarine
4 chicken breast halves, skinned
    and boned
1 to 2 medium tomatoes, wedged
1 medium zucchini, cut into strips
1/4 teaspoon pepper, freshly ground

Melt margarine in a large skillet over medium heat. Add chicken and cook over medium-high heat for 10 to 12 minutes or until brown on both sides. Add tomato, onion, and zucchini, then sprinkle with pepper. Cover, reduce heat, and cook over low heat for 5 to 7 minutes or until vegetables are tender-crisp. Makes 4 servings.
➤ Approx. per serving: 193 calories; 6 grams of fat

Poultry

Chicken Sukiyaki

1 tablespoon corn oil or safflower oil
3 chicken breasts, skinned, boned,
    and sliced
1 small onion, sliced
1 cup water chestnuts, sliced
2/3 cup celery, sliced diagonally
2/3 cup red bell pepper, sliced diagonally
1 cup bamboo shoots, sliced diagonally
2/3 cup fresh mushrooms, sliced
1-1/2 cups fresh spinach
2/3 cup white wine
2/3 cup water
1/3 cup light soy sauce
1 3-ounce can Chinese noodles

Heat oil over medium-high heat in a large nonstick skillet, cast iron skillet, or wok. Add chicken and onion and stir-fry until chicken is cooked through. Heat a serving plate in a warm oven and spoon chicken mixture onto warm plate. Add water chestnuts, celery, red pepper, bamboo shoots, mushrooms, and spinach to skillet one at a time in order listed, stir-frying for several seconds after each addition. In a small bowl, mix wine, water, and soy sauce. Stir mixture into vegetables, then add chicken mixture. Reduce heat to medium and cook for 5 to 6 minutes. Spoon sukiyaki onto a serving plate over rice. Sprinkle with noodles. Makes 6 servings.

➤ Approx. per serving: 285 calories; 9 grams of fat

Fruited Chicken Breasts

6 chicken breast halves, skinned
    and boned
1 tablespoon corn oil margarine
1/4 teaspoon cardamom
1/4 teaspoon salt (optional)
Dash of pepper
2-1/2 to 3 cups firm baking apples,
    unpeeled and thinly sliced
1/3 cup cider
1/4 cup granulated sugar
1 tablespoon fresh lemon juice
1-1/2 teaspoons grated lemon rind
1 teaspoon Worcestershire sauce
1 teaspoon prepared cream-style
    horseradish (optional)

Preheat oven to 350°. Arrange chicken in a shallow baking pan, dot with margarine, then sprinkle with cardamom, salt, and pepper. Bake for 1 hour or until tender. Combine apples, cider, sugar, lemon juice and rind, Worcestershire sauce, and horseradish in a medium saucepan. Simmer over medium-low heat until apples are tender. Pour over chicken and bake just until heated through. Makes 6 servings.

➤ Approx. per serving: 236 calories; 5 grams of fat

Chicken-Vegetable Stir-Fry

6 chicken breast halves (8 ounces
 each), skinned, boned, and cut
 into 1-1/2-inch pieces
1/4 cup plus 1 tablespoon light soy
 sauce
2 small green bell peppers, cored,
 seeded, and cut into 1-inch strips
1 large onion, coarsely chopped
1/2 cup fresh mushrooms or
 1 4-ounce can mushrooms,
 sliced
1 8-ounce can water chestnuts,
 drained and sliced
1 teaspoon cornstarch
3/4 teaspoon granulated sugar
1/8 teaspoon red pepper
3 cups cooked rice
Nonfat cooking spray

Spray wok or skillet with vegetable cooking spray. Heat over medium-high heat for 1 to 2 minutes. Add chicken and soy sauce. Stir-fry for 3 to 4 minutes or until light brown, then remove chicken from wok with slotted spoon. Add green peppers and onion to wok and stir-fry for 4 minutes or until tender-crisp. Drain mushrooms, reserving any liquid. Add chicken, mushrooms, and water chestnuts to stir-fried vegetables. In a small bowl, combine reserved mushroom liquid, cornstarch, sugar, and red pepper, and mix well. Stir into chicken mixture. Reduce and simmer for 2 to 3 minutes or until slightly thickened, stirring constantly. Serve over rice. Makes 6 servings.

➤ Approx. per serving: 469 calories; 7 grams of fat

Joan Lunden

Joan Lunden is one of television's most recognizable faces. As the longest-running cohost on early morning TV, Joan cohosted **Good Morning America** for 17 years. Joan has hosted several prime-time specials and programs on parenting, as well as a parenting video. A celebrated author, Joan's book, **A Bend in the Road Is Not the End of the Road**, details 10 positive principles for dealing with change.

Chicken Yucatán

3 tablespoons fresh orange juice
2 tablespoons canned unsweetened
    pineapple juice
2 tablespoons fresh lime juice
2 tablespoons fresh oregano, chopped
1 tablespoon olive oil
1 teaspoon cumin, ground
1 teaspoon chili powder
1 garlic clove, chopped
4 to 6 dashes hot pepper sauce
Salt and pepper to taste
6 skinless bone-in chicken breasts

Preheat oven to 375°. In a food processor or blender, combine all the ingredients except the chicken, add salt and pepper to taste, and purée until smooth. Arrange chicken in an 8 x 11-1/2-inch baking dish and brush with half the citrus-herb mixture. Bake the chicken in preheated oven, turning once, and brushing with the remaining mixture for 30 to 35 minutes or until chicken is no longer pink in the center. Season with salt and pepper to taste. Serve hot. Makes 6 servings.

➤ Approx. per serving: 157 calories; 4 grams of fat

Recipe courtesy of John Willoughby

Peachy Chicken

1/2 cup peach preserves
1/2 cup water
Juice of 1/2 lemon
6 chicken breasts, skinned and boned
3 cups cooked rice

Combine peach preserves, water, and lemon juice in a small bowl and mix well. Arrange chicken in a shallow dish and pour preserve mixture over chicken. Marinate in refrigerator overnight. Preheat oven to 350°. Drain chicken, reserving marinade. Arrange chicken in a baking dish and bake for 45 minutes or until chicken is tender, basting frequently with reserved marinade. Serve with rice. Makes 6 servings.

➤ Approx. per serving: 217 calories; 3 grams of fat

Chicken with Grapes and Mushrooms

1 tablespoon unbleached flour
2 pounds chicken breasts, boned, skinned, and cut into bite-sized pieces
2 tablespoons corn oil margarine
1/4 cup onion, minced
1/2 pound small fresh mushrooms
3/4 cup chicken broth, either home-made or canned
1/2 cup white wine
1/2 cup 1% low-fat milk
1 tablespoon cornstarch
1 tablespoon water
1 cup seedless grapes
Salt and pepper to taste

Preheat oven to 325°. Combine flour, salt, and pepper in a bag, add chicken, and shake to coat. In a skillet, heat margarine over medium heat. Add chicken and sauté until light brown. Spoon chicken into a casserole with slotted spoon. Add onion to skillet and cook over low heat until onion is tender. Add mushrooms and cook for 3 minutes. Spoon mixture over chicken. Add broth and wine to skillet and bring to a boil over medium heat. Add milk, return to boiling point, and simmer over medium-high heat for 5 minutes. Blend cornstarch and water in a small bowl, then stir into simmering sauce. Cook until thickened, stirring constantly. Pour mixture over chicken. Cover casserole and bake for 20 minutes. Add grapes and bake for 10 minutes longer. Serve immediately. Makes 8 servings.

➤ Approx. per serving: 211 calories; 6 grams of fat

Herb-Baked Chicken

1 (3-pound) broiler-fryer, skinned
    and cut up
2 teaspoons fresh rosemary or
    1 teaspoon dried rosemary
Pepper to taste
1/2 cup unsweetened pineapple juice
1/4 teaspoon ginger, ground
5 shallots, minced
Paprika

Preheat oven to 350°. Rub chicken with rosemary and pepper, then arrange in a 9-inch baking dish. Combine pineapple juice and ginger in a bowl and pour over chicken. Sprinkle with shallots and paprika. Cover and bake for 30 minutes. Uncover and bake for an additional 25 to 30 minutes or until tender. Makes 6 servings.

➤ Approx. per serving: 325 calories; 7 grams of fat

Chicken-Apple Sauté

1 tablespoon corn oil or safflower oil
1 pound chicken breasts, skinned,
    boned, and cut into strips
1 cup celery, diagonally sliced
1 medium green bell pepper, cored,
    seeded, and sliced lengthwise
1 medium onion, sliced lengthwise
1 Golden Delicious apple, cored
    and sliced
1/2 cup apple juice
1 tablespoon white wine vinegar
1 tablespoon cornstarch
1 teaspoon light soy sauce

Heat oil over medium heat in a wok or nonstick skillet. Add chicken and sauté over medium-high heat until cooked through, then remove chicken. Add celery, green pepper, onion, and apple and stir-fry for 1 minute. Combine apple juice, vinegar, cornstarch, and soy sauce in a small bowl, then add to chicken. Cook until thickened, stirring constantly. Makes 4 servings.

➤ Approx. per serving: 238 calories; 7 grams of fat

Poultry

Chicken Picatta

8 chicken breast halves, skinned
   and boned
1/2 cup all-purpose flour
Salt and pepper to taste
Paprika to taste
2 tablespoons corn oil margarine
1 tablespoon olive oil
2 to 4 tablespoons dry Madeira
   or Sherry
3 tablespoons fresh lemon juice
3 to 4 tablespoons capers

With a meat mallet or heavy plate, flatten chicken breasts between sheets of waxed paper. Combine flour, salt, pepper, and paprika in a bowl, then coat chicken with seasoned flour, shaking off excess. Melt margarine and olive oil in a large skillet over medium heat. Add chicken and sauté over medium-high heat for 2 to 3 minutes on each side. Remove chicken; drain on paper towel. To the skillet add Madeira, stirring to deglaze. Add lemon juice. Cook until heated through. Add chicken and heat to serving temperature. Arrange chicken on a heated serving plate. Garnish with capers. Makes 8 servings.

➤ Approx. per serving: 293 calories; 10 grams of fat

Paprika Chicken

1-1/2 tablespoons corn oil or
   safflower oil
2 whole chicken breasts, skinned,
   boned, and cut into 1-1/2-inch
   pieces
1 cup fresh mushrooms, sliced
1/2 cup onion, chopped
1/2 cup chicken broth, either homemade or canned
1 tablespoon paprika
1 teaspoon fresh dill or 1/2 teaspoon
   dried dillweed
1/4 teaspoon pepper
2-1/2 cups uncooked egg noodles
2 tablespoons cold water
2 tablespoons cornstarch
1 cup low-fat plain yogurt

Heat oil over medium heat in a large skillet. Add chicken, mushrooms, and onion and sauté over medium-high heat until tender. Add broth, paprika, dill, and pepper. Cover, reduce heat, and simmer for 10 minutes or until chicken is tender. Cook noodles according to package directions using unsalted water, then drain. Blend water and cornstarch in a small bowl, then stir into chicken mixture. Cook for 1 minute, stirring constantly. Remove from heat. Stir in yogurt. Serve over noodles. Makes 4 servings.

➤ Approx. per serving. 486 calories; 10 grams of fat

Ted Danson

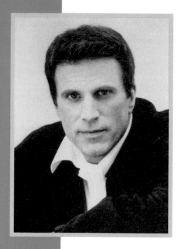

There's more to versatile actor Ted Danson's career than just his well-known Emmy and Golden Globe Award winning portrayal of **Cheers** bar owner Sam Malone. Ted's career includes plenty of drama and film roles, in addition to his television work. Moviegoers have enjoyed Ted in **Three Men and a Baby** and its sequel. Other notable movie roles include **Mumford**, **Cousins**, **Made in America**, and **Saving Private Ryan**. His television work includes the sit-com **Ink**, in which he starred opposite his wife Mary Steenburgen, and **Becker**.

Tex/Mex Chicken Fajitas

1-1/2 pounds chicken breasts, skinned and boned
1 cup onion, thinly sliced
2 cups green and red bell peppers, cored, seeded, and sliced
1/4 cup picante sauce
2 cups fresh tomatoes, cubed
Dash of salt
Pinch of pepper
8 large flour tortillas
1/2 cup fat-free sour cream
1/2 cup guacamole

Spray bottom of a nonstick skillet with vegetable cooking spray. Add onions and green and red peppers and sauté over medium-high heat until soft. Cut chicken breasts into thin strips and add to skillet, along with 1 cup of tomatoes, picante sauce, and black pepper. Sauté until chicken is cooked, stirring frequently. Set mixture aside. Heat tortillas between damp paper towels in a microwave on high for 1 minute. Spread mixture into warm tortillas and top with cheese, sour cream, guacamole, and fresh tomatoes from remaining 1 cup. Roll tortillas and serve. Makes 8 servings.

➤ Approx. per serving: 275 calories; 6 grams of fat

Chicken Scaloppine

2 tablespoons corn oil margarine
1 pound boneless chicken breasts,
    cut into thin slices
1/4 cup dry white wine
2 tablespoons chicken broth, either
    homemade or canned
1 tablespoon fresh lemon juice
2 teaspoons capers
2 cups brown rice, cooked

Melt margarine in a skillet over medium heat. Add chicken and sauté over medium-high heat for 1 minute on each side. Remove chicken and keep warm. Add wine, broth, and lemon juice to skillet. Bring to a boil over medium heat and cook for 3 minutes, stirring to deglaze skillet. Add capers and chicken, turning chicken to coat with sauce. Reduce heat and simmer for 5 minutes, or until chicken is cooked. Serve over rice. Makes 4 servings.

➤ Approx. per serving: 320 calories; 9 grams of fat

Chicken with Pasta and Snow Peas

1 pound tomato rotelle (corkscrew
    pasta)
1 chicken, skinned, boned, and boiled,
    poached, or baked
4 ounces snow peas
1 bunch green onions, finely chopped
1 slice (1 inch) fresh ginger root, grated
1/4 to 1/2 cup red wine vinegar
3 tablespoons extra virgin olive oil
Salt and pepper to taste

Cook rotelle using package directions for 8 minutes or until al dente. Rinse with cold water, then drain. Shred chicken. In a saucepan over medium-high heat, blanch snow peas in a small amount of boiling water. Place snow peas into a bowl of ice water, then drain. Combine rotelle, chicken, snow peas, green onions, and ginger root in bowl. Combine vinegar, olive oil, salt, and pepper in a separate small bowl and mix well. Pour over rotelle mixture, mixing gently. Garnish with additional snow peas. Makes 4 to 6 servings.

➤ Approx. per serving: 565 calories; 15 grams of fat

Poultry

Crispy Herbed Chicken

6 chicken pieces, about 2 pounds,
    skinned and boned
1/2 cup all-purpose flour
4 teaspoons fresh basil or
    2 teaspoons dried basil
4 teaspoons fresh thyme or
    2 teaspoons dried thyme
2 teaspoons salt (optional)
2 teaspoons fresh oregano or
    1 teaspoon dried oregano
2 teaspoons fresh tarragon or
    1 teaspoon dried tarragon
1 teaspoon paprika
1/2 teaspoon pepper
1/3 cup warm water

Preheat oven to 375°. Place chicken in a single layer into a lightly greased shallow roasting pan. Combine flour, basil, thyme, salt, oregano, tarragon, paprika, and pepper in a small jar. Cover and shake well. Sprinkle 2 tablespoons of the herb-seasoned flour mixture on top of chicken. Store remaining herb-seasoned flour in covered jar at room temperature. Pour warm water down side of pan. Do not pour directly on the chicken. Bake for 40 to 50 minutes or until tender, basting with pan juices occasionally. Makes 6 servings.

➤ Approx. per serving: 257 calories; 5 grams of fat

Glazed Cornish Hens

2 Cornish game hens, cut in half
    and skinned
1/3 cup light corn syrup
1/4 cup prepared mustard
2 teaspoons curry powder
1 clove garlic, minced

Preheat oven to 350°. Wash Cornish hens, pat dry, and place onto a rack in a roasting pan. Combine corn syrup, mustard, curry powder, and garlic in a small bowl and mix well. Brush Cornish hens with corn syrup mixture. Bake for 1-1/2 hours, basting occasionally. Makes 2 to 4 servings.

➤ Approx. per serving: 461 calories; 9 grams of fat

Cornish Game Hens with Spicy Rice

2 Cornish game hens
2 tablespoons olive oil
1/2 cup paprika
4 tablespoons crushed, dried oregano
4 teaspoons chili powder
2 teaspoons dry mustard
2 small boxes of raisins, chopped
6 dried apricot halves, chopped
1-1/3 cups white rice, uncooked
2 14-1/2-ounce cans fat-free chicken broth

Preheat oven to 350°. Rub oil over the outside of the hens. In a small bowl, combine the paprika, oregano, chili powder, mustard, raisins, apricots, rice, and broth. Place each hen in the middle of a piece of 1-1/2-foot square piece of foil. Fold up the top and sides but do not close the packet. Add half of the rice mixture to each packet, spooning the rice around the bottom of each hen. Fold all edges of the packets tightly so the liquid and steam will not escape. Alternatively, add the hens and rice mixture to commercially available oven bags, such as Reynolds brand oven bags. Close the cooking bags with twist ties. Snip three or four tiny holes in the top of each bag (this will keep steam in the bags but prevent the bags from popping). Place the foil packets or oven bags in a large casserole dish. Bake for 45 minutes. Makes 4 servings.

➤ Approx. per serving: 317 calories; 13 grams of fat

Ross Browner

As the oldest of eight children, Ross Browner is part of a notable family that includes four brothers who played in the NFL. Ross, Jimmie, Joey, and Keith's work on the football field earned their mother the first and only NFL Mother of the Year award in 1987. Ross is a Heisman Trophy winner from Notre Dame. As a first-round draft pick for the Cincinnati Bengals, he went on to be part of the celebrated AFC Championship Team at the 1981 Super Bowl. Ross was inducted into the Gatorbowl Hall of Fame on New Year's Day 1999.

Turkey Polynesian

1 tablespoon cornstarch
2 teaspoons water
1 teaspoon light soy sauce
1 teaspoon salt (optional)
1 to 1-1/2 pounds uncooked turkey breast, skinned, boned, and cubed
1 cup onion, sliced
1-1/2 tablespoons corn oil or safflower oil, divided
1 cup celery, diagonally sliced
1 8-ounce can water chestnuts, drained and sliced
1 cup juice-pack pineapple chunks or tidbits
1/4 cup pineapple juice
Hot cooked rice

Combine cornstarch, water, soy sauce, and salt in a small bowl and mix well. Coat turkey cubes with cornstarch mixture. In a skillet over medium-high heat, sauté onion in 1/2 of tablespoon oil. Cook for 2 minutes. Add celery and water chestnuts and sauté 2 minutes. Remove vegetables from skillet. Add remaining 1 tablespoon of oil and turkey to skillet and sauté until brown. Add sautéed vegetables, pineapple, and juice. Simmer for 10 minutes. Serve with hot rice. Makes 6 servings.

➤ Approx. per serving: 188 calories; 4 grams of fat

Turkey Breast with Lemon and Cauliflower

1 cup uncooked brown rice
2 cups chicken or turkey broth,
  either homemade or canned
1-1/2 pounds turkey breast, skinned,
  boned, and cut into bite-sized
  pieces
1 large head cauliflower, broken
  into florets
2 tablespoons corn oil margarine
1/4 cup unbleached flour
2 cups 1% low-fat milk
1/4 cup fresh lemon juice
1 teaspoon fresh thyme or
  1/2 teaspoon dried thyme
1/2 teaspoon salt (optional)
1/2 teaspoon pepper
1 cup fresh parsley, chopped

Cook rice according to package directions and keep warm. Bring broth to a boil in a medium saucepan over medium heat. Add turkey to broth and simmer for 5 minutes or until heated through, then drain. Heat 2 baking dishes in a warm oven and place turkey into one dish to keep warm. In a saucepan, steam cauliflower in a small amount of water for 5 to 10 minutes or until tender. Place into second heated baking dish to keep warm. Melt margarine in a medium saucepan over medium heat. Blend in flour and cook until golden brown, stirring constantly. Stir in milk gradually and cook over medium heat until thickened, stirring constantly. Whisk in lemon juice, thyme, salt, and pepper, then add turkey. Spoon rice onto center of a serving platter, then arrange cauliflower around rice. Spoon turkey mixture over rice, drizzling a small amount of sauce over cauliflower. Sprinkle with parsley. Pour remaining sauce into a small serving dish. Serve with turkey. Makes 6 servings.

➤ Approx. per serving: 411 calories; 7 grams of fat

Rhea Perlman

Before she broke into acting, Rhea Perlman held a variety of jobs including waitress at New York's famed Rainbow Room. She's best known for her role as the scrappy waitress Carla on the long-running sitcom **Cheers**, which earned her four Emmys. Rhea has also starred in the television shows **Kate Brasher** and **Pearl**, in which she was the show's executive producer. Her career also includes movie roles in **Matilda**, **Sunset Park**, **Final Analysis**, and **Love in Venice**. Rhea is married to actor Danny DiVito, and they have been involved in many projects together.

Rhea's Favorite Turkey Burgers

2 pounds ground turkey breast
1/3 cup ketchup
2 tablespoons Worcestershire sauce
1/2 cup Italian-style bread crumbs
2 teaspoons garlic powder
Salt and pepper to taste

Mix all ingredients together well and form into eight round patties. Grill patties over hot coals, turning once – approximately 12 to 15 minutes, until the patties are no longer pink. Makes 8 servings.
➤ Approx. per serving: 159 calories; 1.4 grams of fat

Tangy Turkey Meatloaf

1 pound ground turkey breast
1 cup cooked rice
1 small onion, finely chopped
1 egg
1/3 cup ketchup
1/4 cup pineapple, chopped
2 tablespoons brown sugar

Preheat oven to 350°. In a bowl combine the turkey breast, rice, onion, and egg. Mix well and place in a small loaf pan. Bake at 350° for approximately 30 minutes. In a small bowl combine ketchup, pineapple, and brown sugar. Pour over meatloaf and continue to cook for an additional 30 minutes or until meat is cooked through. Makes 6 servings.

➤ Approx. per serving: 200 calories; 7 grams of fat

Seafood

Seafood

Lemon Barbecued Shrimp

2-1/2 pounds large fresh shrimp,
   peeled and deveined
1/2 cup fresh lemon juice
1/3 cup reduced-calorie Italian salad
   dressing
1/4 cup water
1/4 cup light soy sauce
3 tablespoons fresh parsley, minced
3 tablespoons onion, minced
1 clove garlic, crushed
1/2 teaspoon pepper, freshly ground

Arrange shrimp in a large shallow dish. Combine lemon juice, salad dressing, water, soy sauce, parsley, onion, garlic, and pepper in a jar, then cover tightly. Shake jar vigorously. Pour mixture over shrimp, cover, and marinate for 4 hours. Drain, reserving marinade. Thread shrimp onto skewers. Preheat broiler or grill. Arrange skewers on broiler pan or grill and cook 5 to 6 inches from medium heat source for 3 to 4 minutes on each side, basting frequently with reserved marinade. Makes 6 servings.

➤ Approx. per serving: 176 calories; 3 grams of fat

Shrimp Dijon

2 pounds fresh medium shrimp
2 tablespoons corn oil margarine
1/2 cup dry white wine
2 tablespoons fresh lemon juice
1 tablespoon fresh parsley, minced
1 teaspoon garlic, minced
1/2 teaspoon Dijon mustard
1/4 teaspoon salt (optional)
Hot cooked brown rice
Parmesan cheese, freshly grated
Fresh parsley for garnish

Peel and devein shrimp, then pat dry with paper towels. Melt margarine in a heavy skillet over low heat. Add shrimp and sauté for 5 minutes or until pink. Warm a baking dish in oven, then place shrimp in dish to keep warm. Add wine, lemon juice, parsley, garlic, mustard, and salt to skillet and cook for 3 minutes. Place shrimp into skillet and heat just to serving temperature. Do not overcook. Serve over brown rice. Garnish with Parmesan cheese and fresh parsley. Makes 4 to 6 servings.

➤ Approx. per serving: 227 calories; 6 grams of fat

Hank Aaron

Fans of baseball will remember where they were on April 8, 1974 – the night Atlanta Braves' Hank Aaron broke Babe Ruth's home run record with number 715. Hank still holds more major league batting records than any other player in the game's history, including most home runs lifetime – 755, and most runs batted in lifetime – 2,297. He was inducted into the Baseball Hall of Fame in 1982. Today, Hank serves as Senior Vice President of Atlanta National League Baseball Club and with his wife Billye, he is founder of the Hank Aaron Chasing the Dream Foundation.

Lemon Garlic Broiled Shrimp

2 pounds medium shrimp, peeled and deveined
1-1/2 tablespoons corn oil margarine
2 cloves garlic, halved
3 tablespoons fresh lemon juice
1 tablespoon Worcestershire sauce
1/2 teaspoon salt (optional)
3 drops hot pepper sauce
Coarsely ground pepper to taste
3 tablespoons fresh parsley, chopped

Arrange shrimp in a single layer in a 10 x 15-inch baking pan. Melt margarine in a small saucepan over low heat. Add garlic and sauté for several minutes. Remove and discard garlic. Add lemon juice, Worcestershire sauce, salt, hot pepper sauce, and pepper and mix well. Pour mixture over shrimp. Preheat broiler. Broil 4 inches from heat source for 8 to 10 minutes, basting once. Sprinkle with parsley. Makes 6 servings.

➤ Approx. per serving: 206 calories; 5 grams of fat

Seafood

Shrimp Cacciatore

2 pounds fresh shrimp, peeled
    and deveined
1 tablespoon olive oil
1/2 cup onion, minced
1/2 cup green pepper, chopped
2 cloves garlic, minced
1 20-ounce can tomatoes
1 8-ounce can tomato sauce
1/2 cup red wine
1/2 teaspoon salt (optional)
1/2 teaspoon allspice
1/2 teaspoon fresh thyme or
    1/4 teaspoon dried thyme
1/4 teaspoon black pepper
1 bay leaf, crumbled
Dash of cayenne pepper

In a large saucepan, combine shrimp and boiling water to cover. Simmer for 3 minutes or until shrimp turn pink, then drain. Heat olive oil over medium heat in a skillet. Add onion, green pepper, and garlic and sauté until onion is tender. Add tomatoes, tomato sauce, wine, salt, allspice, thyme, black pepper, bay leaf, and cayenne pepper, and mix well. Simmer for 20 minutes. Add shrimp and heat to serving temperature. Makes 6 servings.

➤ Approx. per serving: 250 calories; 4 grams of fat

Chinese Shrimp

1 pound uncooked shrimp, peeled
    and deveined
1 tablespoon corn oil
1 small onion, chopped
4 cloves garlic, minced
1 teaspoon fresh ginger root, grated
1 cup fresh or frozen peas
6 Chinese dried black mushrooms,
    soaked for 30 minutes and sliced,
    or fresh mushrooms, sliced
1/2 cup chicken broth, either home-
    made or canned
2 tablespoons light soy sauce
2 tablespoons water
1 tablespoon cornstarch

Heat oil in a wok over high heat. Add onion, garlic, and ginger root and stir-fry for 2 minutes. Add peas and mushrooms and continue to stir-fry for 5 more minutes. Add shrimp and stir-fry until shrimp turn pink. Combine broth, soy sauce, water, and cornstarch in a small bowl. Add to wok and cook until sauce comes to a boil and thickens, stirring constantly. Serve immediately. Makes 4 to 6 servings.

➤ Approx. per serving: 202 calories; 5 grams of fat

Lyn Vaughn

Lyn Vaughn is a former CNN Headline News anchor, working on-air for CNN for over 13 years. She began her career on the radio in New York and worked in radio and television in Boston before moving to Atlanta as a local news anchor. Lyn was twice named Outstanding TV Newsjournalist of the Year by the National Association of Media Women. Lyn is also busy on the lecture circuit and especially enjoys addressing student groups. In 1995 she had an academic scholarship named in her honor at College of St. Rose in Albany, NY.

Shrimp Creole

1 cup onion, chopped
1 cup green bell pepper, cored, seeded, and chopped
1 cup celery, chopped
1/4 cup butter or olive oil
2 cloves of garlic, finely minced
1/4 cup all-purpose flour
1 teaspoon salt
Pepper to taste
1 bay leaf
2 cups canned tomatoes with liquid, diced
1-1/2 pounds shrimp, cleaned and deveined
Hot cooked rice

In a saucepan over medium heat, sauté onion, green pepper, celery, and garlic in butter or oil until tender. Blend in flour and stir until browned. Add salt, pepper, and bay leaf. Stir in tomatoes and liquid until thick. Lower heat, add shrimp, and simmer half-covered for 10 minutes until shrimp are done, but not overcooked. Serve with rice. Makes 6 to 8 servings.

➤ Approx. per serving: 443 calories; 9 grams fat

Seafood

Fresh Sole Fillets

1 tablespoon corn oil margarine,
1 pound sole fillets
2 fresh nectarines, pitted and thinly
    sliced
2 tablespoons fresh lemon juice
2 tablespoons fresh parsley

Melt margarine in a large skillet over medium heat. Cook fillets for 2 to 3 minutes on each side or until brown. Remove fillets and place on a warm platter. Add nectarines and lemon juice to skillet and heat to serving temperature. Spoon over fillets. Sprinkle with parsley. Makes 2 to 3 servings.

➤ Approx. per serving: 241 calories; 8 grams of fat

Fillet of Sole with Dill Sauce

4 sole fillets (4 ounces each)
1 small zucchini, julienned
1 medium carrot, julienned
2 green onions
1/2 teaspoon salt (optional)
1 cup water
2 teaspoons cornstarch
1/4 cup low-fat plain yogurt
1/2 teaspoon fresh dill or
    1/4 teaspoon dried dillweed
Non-fat cooking spray

Preheat oven to 400°. Arrange sole in a shallow baking dish that has been sprayed with nonfat cooking spray and bake for 10 minutes or until fish flakes easily. Cut vegetables into strips. Spray a large skillet with vegetable cooking spray. Add vegetables and salt, then stir-fry over medium-high heat for 2 minutes. Add water, cover, and simmer for 5 minutes. Remove vegetables with a slotted spoon. In a small bowl, dissolve cornstarch in 1 tablespoon of cold water. Stir into skillet juices. Cook until thickened, stirring constantly. Blend yogurt and dill in a small bowl. Layer half the yogurt mixture, sole and vegetables onto a serving platter. Blend remaining yogurt mixture into fish pan juices. Pour mixture into a sauce boat and serve over fillets. Makes 4 servings.

➤ Approx. per serving: 107 calories; 2 grams of fat

Seafood

Sole with Fresh Tomato Sauce

6 4-ounce sole fillets
1 teaspoon corn oil margarine
3 tablespoons shallots, minced
3 tomatoes, peeled and chopped or
    2 cups canned tomatoes
4 fresh basil leaves
Salt and pepper to taste
Nonfat cooking spray

Heat margarine in a heavy saucepan over medium heat. Add shallots and cook for 2 minutes. Add tomatoes, bring to a boil, then add basil, and salt and pepper. Simmer for 10 minutes or until thickened. Preheat oven to 500°. Pour sauce into a blender and process until smooth, then strain. Keep sauce warm. Lightly brush a baking sheet with oil. Arrange fillets in a single layer on baking sheet and sprinkle with salt and pepper. Place baking sheet onto lowest oven rack and bake for 2 to 3 minutes, or just until fish is opaque and flakes easily. Heat a serving plate in a warm oven, then spoon sauce on hot plate. Arrange fillets in sauce. Makes 6 servings.

➤ Approx. per serving: 140 calories; 2 grams of fat

Sole with Tomatoes

1 tablespoon corn oil margarine
1-1/2 cups fresh mushrooms,
    thickly sliced
1 clove garlic, minced
3 tomatoes, seeded and cut
    into chunks
1 teaspoon fresh basil or
    1/2 teaspoon dried basil
2 pinches of fresh thyme or
    1 pinch of dried thyme
1 pound sole fillets
1 14-ounce can artichoke hearts,
    drained and halved
Salt and pepper to taste

Sauté mushrooms in melted margarine over medium-high heat. Add garlic, tomatoes, basil, and thyme and turn down heat. Add artichokes and sole and simmer covered for 3 minutes. Remove cover and cook 5 minutes more. Add seasonings and serve. Makes 4 servings.

➤ Approx. per serving: 197 calories; 4 grams of fat

Seafood

Lemon Sole Fillets

1 pound sole fillets
2 tablespoons butter, melted
2 tablespoons fresh parsley, chopped
1 tablespoon lemon juice
Salt and pepper to taste
Nonfat cooking spray

Preheat oven to 450°. Place fillets in a single layer into a lightly-oiled baking dish. Season with salt and pepper. Combine butter, parsley, and lemon juice in a small bowl and drizzle over fish. Bake uncovered until fish is opaque and flakes easily. Makes 4 servings.

➤ Approx. per serving: 155 calories; 7 grams of fat

Swordfish Steaks in Lime-Soy Marinade

6 swordfish steaks (5-1/3 ounces each)
2 tablespoons fresh lime juice
2 tablespoons scallion, minced
1-1/2 tablespoons light soy sauce
1 tablespoon corn oil or safflower oil
1-1/2 teaspoons Dijon mustard
1 teaspoon lime rind, grated
1 clove garlic, peeled and minced
1/4 teaspoon pepper, freshly ground
1 scallion, cut into julienne strips
Lime rind (zest), cut into julienne strips

Place swordfish steaks into a glass dish. In a small bowl, combine next 8 ingredients and mix well. Pour mixture over swordfish. Cover and marinate in refrigerator for 2 to 4 hours. Preheat broiler or grill. Place swordfish onto a broiler pan or grill and cook for 4 to 5 minutes on each side or until fish flakes easily. Serve with pan juices or heated marinade. Garnish with scallions and lime zest. Makes 6 servings.

➤ Approx. per serving: 273 calories; 11 grams of fat

Baked Salmon with Carrot-Zucchini Stuffing

4 4-ounce salmon steaks
1 tablespoon corn oil margarine
1 small onion, finely chopped
3 cups zucchini, shredded
1 cup carrot, shredded
1/4 cup parsley, minced
1 to 2 tablespoons fresh basil or
    tarragon, minced, or
    1/2 to 1 teaspoon dried basil
    or tarragon
1 teaspoon fresh lime juice
Salt and pepper to taste

Preheat oven to 350°. Melt margarine in a skillet over medium heat. Add onion and sauté until tender. Add zucchini, carrot, parsley, and basil, mixing lightly. Place vegetable mixture into a lightly greased 10 x 10-inch baking dish. Coat salmon steaks with lime juice. Arrange over vegetable mixture, then sprinkle with salt and pepper. Cover and bake for 30 minutes. Uncover and bake for 10 minutes longer or until fish flakes easily. Makes 4 servings.

➤ Approx. per serving: 241 calories; 9 grams of fat

Seafood Casserole

1 medium green bell pepper, chopped
1 medium onion, chopped
1 cup celery, chopped
1/2 pound fresh crab meat
1/2 pound fresh shrimp, cooked
1/8 teaspoon pepper
1 teaspoon Worcestershire sauce
1 cup fat-free mayonnaise
1 cup bread crumbs
Dash of paprika
Nonfat cooking spray

Preheat oven to 350°. Combine green pepper, onion, celery, crab meat, shrimp, pepper, Worcestershire sauce, and mayonnaise in a large bowl and mix well. Spray a 3-quart casserole dish with nonfat cooking spray and spoon in mixture. Spread bread crumbs over top, sprinkle with paprika, and bake for 30 minutes. Makes 4 servings.

➤ Approx. per serving: 282 calories; 3 grams of fat

Seafood

Grecian Fish

4 boneless fish fillets (snapper,
    grouper, catfish, etc.)
1 large onion, finely chopped
2 medium tomatoes, finely chopped
1 bell pepper, sliced
1 small can mushrooms, chopped
2 tablespoons margarine, melted
Salt and pepper to taste
4 ounces mozzarella cheese, shredded
4 ounces reduced-fat sharp cheddar
    cheese, shredded

Preheat oven to 350°. Wash fillets, pat dry, and place on a baking dish. Salt and pepper lightly, then place onion, tomatoes, pepper, and mushrooms on top of fillets. Pour melted margarine over fillets and bake for 10 minutes, then broil for 5 minutes. Remove fillets from oven, sprinkle cheeses over top, and return to broiler to melt cheese. Serve immediately. Makes 4 servings.

➤ Approx. per serving: 425 calories; 16 grams of fat

Seafood Au Gratin

1 pound white lump crabmeat
1 pound shrimp, peeled
1 pound crawfish, peeled
1/4 cup margarine
1 cup celery, chopped
1 cup green onion, chopped
2 cans low-fat cream of mushroom
    soup
1 cup Italian bread crumbs
6 ounces reduced-fat sharp cheddar
    cheese, grated
4 ounces Romano cheese, grated
2 tablespoons Worcestershire sauce
Salt and pepper to taste

In a large pot, boil shrimp and crawfish over medium-high heat, then drain and peel. Melt margarine in a large saucepan over medium heat. Add celery and onions and sauté until soft. Add cheddar and Romano cheeses slowly, then add mushroom soup and bread crumbs. If mixture is too thick, add 1/2 cup of water or fat-free milk. Fold in seafood, Worcestershire sauce, and salt and pepper to taste. For a creamier texture, add 1/2 cup of low-fat sour cream. Preheat oven to 400°. Pour mixture into baking dish and bake for 30 minutes. Makes 12 to 15 servings.

➤ Approx. per serving: 210 calories; 8 grams of fat

John Ratzenberger

Best known for portraying Cliff on **Cheers**, John Ratzenberger's activities and interests take him far beyond acting. As president of his own production company, Fiddlers Bay Entertainment, John is involved in the creation, development, acquisition, and production of a variety of projects. He's been featured in movies, **One Night Stand** and **Under Pressure** and as a voice over in the animated movies **A Bug's Life** and **Toy Story**. John is also an environmentalist, founding Eco-Pac Industries in 1989, which creates environmentally safe products.

Shrimp Pierre

3 cloves garlic, finely chopped
1 medium onion, finely chopped
1/4 cup parsley, chopped
1 teaspoon fresh basil or
   1/2 teaspoon dried basil
1 teaspoon dry mustard
1 teaspoon salt
1/2 cup olive oil or peanut oil
Juice of 1 lemon
2 pounds jumbo shrimp, peeled
   and deveined

Combine garlic, onion, parsley, basil, dry mustard, salt, oil, and lemon juice in a large bowl, mixing well. Add shrimp and marinate at room temperature for several hours. Preheat broiler or grill. Broil shrimp in oven or over charcoal for 4–5 minutes, turning once. Makes 6 to 8 servings.

➤ Approx. per serving: 142 calories; 5 grams of fat

Seafood

Poached Snapper

1 (1-1/2-pound) red snapper,
    dressed and with head intact
1 1/4 cups Chablis or other dry
    white wine
1/2 to 1 cup water
1 lemon, sliced
6 sprigs fresh parsley
1/2 teaspoon salt (optional)
4 peppercorns
2 bay leaves

Combine wine, water, lemon slices, parsley, salt, peppercorns, and bay leaves in a fish poacher or large skillet. Bring to a boil over medium-high heat, then add snapper. Cover, reduce heat, and simmer for 20 minutes or until fish flakes easily. Remove snapper carefully and place on a serving plate. Garnish with additional lemon slices. Makes 3 servings.

➤ Approx. per serving: 158 calories; 2 grams of fat

Red Snapper in Foil

8 8-ounce red snapper fillets, skins
    removed
2 tablespoons corn oil margarine,
    melted
3 tomatoes, peeled, seeded, and cut
    into 1/2-inch cubes
8 large fresh mushrooms, sliced
3/4 teaspoon salt (optional)
1/2 teaspoon freshly ground pepper
2 leeks, white and tender green part
    only, cut into 2-inch julienne strips
3/4 cup fresh parsley leaves, loosely
    packed

Preheat oven to 450°. Cut heavy-duty aluminum foil into eight 18-inch squares. Fold each square in half. Brush each square on 1 side of fold lightly with margarine. Place some of the tomatoes and mushrooms onto each margarine-brushed area. Top with 1 fillet. Season lightly with salt and pepper, then add some of the leeks and parsley. Fold foil half over to enclose filling, joining edges. Fold edges again to seal packet tightly. Place packets onto a baking sheet and bake for 8 minutes. Remove each packet with a large spatula and place on a plate. Carefully cut a large X in top of each packet with scissors or a sharp knife, then fold open. If fillets are over 1/2-inch thick, add three minutes to baking time. Makes 8 servings.

➤ Approx. per serving: 268 calories; 5 grams of fat

Scallops Florentine

1 pound scallops, rinsed and trimmed
2 cloves garlic, pressed or minced
1 small shallot or green onion, minced
1 teaspoon lemon rind (zest)
Juice from 1/2 lemon
1 cup spinach, chopped
1/4 cup white wine
1 cup fat-free chicken broth, either
    homemade or canned
Salt and pepper to taste
2 cups rice, cooked
Nonfat cooking spray

Spray a nonstick sauté pan with vegetable spray and heat on high. Add scallops and sauté for 1 minute or until slightly brown on each side. Remove scallops and set aside. Spray pan and add garlic, onion, and lemon zest, and sauté over low heat until soft. Raise heat to high and add spinach and wine. Add seasoning, broth, and lemon juice. Add scallops and simmer for 1 minute to heat through. Serve over cooked rice. Makes 4 servings.

➤ Approx. per serving: 246 calories; 1 gram of fat

Fish Fillets Florentine

1-1/2 tablespoons corn oil margarine
1-1/2 tablespoons all-purpose flour
1/2 teaspoon salt (optional)
1/8 teaspoon pepper
1 cup 1% low-fat milk
1/2 cup low-fat cheddar cheese
2 10-ounce packages frozen chopped
    spinach, cooked and drained
2 pounds fish fillets

Preheat oven to 375°. Melt margarine in a saucepan over medium heat. Add flour, salt, and pepper, blending well. Stir in milk gradually. Cook until thickened, stirring constantly. Add cheese and cook over very low heat until cheese is melted, stirring constantly. Spread a layer of spinach in a 9 x 13-inch baking dish, cover with cheese sauce, then arrange fillets. Bake for 15 to 20 minutes or until fish flakes easily. Makes 6 servings.

➤ Approx. per serving: 254 calories; 8 grams of fat

Seafood

Microwave Fish Fillets

1 pound fish fillets
1 can tomatoes, drained and coarsely
    chopped
Salt and pepper to taste
1/4 cup fresh parsley, chopped
1/4 cup fine fresh bread crumbs
2 tablespoons green onion with top,
    minced
1 tablespoon corn oil margarine
2 cloves garlic, minced

Spoon half the tomatoes into a large microwave-safe dish. Arrange fillets in a single layer in prepared dish and sprinkle with salt and pepper. Cover with remaining tomatoes. Combine parsley, crumbs, green onion, margarine, and garlic in a small bowl and mix well. Sprinkle mixture over tomatoes. Cover loosely and microwave on High for 9 to 12 minutes or until fish is opaque. Let stand for 3 minutes before serving. Makes 4 servings.

➤ Approx. per serving: 183 calories; 5 grams of fat

Grilled Monkfish

1 pound monkfish fillets or medallions,
    cleaned and trimmed
Juice of 1/2 lemon and 1/2 lemon cut
    into thin wedges
Seafood seasoning and pepper to taste
1 tablespoon fresh dill
Nonfat cooking spray

In a small bowl, combine lemon, dill, seafood seasoning, and pepper, mixing well. Pour over monkfish and let marinate. Spray grill or broiler with vegetable cooking spray and heat. Cook for 3 to 5 minutes depending on thickness, then turn and cook an additional 3 to 5 minutes until done or fish turns completely opaque. Do not overcook. Serve with lemon wedges. Makes 3 to 4 servings.

➤ Approx. per serving: 147 calories; 3 grams of fat

Ed Begley Jr.

Ed Begley, Jr. credits his Academy Award winning father, Ed Begley, Sr., for the inspiration to become an actor. But while the senior Begley is widely known for playing big screen "heavies," the younger Begley is best known for his Emmy nominated performance as Dr. Victor Ehrlich on the long running series **St. Elsewhere**. *In addition to the series, he has appeared on* **7th Heaven**, **Roseanne**, **The Drew Carey Show**, *and* **Star Trek**. *On the big screen, he has appeared in* **Addams Family Reunion**, **Batman Forever**, **Pagemaster**, **The Accidental Tourist**, *and* **She Devil**, *among others.*

New Orleans Catfish

1 pound farm-raised catfish fillets, cut into four portions
Dash of pepper
2 cups brown rice, cooked
2 tablespoons onion, grated
1/2 teaspoon curry powder
Lemon slices
1 tablespoon margarine
Hot pepper sauce to taste

Preheat oven to 350°. Grease a 9 x 13-inch baking dish. Arrange fillets in dish and sprinkle with pepper. In a bowl, combine rice, onion, and curry powder, mixing well. Spoon mixture over fillets. Top with lemon slices and dot with margarine. Cover and bake for 25 to 35 minutes or until fish flakes easily, removing cover for last few minutes to permit slight browning. Sprinkle with parsley. Serve with hot pepper sauce. Makes 4 servings.

➤ Approx. per serving: 255 calories; 5 grams of fat

Seafood

Teriyaki Flounder

2 pounds flounder fillets
1/4 cup Chablis or other dry white wine
2 tablespoons teriyaki sauce
1/2 cup green onions, thinly sliced
2 teaspoons fresh basil or
    1 teaspoon dried basil

Arrange fillets in a shallow 2-quart glass baking dish. Mix wine and teriyaki sauce in a small bowl, then pour over fillets. Sprinkle with green onions and basil. Cover loosely with plastic wrap and microwave on high for 8 to 9 minutes or until fish flakes easily, turning dish 1/2 turn after 4 minutes. Makes 6 servings.

➤ Approx. per serving: 153 calories; 1 gram of fat

Flounder Creole

1 cup uncooked brown rice
1 pound flounder or sole fillets
1 cup onion, chopped
1 cup green bell pepper, cored,
    seeded, and chopped
1 cup tomatoes, chopped
1/4 cup white wine
1 teaspoon fresh basil or
    1/2 teaspoon dried basil
1/2 teaspoon salt (optional)
1/4 teaspoon pepper

Cook brown rice according to package directions, starting 15 minutes before preparing flounder. Place fillets in a large pan with a cover. Place onion, green pepper, and tomatoes around fillets. Pour wine over fillets, then sprinkle with basil, salt, and pepper. Cover and cook over medium-low heat for 10 minutes or until fish flakes easily. Arrange fillets onto a serving platter and spoon rice around fillets. Spoon vegetables and sauce over fillets and rice. Makes 4 servings.

➤ Approx. per serving: 315 calories; 2 grams of fat

Meats

Cuban Beef Pot

1 pound sirloin tips, cut in cubes
Fat-free cooking spray
4 cloves garlic, finely chopped
2 onions, chopped
2 red peppers, cored, seeded,
    and thinly sliced
1/2 teaspoon ground cumin
1 teaspoon dried oregano
2 bay leaves
1 8-ounce can tomato sauce
2 tablespoons red wine vinegar
1/2 cup sherry
2 tablespoons capers
6 potatoes, peeled and cut in
    large cubes
1/4 cup raisins
Freshly ground pepper

Spray the bottom of a large sauce pan with cooking spray. Sauté onions, garlic, and red pepper until soft, stirring frequently. Add meat cubes to pan and continue to cook until browned. Stir in cumin, oregano, and bay leaves and cook for 3 more minutes. Add tomato sauce, red wine vinegar, and sherry, and then enough water to cover the meat and simmer for approximately 1 hour on medium heat. Add capers, potatoes, and raisins to the stew and continue to cook until the potatoes are soft. Remove bay leaves before serving. Makes 8 servings.

➤ Approx. per serving: 270 calories; 3.5 grams of fat

Steve Harvey

Comedian Steve Harvey says he doesn't make jokes – just observations about life, given a funny twist by his comedic talents. In addition to playing the top comedy clubs in the nation, Steve has starred on television in the **Steve Harvey Show,** hosted **Showtime at the Apollo,** and had a special on the HBO Comedy Hour called **Steve Harvey: One Man.** Recently, Steve created the King Love Center, named in honor of Dr. Martin Luther King, Jr., as a place young people can go to learn about the importance of positive mental attitude, character building, and making dreams come true.

Steak Stir-Fry

1 pound flank steak, fat trimmed
1/2 cup water
1/4 cup light soy sauce
1 tablespoon cornstarch
1-1/2 teaspoons granulated sugar
1 medium onion
3 stalks celery, diagonally sliced
1/2 pound fresh mushrooms, sliced
1/2 cup water chestnuts, sliced
1/2 pound fresh snow peas
3 cups rice, cooked
Nonfat cooking spray

Partially freeze steak. Slice across grain into 1/4 x 2-inch strips, then set aside. Combine water, soy sauce, cornstarch, and sugar in a small bowl, then set aside. Peel onion, slice 1/4-inch thick, and cut each slice into quarters and set aside. Spray a wok with vegetable cooking spray and heat over medium-high heat for 2 minutes. Add steak to wok and stir-fry for 3 minutes. Remove steak with a slotted spoon and set aside. Add onion, celery, mushrooms, and water chestnuts to wok and stir-fry for 2 to 3 minutes. Add steak and snow peas. Cover, reduce heat to medium, and simmer for 2 to 3 minutes. Stir in soy sauce mixture and cook over medium-high heat until thickened and bubbly, stirring constantly. Serve over rice. Makes 6 servings.

➤ Approx. per serving: 277 calories; 4 grams of fat

Meats

Ginger-Orange Beef

3 pounds flank steak
1 tablespoon corn oil or safflower oil
1/4 cup fresh ginger root, freshly grated
3 cups carrots, diagonally sliced
3 cups red bell peppers, cored,
    seeded, and chopped
3 cups green bell peppers, chopped
2 cups water chestnuts, sliced
8 ounces fresh snow peas, trimmed
2 tablespoons orange rind, grated
1 tablespoon cinnamon
1/3 cup light soy sauce
1 tablespoon cornstarch
2 heads iceberg lettuce, shredded

Slice steak into 1/4-inch thick strips. Heat oil in a large skillet or wok over medium heat. Add ginger root and stir-fry for 1 minute. Add steak and stir-fry for 3 minutes or until steak is cooked through. Remove steak and keep warm. Add red and green peppers, water chestnuts, snow peas, orange rind, and cinnamon. Stir-fry for 3 minutes or until vegetables are tender-crisp, then add steak. In a small bowl, mix soy sauce and cornstarch. Stir into steak and vegetable mixture and cook until thickened, stirring constantly. Place lettuce onto serving plate and spoon steak mixture onto lettuce. Makes 12 servings.

➤ Approx. per serving: 235 calories; 7 grams of fat

Savory Pepper Steak

1 tablespoon corn oil or safflower oil
1 pound round steak, cut into strips
3 medium tomatoes, peeled, seeded,
    and cored
2 green bell peppers, cored, seeded,
    and cut into strips
1 cup fresh mushrooms, sliced
1 medium onion, sliced
2 tablespoons light soy sauce
1 teaspoon salt (optional)
1/2 teaspoon ginger
1/2 teaspoon granulated sugar
1/4 teaspoon pepper
2 tablespoons all-purpose flour
3 cups cooked rice

Heat oil in a large skillet over medium heat. Add steak and sauté until brown. Add tomatoes, green peppers, mushrooms, and onion. Stir in soy sauce, salt, ginger, sugar, and pepper. Cover and simmer for 30 minutes. In a small bowl, blend a small amount of pan juices with flour. Stir mixture into skillet and cook until thickened, stirring constantly. Serve over rice. Makes 6 servings.

➤ Approx. per serving: 330 calories; 9 grams of fat

Meats

Beef with Broccoli

1 pound lean flank steak, thinly sliced
Nonfat cooking spray
1/4 cup green onions, sliced
1 pound fresh broccoli florets (about
     6 cups)
1/4 cup water

Sauce:
3 tablespoons oyster sauce
1 tablespoon soy sauce
1 tablespoon sherry
1 tablespoon water
2 teaspoons sugar
1 teaspoon cornstarch

Combine sauce ingredients and set aside. Spray large pan with cooking spray and sauté meat over high heat for 2 minutes. Remove from pan and set aside. Add more cooking spray and add onion and stir-fry for 1 minute further. Stir in broccoli and water and cover. Cook on high heat for 3 minutes. Return steak to pan and add sauce mixture. Cook for an additional 3 minutes. Serve over rice. Makes 6 servings.

➤ Approx. per serving: 190 calories; 8 grams of fat

Venetian Liver

1 tablespoon olive oil
1 cup onion, thinly sliced
1 clove garlic, minced
1/4 teaspoon fresh sage or
     1/8 teaspoon dried sage
1 pound calves liver, sliced into
     1/4-inch strips
1/2 teaspoon salt (optional)
1/2 teaspoon pepper
1/4 cup white wine
1/4 cup fresh parsley, chopped
6 cups brown rice, cooked

Heat oil in a heavy skillet over medium heat. Add onion, garlic, and sage, and sauté for 5 minutes. Remove onion with a slotted spoon, then set aside. Pat liver slices dry with paper towels, then sprinkle with salt and pepper. Add liver to hot skillet and cook for 2 to 3 minutes or until liver is no longer red. Return sautéed onion to skillet and mix lightly. Remove liver and onion with a slotted spoon, then set aside. Add wine to skillet and boil for 2 minutes, stirring to deglaze skillet. Return liver and onion to skillet, spoon sauce over liver, and heat to serving temperature. Sprinkle with parsley. Serve over brown rice. Makes 5 servings.

➤ Approx. per serving: 446 calories; 7 grams of fat

Meats

Creole Pork Chops

6 center cut pork chops, trimmed
1 small onion, sliced
Juice of 1 lemon
1 8-ounce can tomato sauce
1 8-ounce can stewed tomatoes
1/2 cup water
Oregano to taste
3 cups rice, cooked

Brown pork chops in a large skillet over medium-high heat, then remove from skillet. Add onion and sauté until tender. Add tomato sauce, stewed tomatoes, water, and pork chops. Cover and simmer for 2 hours over low heat. Sprinkle lightly with oregano and squeeze lemon juice over mixture. Cover and simmer until done. Cook rice according to package directions. Serve over rice. Makes 6 servings.

➤ Approx. per serving: 315 calories; 7 grams of fat

Lee Majors

As the star of TV's **The Six Million Dollar Man**, Lee Majors wowed viewers week after week with amazing feats. Lee also starred in four other highly rated television shows, including **The Fall Guy**, **Owen Marshall**, **The Men from Shilo**, and **The Big Valley**. In addition to series roles, he has starred in a number of made-for-TV movies and has been a guest star in a number of television shows, including **Lonesome Dove** and **Walker Texas Ranger**.

Lee's Liver and Onions

1 pound calves liver, sliced
    (1/4–1/2-inch)
1/2 pound turkey bacon
2 large onions, sliced thinly
Salt and pepper to taste

Cook turkey bacon in heavy frying pan until done to taste. Add the liver and onions, browning the liver until done. Be careful not to overcook the liver. Liver is best when it is lightly cooked. Serve liver and onions on a platter, garnished with bacon. Serves 4.

➤ Approx. per serving: 306 calories; 12 grams of fat

Chinese Pork and Vegetables

1 tablespoon corn oil or safflower oil
1 pound lean boneless pork, cut into
   thin strips
5 stalks celery, diagonally sliced
4 carrots, diagonally sliced
1 medium onion, sliced
1 tablespoon fresh ginger root, grated
2 cloves garlic, minced
1 cup hot vegetable broth, either
   homemade or canned
2 tablespoons light soy sauce
1/4 teaspoon freshly ground pepper
1 small head cabbage, about 4 cups
2 tablespoons cold water
1 tablespoon cornstarch
Fresh lemon juice to taste
Salt and freshly ground pepper to taste
2-1/2 cups rice, cooked

Heat oil in a wok or large heavy skillet over high heat. Add pork and stir-fry until no longer pink. Add celery, carrots, onion, ginger root, and garlic. Stir-fry until onion is tender. Add broth, soy sauce, and pepper. Cover and simmer for 5 minutes. Shred cabbage and measure 4 cups packed cabbage. Stir into wok and cook for 3 to 4 minutes or until vegetables are tender-crisp. In a small bowl, mix cold water and cornstarch. Stir into wok and cook until thickened, stirring constantly. Add lemon juice, salt, and pepper to taste. Serve over rice. Makes 5 servings.

➤ Approx. per serving: 486 calories; 14 grams of fat

Edwin Moses

Olympic champion Edwin Moses is one of America's most respected track athletes both on and off the field. As a premier hurdler, Edwin collected 122 straight victories from 1977 to 1987, including gold in the 1976 and 1984 Olympic Games in the 400-meter hurdles. He has also worked to ensure adequate financial support for athletes in training, as well as fostering the development of drug-free sports. A trained physicist who graduated from Morehouse College, he is currently a financial consultant in Atlanta.

Lamb with Fine Herbs

Nonstick cooking spray
16-ounce boneless loin of lamb
Salt and pepper to taste
1 tablespoon dry shallots, chopped
2 sprigs fresh thyme, chopped
1/2 cup dry red wine
1 cup fat-free chicken broth, home-
     made or canned
1 teaspoon Dijon mustard

Spray heavy skillet with nonstick cooking spray and add lamb. Braise the lamb for 10 minutes until cooked. Remove from the skillet and keep warm. Remove fat from pan and add shallots and thyme sprigs. Add wine, broth, and mustard. Reduce the sauce by a third. Slice the lamb. Spoon the sauce onto the serving dish; add lamb slices and garnish with fresh thyme. Makes 4 servings.

➤ Approx. per serving: 416 calories; 25 grams of fat

Portuguese Beef Rolls

1 head cabbage
2 tablespoons beef broth, either
    homemade or canned
1 cup carrots, grated
1 cup onion, chopped
1 pound lean ground beef
2 cups brown rice
1 tablespoon fresh lemon juice
1 teaspoon fresh oregano or
    1/2 teaspoon dried oregano
1 teaspoon fresh thyme or
    1/2 teaspoon dried thyme
1/2 teaspoon salt (optional)
1/4 teaspoon pepper
1 28-ounce can tomatoes, drained
    and coarsely chopped
2 cups beef broth, either homemade
    or canned

Preheat oven to 375°. Remove core from cabbage, leaving head intact. Place cabbage head into a large pan of boiling water, cover loosely, and cook for 10 minutes. Lift out carefully, then drain. Remove 16 to 20 outer leaves and pat dry. Add 2 tablespoons of broth to a skillet over medium heat. Add carrots and onion and sauté over medium-high heat for 5 minutes. Add ground beef, rice, lemon juice, oregano, thyme, salt, and pepper. Cook for 10 minutes or until ground beef is brown and crumbly, stirring frequently. Trim thick center ribs from cabbage leaves and spoon 3 to 4 tablespoons ground round mixture onto each leaf. Roll cabbage leaf to enclose filling, tucking in ends, then secure with thread or toothpicks. Arrange cabbage rolls in a 9 x 13-inch baking pan. In a bowl, mix tomatoes and 2 cups of beef broth, then pour over rolls. Cover and bake for 1 hour. Uncover and bake for 30 minutes longer, basting frequently. If rolls begin to brown, cover with foil. (For thicker sauce, pour sauce into saucepan and bring to a boil over medium heat. In a small bowl, blend 2 tablespoons of cornstarch in 2 tablespoons of water. Stir mixture into sauce and cook until thickened, whisking constantly.) Makes 8 servings.

➤ Approx. per serving: 212 calories; 8 grams of fat

Meats

Beef Stuffed Peppers

1 pound lean ground beef
1-1/2 cups cooked brown rice
1 egg
2 teaspoons fresh oregano or
    1 teaspoon dried oregano
1/2 teaspoon salt (optional)
1/2 teaspoon pepper
8 medium green bell peppers
2 cups fresh tomatoes, chopped
1 cup tomato sauce
1/2 cup onion, finely chopped
1 tablespoon fresh lemon juice

Preheat oven to 350°. Combine ground beef, rice, egg, carrots, oregano, salt, and pepper in a bowl and mix well. Cut peppers into halves lengthwise, removing membrane and seed. Spoon mixture into pepper shells. Place stuffed peppers into a large baking dish. Do not crowd. Combine tomatoes, tomato sauce, onion, and lemon juice in a medium bowl and mix well. Spoon over and around peppers. Cover with foil and bake for 1 hour. Serve immediately. Makes 8 servings.

➤ Approx. per serving: 203 calories; 8 grams of fat

Salad Burgers on the Grill

8 ounces extra lean ground beef
1 cup spinach, finely chopped
1 cup garbanzo beans, mashed
1/4 cup chopped onion
1 egg
Salt and pepper to taste

Combine all ingredients in a bowl and mix until thoroughly blended. Sep-arate the mixture into four even portions and form into round patties. Refrigerate for at least one hour before grilling. Cook patties on grill until done throughout, turning once. Makes 4 servings.

➤ Approx. per serving: 216 calories; 10 grams of fat
➤ Approx. per serving with bun: 345 calories; 13 grams of fat

Pastas

Pastas

Pasta dishes are a popular and healthy choice for the main course. Here is a quick guide to pasta shapes and types. In general, thin, delicate pastas (capellini, thin spaghetti) call for light sauces, while thicker pasta shapes (fettuccine, rotini) work better with heavier sauces. Chunky sauces mix well with pasta with ridges, such as mostaccioli or radiatore.

Alphabet – usually found in soups, these fun shapes are a hit with kids

Bucatini – long, hollow tubes used in casseroles or tossed with sauce

Cannelloni – large smooth tubes that are stuffed with cheese or meats and baked

Capellini – angel hair pasta; the thin delicate strands work best with lighter sauces, or soups, stir-fry, and even salads

Conchiglie – these shells comes in several sizes and can be stuffed or tossed with sauce

Ditalini – small tubes; make a nice base for a variety of dishes

Farfalle – bow tie pasta; perfect for a thicker sauce, as well as soups and cold salads

Fettuccini – ribbon strands; good for heavier meat, cheese, or tomato sauces

Fusilli – with a shape liked twisted spaghetti, this long spiral is good with most sauces, added to soups and salads, or baked in a casserole

Gnocchi – "little dumplings" made from potato or semolina dough; boiled and served with sauce

Lasagna – wide, flat noodle with a ruffled edge; perfect for casseroles using a variety of ingredients

Linguine – flattened pasta, similar to fettuccini, but thinner; good for any type of sauce, salads, and stir-fry dishes

Macaroni – small tubes; versatile enough for any sauce, or baked in casseroles

Manicotti – large tubes; great for stuffing with meats, cheese, vegetables, and topped with your favorite sauces

Noodles – egg noodles; usually come in medium and wide sizes; perfect hot or cold, baked in casseroles, tossed in salads, or topped with a variety of sauces

Orzo – grain-shaped pasta made from barley; works well as a side dish, baked in casseroles, or topped with sauce

Penne – also known as mostaccioli, this tubular pasta works well with heavier and chunky sauces

Radiatore – ridged and ruffled, this small pasta adds an interesting touch to sauces, casseroles, soups, and salads

Ravioli – little squares of dough filled with a variety of fillings

Rigatoni – another ridged pasta, similar to penne but heavier; goes well with a variety of sauces

Rotini – the twisted, spiral shape works hot or cold in casseroles and salads, with meat, cheese, and vegetables

Ruote – better known as wagon wheels, these small shapes can be added to a variety of soups, salads, and other dishes for a new look

Shells – jumbo shells can be stuffed and baked, while medium shells can be used in salads or in an updated version of macaroni and cheese

Spaghetti – this familiar standby is a traditional favorite and works with almost any sauce

Stelline – tiny little star shapes – great for children's soups

Tortellini –rings of pasta stuffed with meat or cheese fillings

Vermicelli – a thinner version of spaghetti, but just as versatile when topped with your favorite sauces

Ziti – another tubular pasta, good for chunky, meat sauces or in casseroles

Pastas

Bowtie Pasta Portobello

2 tablespoons olive oil
2 cloves garlic, pressed
3 tomatoes, chopped
2 tablespoons chopped fresh basil
1/4 teaspoon salt
1/4 teaspoon black pepper
2 large Portobello mushrooms, sliced
1 tablespoon Worcestershire sauce
1 16-ounce package of farfalle pasta
1/4 cup fresh Parmesan cheese, grated

Sauté garlic in olive oil in large skillet over medium heat for 3 minutes. Add tomatoes, basil, salt, and pepper. Toss in mushrooms and Worcestershire sauce and cook until mushrooms are soft. Prepare pasta according to package directions. Drain. Toss with sauce and sprinkle with cheese. Makes 6 servings.

➤ Approx. per serving: 180 calories; 7 grams of fat

Stuffed Shells with Beef and Tomato Sauce

18 jumbo pasta shells
Nonfat cooking spray
1/2 pound lean ground beef
1 small onion, chopped
Cloves of garlic to taste, minced
1 15-ounce can tomato sauce
1 6-ounce can tomato paste
1-1/2 teaspoons fresh oregano or
    3/4 teaspoon dried oregano
1/2 teaspoon pepper
1-1/2 cups low-fat cottage cheese
3 tablespoons Parmesan cheese,
    grated
1 egg, beaten
2 tablespoons fresh parsley, minced
Dash of nutmeg

Preheat oven to 350°. Cook pasta shells according to package directions, omitting salt, then drain, and set aside. Spray a large skillet with vegetable cooking spray. Place skillet over medium heat, then add ground beef, onion, and garlic. Cook until brown and crumbly, stirring frequently. Place mixture into colander. Drain well then pat dry with paper towels. Wipe skillet with fresh paper towels. Place ground beef mixture into skillet and add tomato sauce, tomato paste, oregano, and pepper, and mix well. Bring to a boil over medium heat. Reduce heat and simmer, uncovered, for 15 minutes. In a medium bowl, combine cottage cheese, Parmesan cheese, egg, parsley, and nutmeg, mixing well. Stuff 1 rounded tablespoon of cottage cheese mixture into each pasta shell. Spoon sauce into an 8 x 12-inch baking dish and arrange shells. Cover and bake for 40 minutes. Makes 6 servings.

➤ Approx. per serving: 325 calories; 10 grams of fat

Pastas

Cheese Lasagna

12 whole-wheat or white lasagna
noodles, divided
1 cup part-skim ricotta cheese
1 cup low-fat cottage cheese
1/2 cup fresh parsley, finely chopped
2 cloves garlic, minced
1/4 teaspoon nutmeg
Pepper to taste
4 cups Marinara Sauce, divided
(see below)
1/2 pound part-skim mozzarella
cheese, grated, divided
2 tablespoons Parmesan cheese,
freshly grated

Preheat oven to 375°. Cook lasagna noodles al dente according to package directions, then drain. Combine ricotta cheese, cottage cheese, parsley, garlic, nutmeg, and pepper in a small bowl and mix well. Spread 1 cup of Marinara Sauce in a 9 x 13-inch baking dish and arrange 4 noodles over sauce. Spoon in half the cottage cheese mixture. Sprinkle with half the mozzarella cheese. Repeat layers with 4 noodles, remaining cottage cheese mixture, 1 cup of sauce, and remaining mozzarella cheese. Layer remaining 4 noodles and 1 cup sauce on top. Sprinkle with Parmesan cheese. Cover and bake for 35 minutes. Uncover and bake for 10 minutes longer. Let stand for 5 to 10 minutes before serving. Makes 8 servings.

➤ Approx. per serving: 350 calories; 13 grams of fat

Marinara Sauce

1 tablespoon olive oil
1/2 cup onion, chopped
2 cloves garlic, minced
1 14-1/2-ounce can Italian-style
tomatoes
1 15-ounce can tomato sauce
1 6-ounce can tomato paste
1/2 cup red wine
1 tablespoon fresh basil or
1-1/2 teaspoons dried basil
1-1/2 teaspoons granulated sugar
1 bay leaf
1/2 teaspoon fresh oregano or
1/4 teaspoon dried oregano
1/4 teaspoon salt (optional)
1/4 teaspoon pepper

Heat olive oil in a large saucepan over low heat. Add onion and garlic and sauté until transparent. In a blender, purée tomatoes with juice, then add to onion mixture. Add tomato sauce, tomato paste, wine, basil, sugar, bay leaf, oregano, salt, and pepper, mixing well. Simmer, uncovered, for 1 hour. Discard bay leaf. Serve hot over pasta. Makes 5-1/2 cups (1/2 cup per serving).

➤ Approx. per serving: 55 calories; 2 grams of fat

Vegetable Lasagna

16 whole-wheat lasagna noodles, cooked
1/4 cup olive oil
1 large onion, diced
1 medium eggplant, peeled and diced
1/4 pound fresh mushrooms, sliced
3 cloves fresh garlic, pressed
1 pound fresh tomatoes, chopped
8 ounces tomato sauce
2 teaspoons oregano
1 teaspoon basil
1/4 teaspoon black pepper
2 cups fat-free ricotta cheese
2 cups low-fat mozzarella cheese, shredded
1/4 cup fresh Parmesan cheese, grated

Preheat oven to 350°. Heat oil in large skillet over medium heat. Add onions, eggplant, mushrooms, and garlic and cook for 15 minutes. Add tomatoes, tomato sauce, oregano, basil, and black pepper. Bring to a boil and reduce heat. Cover and simmer for 30 minutes. Uncover and cook until sauce is thick. In a 9 x 13-inch baking dish, arrange lasagna layers in the following order: sauce, noodles, ricotta cheese, mozzarella cheese. Repeat layers two more times. Cover top with remaining cheese and sprinkle with Parmesan cheese. Bake uncovered for 45 minutes. Cut into squares to serve. Makes 10 servings.

➤ Approx. per serving: 330 calories; 11 grams of fat

Debbie Miller-Palmore

As an All-American basketball standout at Boston University, Debbie Miller-Palmore set records for points scored, rebounds, assists, and steals. After honing her skills at the 1980 Olympic trials, she played professionally and coached for several years overseas. When the American Basketball League was formed, Debbie became general manager for the Atlanta Glory, helping to promote and develop the new league. In addition, Debbie founded a nonprofit organization, Top of the Key, which produces and manages sports events and teaches athletes basketball skills and sportsmanship.

Turkey Lasagna

1 pound ground turkey breast
3/4 cup onion, chopped
1 pound tomatoes, chopped
2 6-ounce cans tomato paste
2 cups water
1 tablespoon parsley, chopped
1 teaspoon granulated sugar
1/4 clove fresh garlic, pressed
1/2 teaspoon pepper
1/2 teaspoon oregano
6 lasagna noodles
1 pound low-fat cottage cheese
8 ounces mozzarella cheese, shredded
1 cup Parmesan cheese, grated

Lightly brown ground turkey breast and onions in a large pan over medium heat. Add tomatoes, tomato paste, water, parsley, sugar, garlic, pepper, and oregano. Simmer uncovered, for 30 minutes, stirring occasionally. Boil water in a large pot over medium-high heat and cook lasagna noodles using package directions, then drain. Preheat oven to 350°. Spread one cup of sauce in a 13 x 9 x 2-inch baking dish. Alternate layers of noodles, sauce, cottage cheese, mozzarella, and Parmesan. Bake for 40 to 50 minutes, until lightly browned and bubbling. Allow to stand for 15 minutes before serving. Makes 10 to 12 servings.

➤ Approx. per serving: 247 calories; 9 grams of fat

Pastas

Angel Hair Vegetable Medley

1 12-ounce box capellini pasta
1 pound of zucchini, sliced
6 ounces mushrooms, sliced
6 ounces snow peas, trimmed
1 clove fresh garlic, pressed
2 cups tomato sauce
2 tablespoons olive oil
Salt to taste
1/4 cup freshly grated Parmesan
 cheese

Heat oil in a large skillet. Stir-fry all vegetables and garlic for 5 minutes. Add tomato sauce and salt to taste. Cook on low heat for an additional 10 minutes. Cook capellini pasta according to box directions. Serve sauce over pasta and sprinkle cheese on top. Makes 6 servings.

➤ Approx. per serving: 190 calories; 7 grams of fat

Spaghetti with Spinach and Mushrooms

1/2 pound fresh mushrooms, trimmed
 and thinly sliced
1 tablespoon fresh lemon juice
1 tablespoon corn oil margarine
2 tablespoons Madeira
2 cloves garlic, minced
1 cup 1% low-fat milk
1/2 teaspoon salt (optional)
1/4 teaspoon pepper
1 10-ounce package frozen chopped
 spinach, thawed and drained
1/2 pound whole-wheat or white
 spaghetti
2 tablespoons Parmesan cheese,
 freshly grated

Combine mushrooms and lemon juice in a small bowl. Melt margarine in a large skillet over low heat. Add Madeira and garlic and cook for 3 minutes. Add mushrooms and cook for 5 minutes. Add milk, salt, and pepper. Bring to a boil over medium heat, stirring constantly. Drain spinach well. Add spinach to mushroom mixture and simmer for 5 minutes. Remove from heat and keep warm. Cook spaghetti al dente using package directions, then drain. Combine spinach mixture and hot spaghetti in a serving dish, tossing well. Sprinkle with Parmesan cheese. Makes 4 servings.

➤ Approx. per serving: 257 calories; 5 grams of fat

Pastas

Orange Asparagus Ziti

1/2 pound mostaccioli, ziti, or other
    medium pasta shape, uncooked
2 teaspoons vegetable oil, divided
12 ounces frozen small shrimp,
    thawed, peeled, and deveined
3 medium carrots, cut diagonally
    and thinly sliced
1 bunch scallions, sliced
1 pound asparagus, cut diagonally
    into 2-inch lengths
1 cup fresh orange juice
Salt and pepper to taste

Boil 4 cups of water in a large saucepan, add pasta, and cook until al dente according to package directions, then drain. Heat oil in a large nonstick skillet or wok over high heat. Add shrimp and stir-fry for 3 minutes until shrimp is firm, opaque, and lightly brown, then set aside. Add remaining oil to pan and stir-fry carrots for 2 minutes. Add asparagus and scallions, stir-fry for 3–4 minutes until asparagus is tender-crisp. Add pasta, shrimp, and orange juice to skillet or wok and toss for 2 minutes, until hot. Season to taste with salt and pepper and serve immediately. Makes 4 servings.

➤ Approx. per serving: 428 calories; 5 grams of fat

Cheese and Spinach Manicotti

8 manicotti shells
1-1/2 cups part-skim ricotta cheese
1 egg
1 10-ounce package frozen chopped
    spinach, thawed and squeezed dry
1/4 cup Parmesan cheese, freshly
    grated, divided
1 teaspoon fresh basil or
    1/2 teaspoon dried basil
1 clove garlic, minced
1/2 teaspoon salt (optional)
1/2 teaspoon pepper
1/8 teaspoon nutmeg
4 cups Marinara Sauce, divided
    (see recipe on page 121)

Preheat oven to 375°. Cook manicotti shells according to package directions. In a bowl, combine ricotta cheese, egg, spinach, 2 tablespoons Parmesan cheese, basil, garlic, salt, pepper, and nutmeg, mixing well. Stuff mixture into manicotti shells. Pour 1 cup of Marinara Sauce into a 9 x 13-inch baking dish and arrange stuffed shells in single layer. Pour over manicotti and sprinkle with remaining 2 tablespoons of Parmesan cheese. Cover pan with foil and bake for 1 hour. Makes 8 manicotti.

➤ Approx. per manicotti: 261 calories; 10 grams of fat

Pastas

Pasta with Peppers and Parmesan

2 tablespoons corn oil margarine

2 tablespoons olive oil

2 red or green bell peppers, cored, seeded, quartered, and thinly sliced

1 clove garlic, minced

1/2 teaspoon salt (optional)

1/4 teaspoon pepper

8 ounces whole-wheat or white fettuccine or other flat pasta

3 tablespoons Parmesan cheese, freshly grated

Combine margarine and olive oil in a large skillet and heat over low heat until margarine melts. Add bell peppers and garlic and sauté for 5 minutes. Add salt and pepper and sauté for 2 minutes. Keep warm. Cook fettuccine al dente according to package directions, then drain. Combine hot fettuccine, sautéed peppers, and cheese in a serving bowl and toss to mix. Serve at once. Makes 6 servings.

➤ Approx. per serving: 204 calories; 3 grams of fat

Cold Pasta Primavera

2 ounces whole-wheat or white small shell or bow tie pasta

1 cup broccoli florets, chopped

1 cup fresh or frozen peas, thawed and drained

1 cup red or green bell pepper, cored, seeded, and thinly sliced

1 cup tomatoes, chopped

1/2 cup fresh parsley, chopped

2 scallions, sliced

2 tablespoons low-fat cottage cheese

1 to 2 tablespoons 1% low-fat milk

1/4 cup low-fat plain yogurt

1 teaspoon fresh oregano or 1/2 teaspoon dried oregano

1 teaspoon fresh basil or 1/2 teaspoon dried basil

1/2 teaspoon salt (optional)

1/4 teaspoon pepper

1/4 cup Parmesan cheese, freshly grated

Cook pasta according to package directions, then drain and cool. In separate saucepans over medium heat, cook broccoli and peas in a small amount of water until tender-crisp, then drain and cool. Combine pasta, broccoli, peas, bell pepper, tomatoes, parsley, and scallions in a medium bowl and toss to mix. Combine cottage cheese and milk in a blender and process until smooth. In a small bowl, combine blended cottage cheese, yogurt, oregano, basil, salt, and pepper, then blend well. Add to pasta, tossing to coat. Add Parmesan cheese, tossing gently until well coated. Chill in refrigerator. Serve chilled. Makes 4 servings.

➤ Approx. per serving: 170 calories; 3 grams of fat

Pastas

Honey-Mustard Rotini and Tuna

1/2 pound rotini, uncooked
3 tablespoons prepared mustard
2 tablespoons honey
1 cup nonfat buttermilk
1/2 cup nonfat mayonnaise
1/2 teaspoon celery seed
12 ounces fresh tuna
1 medium cucumber, peeled, seeded
    and thinly sliced
1 medium red pepper, seeded and
    diced

Boil 4 cups water in a large saucepan. Add pasta and cook al dente according to package directions. In a large bowl, combine mustard, honey, buttermilk, mayonnaise, and celery seed, whisk well, then set aside. Heat grill or broiler and cook tuna until firm and opaque. Transfer tuna onto a cutting board and allow to cool. Combine pasta, mustard sauce, cucumber, and red pepper and toss to mix. Dice tuna and add to pasta mixture. Toss gently and serve. Makes 4 to 6 servings.

➤ Approx. per serving: 301 calories; 2 grams of fat

Pasta with Clam Sauce

2 tablespoons corn oil margarine,
    divided
2 red bell peppers, cored, seeded,
    and cut into thin strips
3 cloves garlic, minced, divided
1 dozen fresh shucked clams or
    1 5-ounce can clams, drained
1 cup dry white wine
1 teaspoon fresh thyme or
    1/4 teaspoon dried thyme
1/2 cup fresh parsley, minced
Salt and freshly ground pepper to taste
1/2 pound fresh or dried capellini
1-1/2 tablespoons Parmesan cheese,
    grated

Melt 1 tablespoon of margarine in a heavy skillet over medium heat. Add peppers and one clove of garlic and sauté for 10 minutes or until peppers are soft. Melt remaining 1 tablespoon of margarine in a saucepan over medium heat. Add remaining garlic and sauté for 1 minute. Add clams, wine, and thyme and simmer for 5 minutes. Add parsley, salt, and pepper to taste. In a large pan of boiling water, cook capellini al dente, then drain. Spoon capellini onto warm plates. Top with clam sauce and arrange sautéed pepper strips around capellini. Sprinkle with Parmesan cheese. Makes 3 main-course or 6 appetizer servings.

➤ Approx. per serving: 406 calories; 11 grams of fat

Peter Carruthers

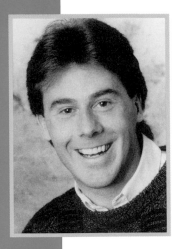

At the 1984 Winter Olympics, Peter Carruthers and his sister Kitty became the first US pairs skaters to win an Olympic Silver Medal since 1952. Before their triumph in Sarajevo, the two had won four consecutive US Figure Skating Championships. Their professional career includes ten years touring with Ice Capades and other shows. Peter has provided sports broadcast commentary for numerous television stations and is currently a figure skating sports analyst for cable and television networks.

Summer Pasta with Feta

*4 large ripe tomatoes, cut into
    1/2-inch cubes
12 ounces feta cheese, crumbled
1 cup fresh basil, chopped
3 to 4 garlic cloves, minced
1/4 cup olive oil
Salt and pepper to taste
9 cups rotelle pasta, cooked
Parmesan cheese*

Combine tomatoes, feta cheese, basil, garlic, olive oil, salt, and pepper in a large bowl and set aside at room temperature. Cook rotelle al dente according to package directions, then drain. Combine with tomato mixture, tossing well to mix. Sprinkle with Parmesan cheese. Makes 6 to 8 servings.

➤ Approx. per serving: 354 calories; 13 grams of fat

Pastas

Creamy Pasta with Vegetables

1 small head cauliflower, trimmed and
    cut into florets
1 small bunch broccoli, trimmed and
    cut into small florets
2 tablespoons olive oil
3 cloves garlic, finely chopped
2-1/2 cups mushrooms, thickly sliced
2-1/2 cups whole-wheat egg noodles
    or spaghetti
1 cup low-fat small curd cottage
    cheese
1/2 cup 1% low-fat milk
1/4 cup low-fat sour cream
1/4 cup Parmesan cheese, grated
Salt and cayenne pepper

In a large pot of boiling water, cook cauliflower and broccoli florets for 5 minutes until tender-crisp. Remove vegetables with a slotted spoon and reserve liquid for cooking pasta. Heat oil in a large skillet over medium-high heat. Add garlic and sauté for 5 minutes. Add mushrooms and sauté for another 5 minutes. Stir in broccoli and cauliflower and sauté for 2 to 3 minutes longer, then set aside. Cook pasta in reserved liquid for 8 to 10 minutes or until al dente, add additional water, if necessary, then drain. In a food processor, combine cottage cheese, milk, sour cream, and Parmesan cheese. Blend until creamy. Pour over broccoli mixture, add drained pasta, and toss until mixed. Season with salt and cayenne pepper to taste. Makes 8 servings.

➤ Approx. per serving: 199 calories; 6 grams of fat

Tomato Basil Fettuccini

6 ounces fettuccini
1 tablespoon olive oil
4 tomatoes, diced
2 cloves garlic, minced
2 teaspoons fresh basil, chopped or
    1/2 teaspoon dried basil
Pinch of granulated sugar
1/4 cup fresh parsley, chopped
Salt and freshly ground pepper to taste
2 tablespoons Parmesan cheese,
    grated

Cook fettuccini in a large pan of boiling salted water, al dente, then drain. Heat oil in a heavy skillet over medium heat. Add tomatoes, garlic, basil, and sugar and cook for 5 minutes, stirring occasionally. Add parsley, salt, and pepper. Add to tomato mixture with cheese, tossing to mix. Makes 2 main-course or 4 appetizer or side-dish servings.

➤ Approx. per serving: 545 calories; 13 grams of fat

Creamy Fettucini with Sun-Dried Tomatoes

1/2 cup sun-dried tomatoes,
    packed without oil
1 12-ounce box fettuccini
1 tablespoon olive oil
1 large onion, thinly sliced
1/2 cup red bell pepper, cored,
    seeded, and sliced
1/2 cup yellow bell pepper, cored,
    seeded, and sliced
1-1/2 tablespoons flour
1-1/3 cup 1% low-fat milk
1/2 teaspoon salt
1/4 teaspoon black pepper
1/4 teaspoon nutmeg
1/2 cup reduced-fat sour cream
1/4 cup Parmesan cheese, grated

Pour boiling water over sun-dried tomatoes and soak for 10 minutes. Then drain. Cook fettuccini according to box directions and drain. In a large pan, sauté onions and peppers in olive oil for about 5 minutes or until soft, stirring frequently. Stir in flour, milk, salt, pepper, and nutmeg and bring to a boil. Reduce heat and simmer for 1 minute. Add sour cream, sun-dried tomatoes, and cheese. Toss together with fettuccini and serve immediately. Makes 4 servings.

➤ Approx. per serving: 113 calories; 3 grams of fat

Nancy Wilson

*Nancy Wilson's spectacular song styling is truly original. And like her music, her personal style is rich with glamour and elegance. Her honors include a Grammy for Best Rhythm & Blues, an Emmy for **The Nancy Wilson Show**, plus her own star on the Hollywood Walk of Fame. To commemorate her 60th birthday, Nancy released her 60th recording, **If I Had My Way,** on Columbia. She has performed throughout the world and captured top honors in music polls, as well as the NAACP Image Award and the Essence Award.*

Vermicelli with Broccoli

1 bunch fresh broccoli
2 tablespoons corn oil margarine
3 scallions, sliced
1 clove garlic, minced
2 tablespoons white wine
1 teaspoon fresh lemon juice
1/2 teaspoon salt (optional)
3/4 pound whole-wheat vermicelli
1 tablespoon olive oil
1/4 cup Parmesan cheese,
  freshly grated

Cut broccoli into florets, then peel and slice stems. In a saucepan or steamer, steam broccoli florets and stems in a small amount of water until tender-crisp. Place broccoli into a colander, rinse gently with cold water, then drain. Melt margarine in a medium skillet over medium heat. Add scallions and garlic and sauté for 2 minutes. Add wine and cook for 5 minutes. Add broccoli, lemon juice, and salt and cook until heated through. Cook vermicelli al dente using package directions, then drain. In a serving bowl, combine hot vermicelli and olive oil, tossing to coat. Add broccoli mixture and toss gently. Sprinkle with Parmesan cheese. Serve immediately. Makes 8 servings.

➤ Approx. per serving: 259 calories; 7 grams of fat

Pastas

Linguine with Tomato, Basil, and Capers

2 pounds tomatoes, peeled, seeded, and coarsely chopped
1 cup fresh basil, coarsely chopped
2 tablespoons olive oil, divided
1/3 cup onion, finely chopped
1/3 cup carrot, finely chopped
1/3 cup celery, finely chopped
2 cloves garlic, crushed
1 3-ounce jar capers, drained and rinsed
2 tablespoons vinegar
Salt and pepper to taste
1 pound spinach or whole-wheat linguine

Mix tomatoes and basil in a bowl, then set aside. Heat 1 tablespoon olive oil in a skillet over low heat. Add onion and sauté just until translucent. Add carrot, celery, and garlic and sauté for 1 minute. Add tomato mixture and simmer, uncovered, for 20 minutes. Add capers, vinegar, salt, and pepper. In a large pan of boiling water, cook linguine al dente, then drain. Add remaining 1 tablespoon olive oil to linguine, tossing to coat. Place linguine onto a large serving platter and top with tomato sauce. Makes 6 servings.

➤ Approx. per serving: 194 calories; 6 grams of fat

Linguine with Shrimp

1/4 pound linguine or whole-wheat noodles
1 tablespoon vegetable oil
1 large clove garlic, finely chopped
2 tablespoons shallots, finely chopped
2 large tomatoes, coarsely chopped
1/4 teaspoon dried basil
1/4 pound small or medium shrimp (raw or cooked)
1 to 2 scallions, chopped
Salt and pepper to taste

Cook linguine until al dente or according to package directions, then drain. Heat oil in a heavy skillet over high heat and add garlic and shallots. Sauté for 30 seconds, stirring constantly. Add tomatoes and basil and continue to cook for 1 minute, stirring constantly. Add shrimp and cook until hot and cooked throughout. Sprinkle with scallions and season with salt and pepper to taste. Spoon over hot linguine. Makes 2 servings.

➤ Approx. per serving: 364 calories; 9 grams of fat

Broccoli-Stuffed Shells

3 cups broccoli florets
1 15-ounce package part-skim
    ricotta cheese
1 egg plus 2 egg whites
2 tablespoons Parmesan cheese
1 teaspoon fresh oregano or
    1/2 teaspoon dried oregano
1/2 teaspoon nutmeg
1/4 teaspoon pepper
24 jumbo pasta shells, cooked
1 cup Marinara Sauce (see recipe
    on page 121)

Preheat oven to 350°. In a saucepan or steamer, cook broccoli over medium heat until tender-crisp, then drain and cool. In a food processor fitted with steel blade or using a sharp knife, mince broccoli. Combine broccoli, ricotta cheese, egg and egg whites, Parmesan cheese, oregano, nutmeg, and pepper in a bowl and mix well. Stuff about 1 tablespoon of mixture into each pasta shell. Pour Marinara Sauce into a baking dish and arrange pasta shells in a single layer. Bake for 30 minutes. Makes 8 servings.

➤ Approx. per serving: 235 calories; 6 grams of fat

Meatless

Meatless

Ratatouille Pizza

1 tablespoon corn oil or safflower oil
1-1/2 teaspoons Italian seasoning
2 cups eggplant, chopped
1 cup zucchini, thinly sliced
1 medium green bell pepper, cored,
    seeded, and cut into 1-inch squares
1 medium tomato, peeled and
    chopped
1/2 cup onion, chopped
1 clove garlic, minced
1 loaf Italian bread, cut in half
    lengthwise
1-1/2 cups part-skimmed mozzarella
    cheese, divided

Preheat oven to 375°. Heat oil and Italian seasoning in a large skillet. Add eggplant, zucchini, green pepper, tomato, onion, and garlic. Sauté until tender-crisp. Lower heat and simmer for 5 minutes. On a baking sheet arrange bread. Sprinkle on half of the cheese and spoon vegetables over cheese. Bake until edges are brown. Sprinkle with remaining cheese. Bake for 3 to 5 minutes longer or until cheese is melted. Makes 8 servings.

➤ Approx. per serving: 249 calories; 5 grams of fat

New Age Pizza

1 cup warm water, 105° to 115°
1 package dry yeast
3 to 3-1/2 cups whole-wheat flour, divided
2 tablespoons olive oil
1/2 teaspoon salt
Cornmeal
1/2 pound part-skim mozzarella
    cheese, thinly sliced
1-1/2 pounds fresh tomatoes, seeded
    and coarsely chopped or 1 cup
    canned tomatoes, drained and
    coarsely chopped
2 cloves garlic, minced
5 to 6 fresh basil leaves, coarsely
    shredded or 1 teaspoon dried basil
    leaves, coarsely shredded or
    1 teaspoon dried basil or oregano
Salt and freshly ground pepper to taste
2 tablespoons Parmesan cheese,
    freshly grated (optional)
2 teaspoons olive oil (optional)

In a medium bowl, combine water and yeast, stirring until dissolved. Add 1 cup of flour, of olive oil, and salt, mixing well with a wooden spoon. Mix in another cup of flour. Sprinkle 1 cup of flour on a working surface and knead dough until smooth and elastic, adding remaining 1/2 cup of flour, if necessary. Lightly flour a 2-quart bowl, place dough, and turn to coat surface. Cover with plastic wrap and let rise for 1 hour or until doubled in bulk. Knead for 1 minute. Preheat oven to 500°. Sprinkle a large pizza pan with cornmeal. Roll or stretch dough into a thin circle and place into prepared pan. Layer mozzarella cheese, tomatoes, garlic, basil, salt, pepper, Parmesan cheese, and olive oil over dough. Bake for 10 to 15 minutes or until crust is golden. Cut into wedges. Makes 12 slices.

➤ Approx. per slice: 193 calories; 7 grams of fat

Vegetable Strata

6 ounces fresh mushrooms, sliced
1/2 cup green onions, diced
1/2 cup onions, chopped
1 red bell pepper, cored, seeded, and
    sliced into thin strips
1 green bell pepper, sliced into thin
    strips or 1/2 cup broccoli, chopped
1 cup reduced-fat cheddar cheese,
    shredded
1/4 cup Parmesan cheese, grated
1 medium loaf Italian bread, cut into
    1-inch cubes
6 eggs
1-3/4 cups skim milk
1/4 teaspoon salt
1/4 teaspoon pepper
Nonfat cooking spray

Spray the bottom of a nonstick skillet with vegetable cooking spray. Sauté mushrooms, green onions, onions, and red and green peppers or broccoli over medium-high heat until tender. Set aside. In a small bowl, combine cheddar and Parmesan cheese. Spread half of the bread cubes in an 11 x 7-inch baking dish sprayed with vegetable cooking spray. Cover with half of vegetable mixture, sprinkle with half of cheese mixture, repeating layers. In a medium bowl, combine eggs, milk, salt, and pepper, then pour over the strata. Cover and chill overnight in refrigerator to set. Preheat oven to 350°. Bake uncovered until set and lightly browned (about 50 to 60 minutes). Garnish with tomatoes and green onion tops, if desired. Makes 6 servings.

➤ Approx. per serving: 377 calories; 11 grams of fat

Tony Lama

You may have heard of the world-famous cowboy boots — now meet the man behind them. Tony Lama, Jr. is the CEO and Chairman of the Tony Lama Boot Company, long recognized for the finest in hand-crafted boots. As the son of the company's founder, Tony has led the company to worldwide brand recognition. He was instrumental in making boots for dignitaries, including former US presidents Truman, Eisenhower, Kennedy, Johnson, Bush, and Reagan. Tony also supports numerous community and civic organizations and in his spare time is an avid golfer.

Green Chile Rice Casserole

3 cups white rice, cooked
2 cups low-fat sour cream
Dash of salt
Non-fat cooking spray
1-1/2 cups Monterey Jack cheese
1/2 cup Jack or Longhorn cheese, grated
4 4-ounce cans green chiles, chopped

Cook rice using package directions. Preheat oven to 350°. In a medium bowl, combine rice, sour cream, and salt, mixing well. Spray a casserole dish with vegetable cooking spray and spoon 1/2 of rice mixture into the pan. Layer with Monterey Jack cheese, then chiles. Top with remaining rice mixture. Sprinkle 1/2 cup Jack or Longhorn cheese on top. Bake 30 minutes. Makes 6 servings.

➤ Approx. per serving: 340 calories; 12 grams of fat

Broccoli Quiche

1 pound fresh broccoli
2 eggs
1/4 cup unbleached flour
2 cups low-fat cottage cheese
2 ounces part-skim mozzarella
    cheese, grated
1/4 cup fresh parsley, finely chopped
1 tablespoon fresh lemon juice
1 teaspoon fresh basil or
    1/2 teaspoon dried basil
1/2 teaspoon fresh oregano or
    1/4 teaspoon dried oregano
1/4 teaspoon salt (optional)
1/4 teaspoon pepper
1/3 cup seasoned Italian bread crumbs
Nonfat cooking spray

Preheat oven to 350°. Cut broccoli into florets, then peel and slice stems. In a saucepan or steamer over medium heat, cook broccoli with a small amount of water until tender-crisp. Drain and chop coarsely. Beat eggs in a bowl with wire whisk. Add flour and continue to whisk until well blended. Add broccoli, cottage cheese, mozzarella cheese, parsley, lemon juice, basil, oregano, salt, and pepper and mix well. Spray 9 x 13-inch baking pan with vegetable cooking spray and pour in broccoli mixture. Top with bread crumbs and bake for 35 to 40 minutes. Cool for 2 to 3 minutes. Cut into squares. Makes 4 servings.

➤ Approx. per serving: 277 calories; 9 grams of fat

Cauliflower Quiche

1 8-ounce package frozen cauliflower
1-1/4 cups low-fat cheddar cheese,
    shredded
1/2 cup green bell pepper, cored,
    peeled, and chopped
1/3 cup onion, finely chopped
1 cup 1% low-fat milk
3/4 cup egg substitute
1/2 cup biscuit mix
1/4 teaspoon paprika
1/8 teaspoon pepper
Nonfat cooking spray

Preheat oven to 375°. Cook cauliflower according to package directions, omitting salt. Drain and coarsely chop cauliflower. Place onto paper towels and squeeze to remove excess moisture. Coat a 9-inch pie plate with vegetable cooking spray and layer cauliflower, cheese, green pepper, and onion. Combine milk, egg substitute, biscuit mix, paprika, and pepper in a blender and process for 15 seconds. Pour mixture over vegetables. Bake for 30 to 35 minutes or until set. Let stand for 5 minutes before serving. Makes 6 servings.

➤ Approx. per serving: 218 calories; 10 grams of fat

Meatless

Stuffed Peppers

3 large bell peppers
2 cups cooked brown rice
1/2 cup chopped almonds
2 scallions, sliced
2 large tomatoes, peeled and chopped
1 cup reduced-fat cheddar cheese,
    shredded
1/4 cup chopped fresh parsley
2 eggs, beaten
2 cloves fresh garlic, pressed
1/2 teaspoon basil
Worcestershire sauce to taste

Preheat oven to 375°. Cut peppers lengthwise. Remove stems and seeds. Drop pepper halves into a pot of boiling water and boil for 2 minutes. Remove and place in cold water. Drain. Stir all remaining ingredients together, saving 1/2 cup of cheese. Fill peppers with mixture. Place peppers in shallow baking dish. Sprinkle remaining cheese over tops. Bake uncovered for 35 minutes. Makes 6 servings.

➤ Approx. per serving: 240 calories; 9 grams of fat

Stuffed Eggplant

3 medium eggplants
1 cup cooked brown rice
1 teaspoon olive oil
1/2 teaspoon salt
1 large scallion, sliced
1 onion, chopped
8-ounce can sliced mushrooms,
    drained
1/2 teaspoon salt
Fresh ground black pepper
1 tablespoon basil
2 tablespoons of bread crumbs

Heat oven to 350°. Puncture the eggplant skin and bake for 45 minutes. Remove from oven and cool. Cut eggplants in half lengthwise, leaving the stem. Scoop out and reserve the insides, leaving 1/2 inch all around. Warm the oil in a medium frying pan. Sauté scallions until softened. Add onion and sauté until it begins to turn golden brown. Add mushrooms, salt, pepper, and basil. Add scooped-out eggplant and cooked rice and cook over low heat for 5 minutes. Fill eggplant shells and place on baking sheet and sprinkle with breadcrumbs. Bake for 15 minutes. Makes 6 servings.

➤ Approx. per serving: 150 calories; 2 grams of fat

Les Brown

*As a noted speaker, best selling author, and radio and television celebrity, Les Brown has reached millions with his high energy message of how to shake off mediocrity and live up to greatness. With no formal education beyond high school, Les rose to the top of his field through sheer persistence and personal determination. He is the author of the highly acclaimed books, **Live Your Dreams** and **It's Not Over Until You Win**.*

Avocado Rolls

1 firm avocado
1 red pepper, seeded
1 carrot, shredded
Juice of one lemon
Alfalfa sprouts
2 scallions, minced
4 Wonton/egg roll wrappers or
 nori sheets
Salt to taste

Peel and slice the avocado. Thinly slice the red pepper. Coat avocado with lemon juice and a sprinkling of salt. Place avocado slices on sheets/wrappers with carrot, sprouts, red pepper, and scallions. Roll, seal, and serve immediately. Makes 4 servings.

➤ Approx. per serving: 230 calories; 5 grams of fat

Eggplant Parmesan

3 medium eggplant, peeled and sliced
1/2 teaspoon salt
1 tablespoon vegetable broth, either
    homemade or canned
1-1/2 cups onion, finely chopped
2 cloves garlic, minced
2 cups low-fat cottage cheese
3 ounces part-skim mozzarella cheese,
    grated
1/2 cup bread crumbs
2 teaspoons fresh oregano or
    1 teaspoon dried oregano
2 teaspoons fresh basil or
    1 teaspoon dried basil
2 teaspoons fresh thyme or
    1 teaspoon dried thyme
1/4 teaspoon pepper
3 fresh tomatoes, thinly sliced
2 cups Marinara Sauce (see recipe
    on page 121)
2 tablespoons Parmesan cheese,
    freshly grated
Non-fat cooking spray

Preheat oven to 350°. Salt eggplant slices lightly. Spray baking sheet with vegetable cooking spray and arrange eggplant slices. Bake for 15 minutes or until tender. Heat vegetable broth in a skillet over medium heat. Add onion and garlic, sauté until soft, then remove from heat. Add cottage cheese, mozzarella cheese, bread crumbs, oregano, basil, thyme, 1/2 teaspoon of salt, and pepper and mix well. Spray a 9 x 13-inch baking pan with vegetable cooking spray and arrange half of the eggplant slices. Spread with cottage cheese mixture, add a layer of remaining eggplant slices, then arrange tomato slices over eggplant. Pour Marinara Sauce over the top and sprinkle with Parmesan cheese. Cover and bake for 25 minutes. Uncover and bake for 10 minutes longer. Let stand for several minutes before serving. Makes 8 servings.

➤ Approx. per serving: 200 calories; 6 grams of fat

Vegetarian Cabbage Rolls with Brown Rice

1 head cabbage
1 tablespoon corn oil margarine
1 cup carrots, chopped
1 cup onion, chopped
1-1/2 cups brown rice, cooked
2 cups vegetable broth, either
   homemade or canned
1 tablespoon fresh lemon juice
1/2 teaspoon salt (optional)
1/4 teaspoon each pepper, cumin
   and celery seed
6 ounces part-skim mozzarella
   cheese, shredded
1 28-ounce can tomatoes, coarsely
   chopped
2 tablespoons cornstarch
2 tablespoons water

Preheat oven to 375°. Remove core from cabbage, leaving head intact. Place cabbage head into a large pot and cover with boiling water. Cover pot partially and cook over medium heat for 10 minutes. Remove cabbage carefully, then drain. Remove 16 to 20 outer leaves, pat dry and set aside. Melt margarine in a large skillet over low heat. Sauté carrots and onion for 5 minutes. Stir in rice, 1/2 cup of broth, lemon juice, salt, pepper, cumin, and celery seed. Cover and simmer for 15 minutes. Remove from heat and allow to cool slightly. Stir in cheese. Trim thick center vein from each cabbage leaf. Place 3 to 4 tablespoons filling into center, roll to enclose filling, folding in sides. Secure with toothpick or thread. Arrange cabbage rolls seam side down in a 9 x 13-inch baking dish. Pour tomatoes with juice and remaining 1-1/2 cups broth over cabbage rolls. Cover and bake for 1 hour. Uncover and bake for 30 minutes longer, basting frequently. Place cabbage rolls onto a serving platter. Pour pan juices into a small saucepan and bring to a boil over medium heat. In a small bowl, blend cornstarch with 2 tablespoons of cold water. Stir into boiling liquid and cook until thickened, stirring constantly. Serve over cabbage rolls. Makes 8 servings.

➤ Approx. per serving: 165 calories; 6 grams of fat

Chinese Meatless Balls

1 14-ounce package meat-flavored
   soy crumbles
2 tablespoons minced fresh ginger
1 clove garlic, finely minced
1 tablespoon cornstarch
1 teaspoon sugar
2 tablespoons vinegar
1 tablespoon soy sauce
1 cup vegetable broth
2 green onions, sliced thinly
1 teaspoon sesame oil
Nonfat cooking spray

In a medium bowl combine soy crumbles, ginger, and garlic. Mix together well and form these into 24 small meatballs. Cover the bottom of a nonstick skillet with cooking spray and cook the balls until brown. Set aside. In a small pan, combine cornstarch, sugar, vinegar, soy sauce, and broth and heat to boiling. Add green onions and sesame oil and remove from heat. Pour mixture over balls and serve immediately. Makes 6 servings.

➤ Approx. per serving: 60 calories; 1 gram of fat

Hickory Smoked Barbecue Tofu Ribs

1 pound light firm tofu
3/4 cup of your favorite hickory
   smoked barbecue sauce
1/2 teaspoon dried mustard powder
2 tablespoons sesame oil
Nonfat cooking spray

Preheat oven to 400°. Squeeze excess liquid from tofu. Cut into 12 rib-like slices. Cover the bottom of a 9 x 13-inch baking pan with cooking spray. Place tofu slices in the pan, keeping them separate so they won't stick. Bake for 10 minutes until brown. Turn and bake another 10 minutes. Mix the barbecue sauce with mustard and sesame oil. Cover all the ribs and bake for an additional 5 to 10 minutes. Ribs can also be cooked on a grill at this point instead. Makes 4 servings.

➤ Approx. per serving: 140 calories; 9 grams of fat

Thanksgiving Tofu Turkey and Stuffing

5 pounds light firm tofu
1 large onion, chopped
2 scallions, chopped
1 bell pepper, cored, seeded,
    and sliced
1 cup mushrooms, sliced
1 cup celery, diced
3 large cloves garlic, pressed
1/4 cup sage
1 teaspoon rosemary
2 teaspoons celery seed
2 teaspoons thyme
1 teaspoon savory
2 teaspoons marjoram
1/4 cup sesame oil, divided
1/2 cup tamari sauce
1 cup packaged stuffing mix
1/2 teaspoon Dijon mustard

Mash tofu until free of lumps. Wrap the tofu in a damp cheesecloth. Drain it in a colander by placing a weight over it to extract all of the liquid. Place in a bowl in the refrigerator for 2 hours. Stir-fry the onion, scallions, bell pepper, mushrooms, and celery in 2 tablespoons of the sesame oil over moderate heat. When tender, add 1/4 cup of tamari sauce, garlic, and spices. Add stuffing and stir well. Remove the cheesecloth from the tofu. Place the tofu on a plate and hollow out the center. Fill the tofu firmly with the stuffing. Cover opening firmly with the remaining tofu. Place stuffed tofu on an oiled baking sheet. Gently smooth the tofu into an oval shape. Make a basting mixture of 1/4 cup of tamari sauce, the remaining sesame oil, and Dijon mustard. Baste the tofu with half of the mixture. Preheat oven to 400°. Cover with foil and bake for 1 hour at 400°. Remove foil, baste again (saving a small portion), and return to oven for another hour until golden brown. Remove from oven and baste with remaining mixture. Serve with cranberry sauce. Makes 8 servings.

➤ Approx. per serving: 289 calories; 10.5 grams of fat

Meatless

Mixed Vegetable Curry

2 tablespoons olive oil
2 large onions, cut in large slices
1 small red bell pepper, cored, seeded, and chopped
1 small yellow bell pepper, cored, seeded, and chopped
2 carrots, peeled and chopped
1 cup fresh mushrooms, sliced
2-1/2 cups vegetable stock, divided
2 large cloves garlic, pressed
1 teaspoon ground cumin
1 teaspoon ground coriander
1 teaspoon chopped fresh cilantro
1/2 teaspoon fresh ginger
1/2 teaspoon ground turmeric
1 pinch allspice
1 pinch cayenne pepper
1 tablespoon tomato paste
2 cups broccoli florets
2 cups cauliflower florets
2 medium new red potatoes, peeled and cut
Juice of one lemon
1 pinch salt
4 cups cooked rice

Warm oil in a large deep skillet. Stir-fry the onions, peppers, carrots, and mushrooms for 2 minutes. Add 1/2 of the stock and then stir in garlic and spices. Reduce heat, simmer, and stir until mixture is thick. Stir in the tomato paste. Purée half of the mixture in a blender and push it through a sieve. Add the purée mixture back to the pan. Add broccoli, cauliflower, and potatoes and mix with the remaining stock. Stir in lemon juice and salt to taste. Cover and simmer until the vegetables are tender. Serve over rice. Makes 8 servings.

➤ Approx. per serving: 201 calories; 4.2 grams of fat.

Sesame Kebobs

2 tablespoons olive oil, divided
2 tablespoons tamari sauce, divided
2 tablespoons lemon juice
2 cloves fresh garlic, pressed
1 tablespoon sesame oil
Salt and pepper to taste
3 small courgettes (zucchini)
6 small pieces of sweetcorn, sliced
16 button mushrooms
12 cherry tomatoes
2 tablespoons sesame seeds
10 ounces light firm tofu, cut in cubes
Cooked rice

Place 1 tablespoon of olive oil, 1 tablespoon of tamari sauce, lemon juice, garlic, sesame oil, salt, and pepper in a blender. Blend until evenly mixed. Place in a small container and refrigerate. Cut each courgette. Blanch in boiling, salted water for 1 minute. Drain. Slide vegetables and tofu onto 4 large skewers, repeating pattern until full. Mix the remaining oil and tamari sauce with the sesame seeds. Brush over kebobs. Grill for 10 minutes, turn, and baste. Serve over rice, using the refrigerated sauce as a garnish. Makes 4 servings.

➤ Approx. per serving: 200 calories; 14 grams of fat

Chili & Stews

Buzz Aldrin

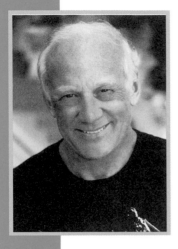

One of NASA's earliest astronauts, Buzz Aldrin had the "right stuff" when he set foot on the moon on July 20, 1969. In addition to his Apollo XI mission, Buzz established a new record for Extra-Vehicular Activity in space on the Gemini XII orbital flight mission in November 1966. Today, Buzz remains active in efforts to insure the USA's leadership in manned space activity. He has created a master plan for sustained exploration in space, and in 1993 received a patent for a permanent space station he designed.

Chicken and Bean Tureen

2 chicken legs
2 chicken breasts
2 onions, chopped, divided
5 carrots, divided
1 stalk celery
2 15-ounce cans Great Northern
*   beans, drained and rinsed*
2 tomatoes, peeled and chopped
1/2 green bell pepper, seeded and
*   chopped*
2 teaspoons fresh thyme or
*   1 teaspoon dried thyme*
2 cloves garlic, minced
Parsley to taste
Salt and pepper to taste

Remove all skin and fat from chicken pieces. Place chicken, half of onion, 1 sliced carrot and celery into a saucepan. Add enough water to cover and cook over medium heat until chicken is tender. Remove chicken, allow to cool, and bone. Strain and reserve 2 cups broth. Preheat oven to 350°. Grease a large casserole dish and place chicken, reserved broth and beans in dish. Cut the remaining 4 carrots into large pieces and add with tomatoes, remaining onion, green pepper, thyme, garlic, parsley, salt, and pepper. Bake for 45 minutes or until mixture simmers gently. Serve in soup bowls. Makes 6 servings.

➤ Approx. per serving: 354 calories; 7 grams of fat

Vegetable Stew

16 small fresh pearl onions
1-1/2 cups water, divided
1 teaspoon fresh thyme or
    1/2 teaspoon dried thyme
1 teaspoon fresh tarragon or
    1/2 teaspoon dried tarragon
Salt (optional)
12 carrots, peeled and cut into
    2-inch pieces
1/2 small bunch broccoli, cut into
    florets
1/2 small cauliflower, cut into florets
6 summer squash, cut into 2-inch
    pieces
4 small zucchini, halved lengthwise
24 green beans, trimmed and cut
    into 2-inch pieces
1 tablespoon mixed fresh basil,
    parsley, thyme, and tarragon or
    1 teaspoon mixed dried herbs
2 cloves garlic, finely chopped
2 tablespoons olive oil
Salt and freshly ground pepper
    to taste

Bring a large saucepan of salted water to a boil. Maintain boil while cooking vegetables. Combine onions, 1 cup of water, thyme, tarragon, and a pinch of salt in a large sauté pan over medium heat. Cover and simmer for 5 minutes. Place carrots into saucepan, cook for 2 minutes, then remove carrots and place into sauté pan. Cover and simmer onions and carrots for 5 minutes. Place broccoli and cauliflower into boiling water and cook for 5 minutes, then remove and place into sauté pan. Add 1/2 cup of water, toss to mix, and cover while continuing to simmer. Add squash and zucchini to boiling water, cook for 3 minutes, then remove and place into sauté pan. Add beans to boiling water, cook for 1 minute, then remove beans to sauté pan. Toss vegetables together and add water, if necessary. Liquid should equal about 1 cup. Cover and cook for 5 minutes Then uncover, turn heat to high, and add mixed herbs, garlic, and olive oil. Cook until sauce thickens slightly, tossing vegetables constantly. Add salt and pepper to taste. Makes 8 servings.

➤ Approx. per serving: 114 calories; 4 grams of fat

Chicken Gumbo

1 pound boneless skinless chicken
    breast, cut into bite-sized pieces
3 cups water
2 cups chicken broth, either home-
    made or canned, divided
1 cup onion, chopped
1 clove garlic, minced
1/2 teaspoon fresh thyme or
    1/4 teaspoon dried thyme
1/4 teaspoon dried red pepper
1/4 teaspoon fresh sage or
    1/8 teaspoon dried sage
1 bay leaf
2 cups fresh okra, sliced
2 cups fresh tomatoes, chopped
2 cups fresh corn
1/2 teaspoon salt (optional)
1/4 teaspoon pepper
2 cups uncooked brown rice
1 tablespoon corn oil margarine
1 tablespoon all-purpose flour

Rinse chicken and place into a large soup pot with water and 1 cup of broth. Bring to a boil over medium-high heat, reduce heat, and skim with slotted spoon. Add onion, garlic, thyme, red pepper, sage, and bay leaf. Cover and simmer for 20 minutes, then skim once again. Add okra, tomatoes, and corn. Cover and simmer for 20 minutes adding salt and pepper. Cook rice according to package directions. Melt margarine in a medium saucepan over low heat. Add flour and cook until golden and bubbly, stirring constantly. Stir in 1 cup broth, bring to a boil, then reduce heat. Whisk until smooth. Stir into chicken mixture and heat to serving temperature. Spoon hot cooked brown rice into large soup bowls and ladle gumbo over rice. Makes 8 servings.

➤ Approx. per serving: 317 calories; 5 grams of fat

Simple Cabbage Stew

1 package dry onion soup mix
2 16-ounce cans tomatoes
2 green bell peppers, seeded
    and chopped
1 cup celery, chopped
2 onions, chopped
1 head cabbage, shredded

Cook onion soup mix in a large sauce-pan or stockpot according to package directions. Add tomatoes, green peppers, celery, onions, and cabbage. Simmer over low to medium heat until vegetables are tender. Makes 6 to 8 servings.

➤ Approx. per serving: 61 calories; 0.6 grams of fat

Chili & Stews

Cabbage Stew

4 cups water
4 cups cabbage, grated
3 cups potatoes, peeled and diced
2 cups carrots, chopped
1 cup onion, chopped
1 cup celery with leaves, chopped
1 teaspoon fresh thyme or
    1/2 teaspoon dried thyme
1 bay leaf
1/2 teaspoon salt (optional)
1/2 teaspoon pepper
2 cups 1% low-fat milk
1 15-ounce can tomato sauce

Bring water to a boil in a large saucepan over medium-high heat. Add cabbage, potatoes, carrots, onion, celery, thyme, bay leaf, salt, and pepper. Bring to a boil, reduce heat, and simmer, uncovered, for 45 minutes or until vegetables are tender. Add milk and tomato sauce. Heat over low heat to serving temperature. Remove and discard bay leaf. Ladle into soup bowls. Makes 8 servings.

➤ Approx. per serving: 119 calories; 1 gram of fat

Beef Stew

1-1/2 cups ditalini or other small
    pasta shape, uncooked
2 tablespoons vegetable oil
1 pound lean beef stew meat,
    cut into 1-inch chunks
3/4 cup onion, chopped
9 cups hot water
3 tablespoons beef-flavored
    instant bouillon
1 large bay leaf
1 teaspoon basil
1/8 teaspoon pepper
1-1/2 cups carrots, sliced
1-1/2 cups celery, sliced
1 14-1/2-ounce can stewed tomatoes
3 tablespoons flour

Heat oil in a large saucepan or Dutch oven over medium-high heat. Coat beef cubes with flour. Add beef and onion to saucepan and cook until beef is browned. Add water, bouillon, bay leaf, basil, and pepper. Bring to a boil, reduce heat, and simmer for 1-1/2 hours, covered, until meat is tender. Add carrots, celery, and tomatoes and cook for 15 minutes longer. Remove bay leaf. Stir in pasta and cook for 10 to 15 minutes until tender, stirring occasionally. Makes 8 to 10 servings.

➤ Approx. per serving: 233 calories; 9 grams of fat

Seafood Gumbo

1 teaspoon corn oil margarine

1 cup onion, chopped

1 clove garlic, minced

7 cups water

1 pound fresh shrimp, peeled and
     deveined

1 10-ounce package frozen okra,
     sliced

1 cup celery, sliced

3/4 cup green bell pepper, seeded
     and chopped

1/2 cup uncooked regular rice

1 16-ounce can whole tomatoes,
     undrained and chopped

1 8-ounce bottle of clam juice

3 tablespoons all-purpose flour

2 teaspoons Worcestershire sauce

1 teaspoon gumbo filé or
     1/2 teaspoon dried whole thyme

3/4 teaspoon salt (optional)

1/4 teaspoon pepper

1/8 teaspoon hot pepper sauce

1 pound fresh crab meat

1 4-ounce jar pimento, diced and
     drained

Nonfat cooking spray

Spray a 5-quart Dutch oven with vegetable cooking spray. Add margarine and melt over medium heat. Add onion and garlic and sauté until tender. Add water, shrimp, okra, celery, bell pepper, and rice. Bring to a boil, reduce heat, and simmer, uncovered, for 30 to 35 minutes. Stir in tomatoes. Combine clam juice, flour, Worcestershire sauce, gumbo filé (or thyme), salt, pepper, and hot pepper sauce in a bowl and mix well. Stir into gumbo mixture and cook over medium heat until thickened, stirring constantly. Add crab meat and pimento. Heat to serving temperature. Makes 17 cups.

➤ Approx. per serving: 102 calories; 1 gram of fat

New Orleans Jambalaya Stew

2 tablespoons corn oil margarine
1/2 cup onion, chopped
1/2 cup scallions, chopped
1/2 cup green bell pepper, seeded
    and chopped
1/2 cup celery, chopped
2 cloves garlic, minced
2 cups chicken broth, either home-
    made or canned
1-1/2 cups fresh tomatoes, chopped
1/4 cup fresh parsley, chopped
1/2 teaspoon salt (optional)
1/2 teaspoon fresh thyme or
    1/4 teaspoon dried thyme
1/8 teaspoon pepper
1/8 teaspoon cayenne pepper
2 bay leaves
1 cup uncooked brown rice
8 chicken breast halves, skinned
    and boned

Heat margarine in a stockpot over medium heat. Add onion, scallions, green pepper, celery, and garlic. Sauté for 5 minutes. Add broth, tomatoes, parsley, salt, thyme, black pepper, cayenne pepper, and bay leaves and cover. Bring to a boil over medium heat. Add rice and chicken, cover and continue to cook over medium-low heat for 45 minutes, stirring occasionally. Remove bay leaves. Serve hot. Makes 8 servings.

➤ Approx. per serving: 276 calories; 7 grams of fat

Chicken Stew

1 (3 to 3-1/2-pound) chicken, skinned,
    and chopped
8 medium potatoes, cut into eighths
1 large onion, cut into eighths
1 large green bell pepper, seeded and
    cut into strips
2 carrots, sliced
Salt and pepper to taste
Nonfat cooking spray

Spray a skillet with vegetable cooking spray and brown chicken over medium-high heat. Add potatoes, onions, green pepper, carrots, salt, and pepper. Simmer for 45 minutes or until chicken is tender. Makes 5 servings.

➤ Approx. per serving: 676 calories; 10 grams of fat

Brian Boitano

*After winning gold at the 1988 Olympic Winter Games in Calgary, Brian Boitano didn't hang up his skates. If anything, he's busier than ever, competing professionally, producing skating shows, and changing the world of professional figure skating. He was the first American male athlete to have his own network television specials, **Canvas of Ice** and **Carmen on Ice** (for which he won an Emmy award). He is also the author of the book, **Boitano's Edge: Inside the Real World of Figure Skating**. Brian has also taken the leadership role in developing a circuit for professional competitions, raising the standard of the professional side of the sport.*

Boardroom Chili

1 tablespoon olive oil
2 large onions, chopped
3 cloves garlic, crushed
1 pound low-fat ground turkey breast
1 teaspoon cinnamon
2 cups mushrooms, coarsely chopped
1 6-ounce can tomato paste
1 can or 12-ounce frozen package corn
1 12-ounce can garbanzo beans,
    drained
1 32-ounce can crushed tomatoes
3 teaspoons fresh oregano, chopped
1 teaspoon salt
1 teaspoon black pepper
4 drops hot pepper sauce

Heat oil in a large soup pot or stockpot over medium heat. Add onion and crushed garlic and sauté for 15 minutes, until browned and wilted. Add turkey and sprinkle with cinnamon. Cook until browned, stirring frequently to mix onions, and to ensure meat cooks evenly. Add mushrooms and simmer for 5 minutes or until mushrooms are dark in color, but still firm. Add tomato paste, stirring in thoroughly, then add corn, beans, crushed tomatoes, and oregano. Add salt, pepper, and hot pepper sauce, seasoned to taste. Cook for 30 minutes partially covered over low heat. Makes 6 to 8 servings.

➤ Approx. per serving: 261 calories; 7 grams of fat

Caribbean Chili

4 cups dried black beans, soaked
8 cups water
2 jalapeño peppers, chopped
1 tablespoon grated fresh ginger
1 bay leaf
1 cup cilantro, chopped, divided
1 teaspoon cumin seeds
1/2 tablespoon mustard seeds
2 tablespoons chili powder
1/2 tablespoon oregano
5 cups of tomatoes, peeled and
    chopped
1/2 cup sun-dried tomatoes
1/3 cup uncooked bulgur wheat
1 teaspoon salt
1 teaspoon black pepper
4 cups cooked rice

Drain beans. Place in large pot with 8 cups of water and bring to a boil. Add peppers, ginger, bay leaf, and 1/2 cup cilantro. Cover and simmer for 1-1/2 hours. Remove from heat. Remove bay leaf and discard. In a separate pot add cumin seeds, mustard seeds, chili powder, oregano, and tomatoes. Simmer on low heat for 1/2 hour, stirring frequently. Combine bulgur wheat with 1/2 cup of boiling water in a separate bowl and let sit for 10 minutes. Take one cup of the cooked beans, along with some of the cooking liquid and purée. Pour this purée back into the bean mixture, along with tomato mixture, bulgur wheat, salt, and pepper. Simmer for 10 minutes. Serve over rice and add remaining cilantro to top of bowl before serving. Makes 8 servings.

➤ Approx. per serving: 486 calories; 2.2 grams of fat

Italian Beef Stew

2 pounds lean stew beef
1 16-ounce can tomatoes
1 cup beef broth, either homemade
    or canned
1/2 cup dry red wine
1/4 cup tapioca
3 cloves garlic, minced
3 bay leaves
2 teaspoons each fresh marjoram,
    oregano and basil or 1 teaspoon
    each, dried
1 teaspoon salt (optional)
1 teaspoon granulated sugar
1 teaspoon fresh thyme or
    1/2 teaspoon dried thyme
1/2 teaspoon pepper
1/2 teaspoon dry red pepper flakes
    (optional)
2 medium onions, cut into chunks
4 stalks celery, cut into chunks
2 to 4 medium potatoes, peeled and
    cut into chunks
4 to 6 carrots, peeled and cut into
    chunks
1/2 pound fresh mushrooms
1 10-ounce package frozen peas,
    thawed

Preheat oven to 275°. Combine beef, tomatoes, broth, wine, and tapioca in a 6-quart Dutch oven and mix well. Add garlic, bay leaves, marjoram, oregano, basil, salt, sugar, thyme, black pepper, and red pepper flakes and mix well. Stir in onions and celery. Cover and bake for 4 hours. Add potatoes and carrots. Cover and bake for 1-1/4 hours or until vegetables are tender. Sauté mushrooms in a skillet over medium heat. Stir mushrooms and peas into stew. Bake or cook over low heat for 15 minutes longer. Discard bay leaves. Makes 6 to 8 servings.

➤ Approx. per serving: 500 calories; 16 grams of fat

Fresh Beef Stew with Vegetables

2 pounds boneless beef roast,
  all fat removed
8 medium potatoes, peeled and
  quartered
8 medium carrots, peeled and
  quartered
1 large onion, sliced
2 cloves garlic, minced
1 teaspoon fresh thyme or
  1/2 teaspoon dried thyme
1/2 teaspoon salt (optional)
1/4 teaspoon pepper
1/2 cup red wine
2 tablespoons corn oil margarine,
  softened
2 tablespoons all-purpose flour
1 cup fresh parsley, chopped

Preheat oven to 250°. Place roast into a Dutch oven and arrange potatoes, carrots, and onion around and over roast. Sprinkle with garlic, thyme, salt, and pepper, then drizzle wine over top. Cover and roast for 4-1/2 hours. Place roast onto a serving platter and slice if desired. Surround with vegetables and keep warm. Place Dutch oven with pan juices over high heat and cook until bubbly. In a small bowl, blend margarine and flour into a smooth paste, then stir into pan juices. Cook until thickened, whisking constantly. Spoon a small amount over roast and vegetables then sprinkle with parsley. Pour remaining gravy into a gravy boat and serve with roast. Makes 8 (3-ounce) servings.

➤ Approx. per serving: 339 calories; 11 grams of fat

Vegetable Medley Stew

4-1/2 cups water, divided
1 medium onion, chopped
1 46-ounce can tomato juice
1 16-ounce package frozen mixed
  vegetables
1 14-1/2-ounce can tomatoes
2 cups celery, chopped
1 cup Napa or green cabbage, shredded
1 cup uncooked brown rice
1/4 cup fresh parsley, chopped
2 teaspoons fresh oregano or
  1 teaspoon dried oregano
1 teaspoon celery seed
1 teaspoon dillseed
1 teaspoon chives, chopped

Heat 1/4 cup of water over low heat in a nonstick skillet. Add onion and simmer until onion is clear. Place onion into a soup pot. Add remaining 4 cups water, tomato juice, mixed vegetables, tomatoes, celery, cabbage, rice, parsley, oregano, celery seed, dillseed, and chives. Bring to a boil over medium-high heat. Reduce heat and simmer for 30 minutes or until rice is tender. Refrigerate overnight. Reheat to serving temperature over low heat. Makes 3 quarts.

➤ Approx. per serving: 112 calories; 0.7 grams of fat

Garden Chili

3 tablespoons corn oil or safflower oil
3 large onions, chopped
3 zucchini, sliced
1 pound fresh mushrooms, chopped
2 or 3 leeks, thoroughly cleaned and
    chopped
1 clove garlic, minced
2 tablespoons chili powder
2 teaspoons mustard seed
1 teaspoon cumin seed
1/4 teaspoon cardamom, ground
1/4 teaspoon cinnamon
2 20-ounce cans whole tomatoes
1 16-ounce can stewed tomatoes
1 6-ounce can tomato paste
1 cup beer or water
1 tablespoon vinegar
1 tablespoon light brown sugar
3 16-ounce cans kidney beans
Part-skim mozzarella cheese, shredded
Low-fat plain yogurt
Green onions, chopped
Red Salsa for topping
Tomatoes, chopped
Lettuce, shredded
Tortilla chips, slightly crushed
Green chilies, chopped

Heat oil in a large kettle over low heat. Add onions, zucchini, mushrooms, leeks, garlic, chili powder, mustard seed, cumin seed, cardamom, and cinnamon. Sauté for several minutes. Cut canned tomatoes into large chunks. Add tomatoes to sautéed vegetables along with tomato paste, beer, vinegar, and brown sugar. Add beans. Cook over low heat for 45 to 60 minutes or until thickened. Ladle chili into soup bowls. Place cheese, yogurt, green onions, salsa, tomatoes, lettuce, tortilla chips, and chilies into individual serving bowls. Garnish chili with desired toppings. Makes 10 to 12 servings.

➤ Approx. per serving: 262 calories; 6 grams of fat

Robert Hooks

Actor and producer Robert Hooks has developed several notable projects for film and television. His credits include co-production of **Voices of Our People**, a PBS special, production of **Songs of the Lusitanian Bogey**, as well as numerous off-Broadway productions. His acting credits include Broadway, Off-Broadway, film, and television. Robert is founder and organizer of Washington, DC's Black Repertory Theatre Company and helped establish the internationally renowned Negro Ensemble Company.

Hooks Hot Hollywood Chili

4 tablespoons extra virgin olive oil
1 large onion, chopped
1 green pepper, seeded and chopped
2 celery stalks, chopped
4 garlic cloves, crushed and chopped
2 pounds lean ground turkey breast
3 teaspoons hot chili powder
1 teaspoon salt
1 teaspoon pepper
1 teaspoon garlic powder
1 packet chili mix
2 28-ounce cans crushed tomatoes
1 can chopped or minced clams
1 can kidney beans, drained
6 ounces fresh mushrooms

In a large deep saucepan, heat olive oil over moderate heat. When oil is hot, add onions, green pepper, celery, and garlic and fry, stirring occasionally for 5 to 7 minutes or until onion is soft and transparent. In a separate frying pan cook ground turkey, adding spices, garlic powder, and chili mix. Add cooked turkey mixture to sauce pan, and mix together. Add canned tomatoes, clams, beans, and mushrooms and stir with a wooden spoon to mix. Reduce heat to low, cover, and simmer for 30 minutes. Remove pan from heat and serve with garlic bread or saltine crackers. Don't forget water to put out the fire! Makes 8 to 10 servings.

➤ Approx. per serving: 344 calories; 9 grams of fat

Hearty Red Beans and Rice Casserole

3/4 pound ham hocks, washed
1 quart water
1 pound dried red beans, sorted and
    washed
1-1/2 cups onions, chopped
1 cup fresh parsley, chopped
1 cup green bell pepper, seeded and
    chopped
1 8-ounce can tomato sauce
1/2 cup green onions, chopped
1 clove garlic, pressed
1 tablespoon Worcestershire sauce
1 teaspoon pepper
1/2 teaspoon red pepper
1/2 teaspoon fresh oregano or
    1/4 teaspoon dried oregano
1/2 teaspoon fresh thyme or
    1/4 teaspoon dried thyme
3 dashes of hot pepper sauce
5 cups rice, cooked

Place ham hocks and water into a large saucepan, bring to a boil over medium-high heat, and cover. Reduce heat to medium-low and simmer for 30 minutes or until tender. Remove and discard ham hocks. Strain broth and chill overnight. Remove surface fat then set broth aside. Place beans and water to cover into a stockpot and let stand overnight. Drain beans and add ham broth. Cover and cook over low heat for 45 minutes. Add onions, parsley, green pepper, tomato sauce, green onions, garlic, Worcester-shire sauce, black and red peppers, oregano, thyme, and hot pepper sauce. Cover and cook over low heat for 2 to 2-1/2 hours, stirring occasionally and adding additional water if desired. Serve over rice. Makes 10 servings.

➤ Approx. per serving: 282 calories; 1 gram of fat.

Relishes & Salsas

Apple Cranberry Relish

1 apple, cored, peeled, and sliced
1 12-ounce bag of cranberries, fresh
   or frozen
3 tablespoons orange juice concentrate
1/2 teaspoon ground ginger
1/2 teaspoon ground cinnamon
3 tablespoons sugar

Place apple slices and cranberries in food processor and chop lightly. Heat orange juice concentrate, ginger, cinnamon, and sugar in pan over medium heat and add berry mixture to pan. Cook over medium heat for 10 minutes, stirring often. This relish can be served warm or chilled, as a side dish for meats and chicken. Makes 6 servings.

➤ Approx. per serving: 78 calories; 0.2 grams of fat

Sweet Corn Relish

2 cups whole kernel corn
1/4 cup fresh red pepper, seeded,
   cored, and finely chopped
1/2 red onion, thinly sliced
6 tablespoons sweet pickle relish
1/4 teaspoon dry mustard
2 tablespoons distilled white vinegar
2 tablespoons sugar
2 tablespoons water
1/2 teaspoon salt

Stir all ingredients into a saucepan. Bring to a boil, reduce heat to simmer, and simmer for 10 minutes. Refrigerate for 1 hour before serving. Makes 16 servings.

➤ Approx. per serving: 36 calories; 0 grams of fat

Relishes & Salsas

Tangy Plum Relish

2 teaspoons fresh lime juice
1 cup fresh plums, finely chopped
1/4 cup fresh tomato, finely chopped
2 tablespoons brown sugar
Dash of salt

Mix all ingredients together in a small bowl and place in refrigerator. Refrigerate overnight to blend flavors. Makes 6 servings.

➤ Approx. per serving: 33 calories; 0.2 grams of fat

Eggplant Salsa

1 large (1-1/4 pounds) eggplant
1 large tomato, peeled and chopped
3 green onions, finely chopped
1/2 stalk celery, finely chopped
1/4 cup green bell pepper, seeded
    and minced (optional)
1 large clove garlic, minced
2 teaspoons corn oil or safflower oil
1 teaspoon fresh lemon juice
1/2 teaspoon salt (optional)
1/2 teaspoon freshly ground pepper

Preheat oven to 400°. Prick eggplant in several places with fork and place onto a baking sheet. Bake until tender, turning eggplant several times. Allow eggplant to cool, then peel and chop finely. Gently mix eggplant, tomato, green onions, celery, green pepper, and garlic into a medium bowl. Toss to mix. Add oil, lemon juice, salt, and pepper and mix well. Cover and refrigerate for 1 hour or more to blend flavors. Makes 12 (1/4 cup) servings.

➤ Approx. per serving: 24 calories; 2 grams of fat

David Cowgill

*To millions of soap opera fans, David Cowgill is best known as "Cliff" on **The Young and the Restless**, but his credits include television and film performances as well as stage rolls. He has appeared in episodes of **J.A.G.**, **Star Trek Voyager**, **Party of Five**, and **Beverly Hills 90210**. Film credits include **Kiss the Girls**, **Child Again**, **Same River Twice**, and **Nine Guys**. His stage work around Los Angeles includes live radio dramas at the **Gene Autry Western Heritage Museum**.*

Dave's Special Salsa

2 tablespoons finely chopped white onions
1 tablespoon finely chopped red onions
8 Roma tomatoes, diced
2 tablespoons finely cored, seeded, and diced bell peppers
2 serrano chilies, finely diced
2 tablespoons finely chopped cilantro leaves
1 teaspoon sugar
1 teaspoon salt
1 tablespoon fresh lime juice
2 teaspoons finely minced garlic
Dash of hot pepper sauce

Place the white onion in a strainer, rinse with hot water and drain. Combine all ingredients in mixing bowl. Chill in the refrigerator for at least 30 minutes to let flavors combine. Makes 2 cups.

➤ Approx. per serving: 18 calories; 0.2 grams of fat

Pineapple, Peach, and Jalapeño Salsa

2 cups pineapple, chopped finely
2 cups peaches, chopped finely
4 pickled jalapeño slices, minced
2 scallions, chopped finely, divided
1/4 teaspoon garlic salt

In a medium bowl, mix all ingredients together except for 1 tablespoon of scallions. Transfer to serving bowl, top with remaining scallions, and chill 1 hour. Makes 8 servings.

➤ Approx. per serving: 48 calories; 0 grams of fat

Sun-Dried Tomato Dip

1 3-ounce package sun-dried
    tomatoes, packed without oil
    (about 2 cups)
1/3 cup fresh basil leaves (do not
    substitute dried basil)
2 tablespoons balsamic vinegar
2 tablespoons Italian-style tomato paste
1 tablespoon olive oil
1/8 teaspoon salt
1/8 teaspoon pepper
1 15-ounce can white beans, drained
1 garlic clove, minced
Pita chips

In a medium bowl, combine dried tomatoes and 1 cup of boiling water. Let stand for at least 15 minutes. Drain tomatoes, reserving 1/2 cup of soaking water. In a food processor, blend softened tomatoes, reserved water, fresh basil, and remaining ingredients (vinegar through garlic); process until smooth. Serve with pita chips. Makes approximately 8 servings.

➤ Approx. per serving: 140 calories; 2 grams of fat

Fat-free Tartar Sauce

1 cup fat-free mayonnaise
2 tablespoons sweet pickle relish
2 tablespoons onion, finely chopped

Combine ingredients in a bowl and stir well. Cover and refrigerate for 1 hour before serving. Makes 16 servings of 1 tablespoon each.

➤ Approx. per serving: 15 calories; 0 grams of fat

Chunky Sweet and Sour Sauce

1 cup mango chutney
2 tablespoons Dijon mustard
2 tablespoons red wine vinegar
2 tablespoons hoisin sauce
2 tablespoons brown sugar
1 teaspoon hot pepper sauce

Combine all ingredients together in a small bowl and mix well. Cover and refrigerate overnight to blend flavors. Makes 16 servings of 1 tablespoon each.

➤ Approx. per serving: 28 calories; 0 grams of fat

Vegetables

Vegetables

Easy Microwave Vegetables

2 pounds fresh broccoli, trimmed
1 small head cauliflower, cut into
    florets
1 carrot, peeled and thinly sliced
1 zucchini, sliced 1/4-inch thick
4 ounces fresh mushrooms, sliced
1 small red bell pepper, seeded
    and cut into wide strips
2 tablespoons corn oil margarine,
    melted
Parmesan cheese (optional)

Place broccoli around the edge of a microwave-safe platter with stems toward center, place cauliflower florets onto center of platter. Add carrot, zucchini, mushrooms, and red pepper strips around the cauliflower. Drizzle with margarine and cover with plastic wrap. Microwave on high for 10 to 12 minutes or until vegetables are tender, turning platter every 4 minutes. Let stand for 5 minutes. Sprinkle with Parmesan cheese if desired. Makes 8 servings.

➤ Approx. per serving: 77 calories; 4 grams of fat

Garden Ratatouille

2 small eggplant, peeled and
    thinly sliced
Salt to taste
2 tablespoons olive oil, divided
4 small zucchini, sliced
2 cups onions, chopped
3 cloves garlic, minced
3 green bell peppers, cored,
    seeded, and cut into cubes
2 cups fresh tomatoes, chopped
1/2 cup fresh parsley, chopped
2 teaspoons fresh oregano or
    1 teaspoon dried oregano
1/2 teaspoon granulated sugar
1/2 teaspoon salt (optional)
1/4 teaspoon pepper
6 cups brown rice, cooked

Preheat oven to 325°. In a colander, sprinkle eggplant with salt. Rinse after 30 minutes and dry with paper towels. Brush a small amount of oil in a nonstick skillet and sauté eggplant over medium heat until softened, brushing skillet with oil as necessary. Remove eggplant. Add remaining oil and zucchini and sauté until tender. Remove zucchini with a slotted spoon. Add onions and garlic and sauté for 5 minutes. Add green peppers, tomatoes, parsley, oregano, sugar, salt, and pepper. Cook for 5 minutes longer. Layer eggplant, zucchini and tomato mixture, half at a time, in a casserole dish. Cover and bake for 1 hour. Serve over hot rice. Makes 8 servings.

➤ Approx. per serving: 270 calories; 4 grams of fat

Vegetables

Microwave Garden Trio

1 tablespoon corn oil margarine
1/2 pound fresh asparagus spears,
    cut into 2-inch pieces
1/2 teaspoon basil
1/2 pound fresh mushrooms, sliced
1 medium tomato, cut into wedges
Salt and pepper to taste

Microwave margarine on high for 30 seconds in a 1-1/2-quart glass baking dish. Add asparagus, and basil and mix well. Cover and microwave for 3 minutes. Add mushrooms. Cover and microwave for 3 minutes. Add tomato. Cover and microwave for 1-1/2 minutes longer. Season with salt and pepper. Cover and let stand for 3 minutes. Makes 4 servings.

➤ Approx. per serving: 73 calories; 2 grams of fat

Greek Zucchini

8 small zucchini, scored lengthwise
    with fork
2/3 cup water
1 tablespoon corn oil margarine
1 medium onion, chopped
1 clove garlic, chopped
4 ripe tomatoes, peeled and chopped
Salt and pepper to taste

In a large saucepan cook zucchini in water over medium heat until tender. Remove pan from heat and set aside. In a skillet, sauté onion and garlic in margarine until tender. Add tomatoes and cook until they are soft. Season to taste with salt and pepper. Drain zucchini and arrange on a serving plate. Spoon tomato mixture over top. Makes 6 to 8 servings.

➤ Approx. per serving: 53 calories; 1 gram of fat

Vegetables

Fresh Stir-Fry Mélange

2 tablespoons olive oil
3-1/2 cups fresh green bell peppers,
    cut into strips
3-1/2 cups fresh red bell peppers,
    cut into strips
2-1/2 cups fresh mushrooms, sliced
1 cup celery, sliced
2 tablespoons onion, chopped
3/4 teaspoon salt (optional)
1/2 clove garlic, crushed
1/2 teaspoon granulated sugar
1/2 teaspoon fresh oregano or
    1/4 teaspoon dried oregano
Dash of pepper
2 tomatoes, cut into wedges
1 teaspoon wine vinegar

Heat olive oil over medium-high heat in a skillet or wok. Add green and red pepper strips, mushrooms, celery, onion, salt, garlic, sugar, oregano, and pepper. Stir-fry until peppers are tender-crisp. Add tomatoes and vinegar. Stir-fry until heated through. Makes 6 servings.

➤ Approx. per serving: 83 calories; 5 grams of fat

Steamed Vegetables

1/2 pound fresh pearl onions
3/4 pound fresh baby carrots
1/2 pound asparagus
2 tablespoons water
1 tablespoon butter
1 bay leaf
1/2 teaspoon salt
Pinch white pepper

In separate pots of boiling water, blanch the carrots and pearl onions for 2 minutes, then drain. Cut off onion root end and remove skin by gentle squeezing. Trim asparagus. Preheat oven to 375°. Place vegetables flat on heavy-duty foil. Sprinkle with water and season with salt and pepper. Add bay leaf and dot with butter. Seal foil around edges and bake until tender (about 30 minutes). Makes 6 servings.

➤ Approx. per serving: 61 calories; 2 grams of fat

Tomatoes Florentine

6 medium tomatoes
2 tablespoons corn oil margarine
1 small onion, finely chopped
1 clove garlic, minced
1 10-ounce package frozen spinach,
    thawed, drained, and chopped
1/3 cup 1% low-fat milk
2 tablespoons fine dry bread crumbs
2 tablespoons fresh parsley, chopped
2 tablespoons Parmesan cheese,
    freshly grated
Salt and freshly ground pepper to taste

Preheat oven to 400°. Slice tops off tomatoes and scoop out half the pulp. Melt margarine in a skillet over medium heat. Add onion and garlic and sauté until tender. Add spinach, milk, salt, and pepper and mix well. Spoon spinach mixture into tomato shell and place in an ovenproof serving dish or on a baking sheet. Combine bread crumbs, parsley, and cheese in a small bowl and mix well. Sprinkle over tomatoes. Bake for 20 minutes or until heated through. Makes 6 servings.

➤ Approx. per serving: 73 calories; 2 grams of fat

Tomato Wedges Provençal

4 medium tomatoes, each cut
    into 8 wedges
1/4 cup fine bread crumbs
1/4 cup onion, finely chopped
1/4 cup parsley, chopped
1 clove garlic, minced
1 tablespoon corn oil margarine
1/2 teaspoon fresh basil or
    1/4 teaspoon dried basil
Salt and pepper to taste

Preheat oven to 425°. Arrange tomatoes in a greased shallow baking dish. Combine bread crumbs, onion, parsley, garlic, margarine, basil, salt, and pepper in a small bowl and mix well. Sprinkle over tomatoes. Bake for 8 to 10 minutes or until tender. Makes 6 servings.

➤ Approx. per serving: 45 calories; 1 gram of fat

Bourbon Orange Sweet Potatoes

4 pounds sweet potatoes, unpeeled
1/3 cup 1% low-fat milk
1/4 cup bourbon
1/4 cup fresh orange juice
1/4 cup light brown sugar, packed
1 tablespoon corn oil margarine
1/2 teaspoon salt (optional)
1/2 teaspoon pumpkin pie spice
1/4 cup pecans, chopped
Non-fat cooking spray

In a large saucepan over medium heat, combine sweet potatoes and water to cover. Cook until tender, drain, and cool. Preheat oven to 350°. Peel sweet potatoes, place into a large mixer bowl, and mash. Add milk, bourbon, orange juice, brown sugar, margarine, salt, and pumpkin pie spice. Beat until fluffy. Spray a baking dish with vegetable cooking spray and spoon in the sweet potato mixture. Sprinkle pecans over the top. Bake for 40 minutes. Makes 8 servings.

➤ Approx. per serving: 322 calories; 5 grams of fat

Sweet Potatoes with Apples

4 large sweet potatoes or yams, peeled and quartered
1/2 cup light brown sugar, packed
1/4 cup fresh orange juice
2 teaspoons orange rind, grated
1/2 teaspoon cinnamon
2 large tart cooking apples, unpeeled, sliced
2 tablespoons corn oil margarine, chilled and cut into small pieces

Steam sweet potatoes in a steamer over medium heat for 15 minutes or just until tender. Allow potatoes to cool slightly and cut into 1/2-inch slices. Combine brown sugar, orange juice, orange rind, and cinnamon in a small bowl and mix well. Preheat oven to 350°. Layer sweet potatoes, apples, and brown sugar mixture one-third at a time in a baking dish and dot with margarine. Bake for 30 minutes or until apples are tender. Makes 8 servings.

➤ Approx. per serving: 159 calories; 3 grams of fat

Spinach Rockefeller

4 pounds fresh spinach, cooked,
    drained and chopped
4 eggs
1/2 cup dry bread crumbs
1/2 cup scallions, minced
1/4 cup Parmesan cheese, freshly
    grated
2 tablespoons corn oil margarine, melted
2 teaspoons fresh thyme or
    1 teaspoon dried thyme
1/2 teaspoon pepper
1/2 teaspoon cayenne pepper
1/2 teaspoon salt (optional)
4 large tomatoes, sliced (1/2-inch thick)
1/2 teaspoon garlic powder

Preheat oven to 350°. Combine spinach, eggs, bread crumbs, scallions, cheese, margarine, thyme, black pepper, cayenne pepper, and salt in a large bowl and mix well. In a shallow baking dish, arrange tomato slices in a single layer and spoon 1/4 cup spinach mixture onto each tomato slice. Sprinkle with garlic powder. Bake for 15 minutes or until spinach is set. Arrange on serving platter. Garnish with halved tomato slices if desired. Makes 12 servings.

➤ Approx. per serving: 103 calories; 4 grams of fat

Creamed Spinach Bake

1-1/2 pounds fresh spinach, cooked,
    drained, and chopped
1 egg, beaten
2 teaspoons corn oil margarine
1 tablespoon chicken broth, either
    homemade or canned
1/2 cup scallions, chopped
1/2 cup fresh mushrooms, chopped
1/2 cup carrots, grated
2 tablespoons unbleached flour
3/4 cup evaporated skim milk
1/2 teaspoon salt (optional)
1/4 teaspoon pepper
1/4 teaspoon nutmeg
Non-fat cooking spray

Preheat oven to 350°. Combine spinach and egg in a bowl and mix well with a fork. In a skillet, heat margarine and broth over medium heat. Add scallions and sauté until tender but not brown. Add mushrooms and carrots. Cook over low heat for 5 minutes or until liquid evaporates. Add flour and continue to stir until vegetables are coated. Add evaporated milk and bring to a boil over medium heat, stirring constantly. Reduce heat and cook for 2 to 3 minutes, stirring constantly, then remove skillet from heat. Stir in spinach mixture and add salt, pepper, and nutmeg. Spray a loaf pan with vegetable cooking spray and spoon spinach mixture into the pan. Bake for 25 minutes or until firm. Cut into squares. Makes 4 servings.

➤ Approx. per serving: 118 calories; 4 grams of fat

Vegetables

Georgia Southern Okra and Tomatoes

1 tablespoon oil
1 cup fresh okra, cut into small slices
1/2 cup onion, chopped
1 16-ounce can stewed tomatoes
   with peppers and celery
1 tablespoon all-purpose flour
2 tablespoons granulated sugar
1 tablespoon molasses (optional)

Heat oil in a medium saucepan over medium-high heat. Sauté okra and onion until tender but not brown. Add stewed tomatoes. In a small bowl, combine flour and sugar, then dissolve in a small amount of tomato juice. Add flour mixture to saucepan and cook gently, stirring until sauce is clear. Add molasses if desired, stirring constantly. Cook for 15 minutes, until tender and thick. Serve with vegetables. Makes 4 to 6 servings.

➤ Approx. per serving: 84 calories; 3 grams of fat

Butternut Squash with Ginger and Lemon

2 butternut squash (2 pounds each)
   or other winter squash
1 tablespoon corn oil margarine
1 tablespoon fresh ginger root, grated
1 tablespoon fresh lemon rind, grated
Salt and freshly ground pepper to taste

Preheat oven to 350°. Puncture several holes in each squash and place onto a baking sheet. Bake for 1 hour or until tender, turning once. Cut squash in half and discard seed. Scoop out pulp and discard peel. Place squash pulp into a food processor or mixer bowl. Add margarine, ginger, lemon rind, salt, and pepper. Process or beat just until mixed. Spoon squash mixture into a serving dish. Serve immediately. Makes 8 servings.

➤ Approx. per serving: 45 calories; 2 grams of fat

Vegetables

Oriental Snow Pea Stir-Fry

1/4 cup chicken broth, either
    homemade or canned
1 teaspoon cornstarch
1 or 2 cloves garlic, minced
2 cups fresh snow peas
1 8-ounce can sliced bamboo shoots,
    drained
1 8-ounce can sliced water chestnuts,
    drained
2 teaspoons light soy sauce
Nonfat cooking spray

Combine chicken broth and cornstarch in a small bowl and mix well. Set aside. Coat a nonstick skillet with vegetable cooking spray and heat skillet over low heat. Add garlic and sauté until light brown. Add snow peas, bamboo shoots, water chestnuts, and soy sauce. Increase heat. Stir-fry over high heat for 1 minute. Reduce heat to medium and stir in broth mixture. Bring to a boil then cook for 1 minute or until thickened, stirring constantly. Makes 4 servings.

➤ Approx. per serving: 66 calories; 0.4 grams of fat

Cabbage and Greens

1/2 cup vegetable broth, either
    homemade or canned
1 head of cabbage, shredded
1 package collard greens, chopped
1 package turnip greens, chopped
3 scallions, chopped
1 green bell pepper, seeded and
    chopped
4 cloves garlic, crushed
1 package of whole miniature carrots
3 tablespoons pickled pepper juice
1 tablespoon thyme
1 tablespoon white pepper

Heat vegetable broth in a large pot over low to medium heat. Add cabbage, greens, and garlic and cook for 3 minutes, continuing to add greens as they cook down. Add carrots, green pepper, and scallions and cook for 2 minutes. Add thyme, white pepper, and pickled pepper juice. Cook for 15 to 20 minutes and season to taste. Makes 6 to 8 servings.

➤ Approx. per serving: 87 calories; 0.8 grams of fat

Vegetables

Apple and Cranberry Acorn Squash

4 small acorn squash
2 medium apples, unpeeled, chopped
1/2 cup fresh cranberries
1/4 cup light brown sugar, packed
2 tablespoons almonds, chopped
1 tablespoon fresh orange juice
1 tablespoon corn oil margarine, melted

Preheat oven to 375°. Cut squash lengthwise into halves and discard seed. Arrange squash cut side down in a baking dish and add 1/2-inch water. Bake for 40 minutes. Combine apples, cranberries, brown sugar, almonds, orange juice, and margarine in a bowl and mix well. Turn squash cut side up and spoon apple mixture into squash cavities. Bake for 30 minutes. Makes 8 servings.

➤ Approx. per serving: 129 calories; 3 grams of fat

Twice-Baked Spinach Potatoes

4 medium baking potatoes, baked
    and cut into halves
1/4 cup 1% low-fat milk
2-1/2 teaspoons fresh lemon juice
1/4 teaspoon pepper
1 pound fresh spinach, cooked
    and drained
Dash of paprika

Scoop out potato pulp and combine with milk, lemon juice, and pepper in a medium bowl. Mash until smooth. Add spinach and mix well. Spoon spinach mixture into potato shells and sprinkle with paprika. Preheat broiler and broil for 10 minutes. Makes 4 servings.

➤ Approx. per serving: 146 calories; 0.4 grams of fat

Oven French Fries

2 pounds potatoes, unpeeled, cut
   into large sticks
2 tablespoons corn oil or safflower oil
1/2 teaspoon pepper
1/2 teaspoon paprika

Preheat oven to 375°. Combine potatoes, oil, pepper, and paprika in a large bowl and toss to coat well. Arrange potatoes in a single layer on a nonstick baking sheet and bake for 20 minutes. Loosen potatoes with a spatula and toss gently. Bake for 20 minutes longer. Remove potatoes to a serving plate. Makes 6 servings.

➤ Approx. per serving: 172 calories; 5 grams of fat

Parsley Potatoes

2 pounds small new potatoes
Salt to taste
2 tablespoons corn oil margarine
1 tablespoon fresh parsley, finely
   chopped

Combine potatoes, salt, and water to cover in a large saucepan. Bring to a boil over medium-high heat. Cook for 18 minutes or until tender, then drain. Add margarine and cook for several minutes longer, shaking saucepan. Add parsley and toss to coat. Makes 6 servings.

➤ Approx. per serving: 124 calories; 4 grams of fat

Vegetables

Lightly Stuffed Potatoes

2 baking potatoes, scrubbed
1 cup low-fat cottage cheese
2 ounces part-skim mozzarella
    cheese, shredded
1/4 cup Parmesan cheese, freshly
    grated
2 tablespoons fresh parsley, chopped
2 tablespoons fresh dill, chopped or
    1 tablespoon dried dillweed
Freshly ground pepper to taste

Preheat oven to 350°. Bake potatoes for 1 hour or until tender. Cut potatoes into halves lengthwise and scoop out pulp, leaving 1/4-inch shells. Place potato pulp into a bowl, add cottage cheese, mozzarella cheese, Parmesan cheese, parsley, dill, and pepper and mix well. Spoon mixture into potato shells. Place stuffed potatoes onto a baking sheet and bake for 15 minutes or until lightly browned. Makes 4 servings.

➤ Approx. per serving: 219 calories; 5 grams of fat

Mashed Potatoes with Onions

6 large potatoes, peeled and cut into
    quarters
2 teaspoons corn oil margarine
2 medium onions, finely chopped
1 tablespoon water
1/2 cup 1% low-fat milk
Salt and pepper to taste

Cook onions in margarine and table-spoon of water in a heavy skillet over low heat until tender but not brown, and set aside. Boil potatoes in a large saucepan until tender. Drain and dry potatoes. Cream potatoes with milk in a large bowl and mash, making potatoes smooth and fluffy. Add onions, salt, and pepper. Makes 6 servings.

➤ Approx. per serving: 158 calories; 2 grams of fat

Vegetables

Baked Potato Chunks with Garlic

4 baking potatoes, peeled or unpeeled
1 bulb garlic (about 10 cloves),
    unpeeled
1-1/2 tablespoons olive oil
Salt and pepper to taste

Preheat oven to 450°. Cut potatoes into chunks and arrange in a shallow baking pan. Add unpeeled garlic cloves. Drizzle olive oil over potatoes, spreading oil to coat cut surfaces. Bake for 30 minutes or until potatoes are brown on the outside and soft inside, stirring every 10 minutes and basting with pan juices. Sprinkle with salt and pepper. Makes 4 servings.

➤ Approx. per serving: 158 calories; 5 grams of fat

Healthy Hash Browns

2 large baking potatoes
2 tablespoons onion, finely chopped
1 clove garlic, finely minced
1/2 teaspoon fresh thyme or
    1/4 teaspoon dried thyme
1/8 teaspoon pepper
Nonfat cooking spray

In a saucepan, cook potatoes in boiling water to cover until tender. Drain, allow to cool slightly, then peel and shred. Combine potatoes, onion, garlic, thyme, and pepper in a bowl and toss to mix. Spray a 10-inch nonstick skillet with vegetable cooking spray and place over medium heat until hot. Pack potato mixture into preheated skillet and cook for 6 to 7 minutes or until browned on the bottom. Invert potato patty onto a plate. Slip potato patty browned side up into skillet and cook for 6 to 7 minutes or until browned. Cut into wedges. Makes 4 servings.

➤ Approx. per serving: 150 calories; 0.2 grams of fat

Vegetables

Quick Green Bean Bake

2 9-ounce packages frozen green
    beans or 2 1-pound cans green
    beans, drained
1 can cream of mushroom soup,
    condensed
1/2 cup 2% milk
1 teaspoon soy sauce
1 can French-fried onions
1 cup low-fat mozzarella cheese,
    shredded

Preheat oven to 350°. In a casserole dish, combine green beans, soup, milk, and soy sauce, and stir well. Bake for 20 minutes and remove. Top with French-fried onions and cheese, and bake again for an additional 10 minutes, or until cheese is lightly brown. Makes 6 servings.

➤ Approx. per serving: 185 calories; 12 grams of fat

Parsnips in Orange Sauce

12 small parsnips
1/2 cup fresh orange juice
2 tablespoons light brown sugar
2 tablespoons light corn syrup
1/2 teaspoon salt (optional)
Pinch of paprika
1 tablespoon corn oil margarine
Freshly grated orange rind

Preheat oven to 400°. Place parsnips into a greased shallow 8 x 12-inch baking dish. Combine orange juice, brown sugar, corn syrup, salt, and paprika in a small bowl, mixing well. Pour mixture over parsnips. Dot with margarine and sprinkle with orange rind. Bake for 20 minutes. Makes 6 servings.

➤ Approx. per serving: 126 calories; 2 grams of fat

Mashed Carrots and Turnip

1 small yellow turnip (rutabaga),
    peeled and cut into 3/4-inch pieces
4 carrots, peeled and cut into
    3/4-inch pieces
2 tablespoons light brown sugar
1 tablespoon corn oil margarine
Pinch of nutmeg
Salt and freshly ground pepper to taste
Fresh parsley, chopped (optional)

Boil turnips and carrots in separate pots (use a small amount of water) until tender, then drain. Process or mash each separately until smooth. Mix turnip, carrots, sugar, margarine, salt, and pepper together well. Garnish with parsley and serve. Makes 8 servings.

➤ Approx. per serving: 54 calories; 2 grams of fat

Marinated Carrots

1-1/2 pounds carrots, sliced
2 tablespoons chicken broth, either
    homemade or canned
1 teaspoon vinegar
2 teaspoons olive oil
2 cloves garlic, peeled and cut in half
1-1/2 teaspoons granulated sugar
1/4 teaspoon salt (optional)
1/8 teaspoon white pepper
1/2 cup fresh watercress, chopped

In a steamer or medium saucepan, steam carrots with a small amount of water until tender-crisp, then drain. Combine broth, vinegar, oil, garlic, sugar, salt, and white pepper in a medium bowl and mix well. Add watercress and carrots, mixing well. Marinate in refrigerator for several hours to overnight. Serve chilled or reheat gently to serve hot. Makes 8 servings.

➤ Approx. per serving: 50 calories; 1 gram of fat

Vegetables

Carrots with Herbs

2 cups carrots, thinly sliced
2 small onions, thinly sliced
2 tablespoons water
1 teaspoon fresh tarragon or
    1/2 teaspoon dried tarragon
Salt and freshly ground pepper to taste
2 teaspoons corn oil margarine

Preheat oven to 350° if not using microwave. Lightly oil a large sheet of foil or a 6-cup glass baking dish. Layer carrots and onions on foil or in dish. Sprinkle water, tarragon, salt, and pepper on onions. Scal foil or cover dish with microwave-safe plastic wrap. Bake foil packet for 30 minutes in oven or microwave dish on high for 10 to 12 minutes or until carrots are tender. Stir in margarine. Makes 4 servings.

➤ Approx. per serving: 62 calories; 2 grams of fat

Lemon Ginger Carrots

1/2 cup granulated sugar
1/4 cup fresh orange juice
1/4 cup chicken broth, either
    homemade or canned
1 teaspoon corn oil margarine
Grated rind of 1 lemon (zest)
1/2 teaspoon ginger, ground
5 whole cloves
1 bunch baby carrots, trimmed
    and peeled

Combine sugar, orange juice, broth, margarine, lemon rind, ginger, and cloves in a saucepan. Simmer for 10 minutes. Add carrots and simmer until tender-crisp. Makes 4 servings.

➤ Approx. per serving: 157 calories; 1 gram of fat

Herbed Corn on the Cob

4 ears fresh corn
3 tablespoons fresh dill, minced or
    1 tablespoon dried dillweed
3 tablespoons fresh thyme, minced or
    1 tablespoon dried thyme
1 tablespoon water
1 tablespoon corn oil or safflower oil
1 clove garlic, minced

Preheat oven to 450°. Remove husks and silk from corn just before cooking. Combine dill, thyme, water, oil, and garlic in a small bowl and mix well. Brush corn with mixture. Place prepared corn ears on squares of aluminum foil and wrap each ear tightly. Bake for 25 minutes, turning several times. Makes 4 servings.

➤ Approx. per serving: 119 calories; 4 grams of fat

Dilled Cabbage

4 cups cabbage, coarsely shredded
1/2 cup carrots, coarsely shredded
1/3 cup chicken broth, either
    homemade or canned
1/4 cup green onions, sliced
1 teaspoon fresh dill or
    1/2 teaspoon dried dillweed
1/4 teaspoon pepper
1 tablespoon corn oil margarine
1/2 teaspoon dry mustard

Combine cabbage, carrots, chicken broth, green onions, dill, and pepper in a large saucepan. Cover and cook over medium heat for 5 minutes or until tender. Melt margarine in a small saucepan and blend in mustard. Drizzle over cabbage mixture. Makes 6 servings.

➤ Approx. per serving: 26 calories; 0.8 grams of fat

Peggy Dillard-Toone

One of the first African-American women to appear on the cover of **Vogue**, Peggy Dillard-Toone is a familiar face to millions of fashion fans. As a top fashion model, she graced the covers of **Cosmopolitan**, **Essence**, **Ebony**, and **Mademoiselle**. After leaving the runway, Peggy turned to running one of New York City's hottest hair care salons, Turning Heads Salon, in Harlem. Together with her husband, artist Lloyd Toone, Peggy created a salon noted for its innovative, safe hair techniques.

Indian Coleslaw

1/2 head of cabbage, shredded
4 medium carrots, grated
1/2 cup plain yogurt
1 tablespoon low-fat mayonnaise
1/2 teaspoon fresh cumin
1/2 teaspoon cardamom
1/2 teaspoon paprika
2 scallions, chopped
1/4 teaspoon sea salt
Juice of 1/2 lemon
1/2 teaspoon parsley

Combine cabbage and carrots in a large bowl, mixing well. Grind cumin and cardamom with mortar and pestle, then sift. Add with remaining ingredients (except parsley) to cabbage and carrot mixture, then sprinkle with parsley. Chill before serving. Makes 4 to 6 servings.

➤ Approx. per serving: 74 calories; 2 grams of fat

Vegetables

Purple Cabbage

1 tablespoon corn oil margarine
1/2 cup onion, chopped
2 pounds red cabbage, shredded
1/3 cup granulated sugar
1/3 cup cider vinegar
1 tablespoon fresh lemon juice
2 teaspoons salt (optional)
Pepper to taste

Melt margarine in a saucepan over medium heat. Add onion and sauté until tender. Add cabbage, sugar, vinegar, lemon juice, salt, and pepper. Cook for 20 to 30 minutes or until cabbage is tender. Makes 6 to 8 servings.

➤ Approx. per serving: 101 calories; 3 grams of fat

Curried Brussels Sprouts

1 pound fresh Brussels sprouts
1 tablespoon corn oil margarine
2 tablespoons all-purpose flour
1 tablespoon onion, minced
1/4 to 1/2 teaspoon curry powder
1/2 teaspoon salt (optional)
1 cup 1% low-fat milk

Cook Brussels sprouts by your choice of method. Drain and set aside. Melt margarine in a small saucepan over medium heat. Add flour, onion, salt, and curry powder and mix well. Stir in milk gradually. Cook until thickened, stirring constantly. Fold in Brussels sprouts. Heat to serving temperature. Makes 4 servings.

➤ Approx. per serving: 110 calories; 4 grams of fat

Vegetables

Herbed Brussels Sprouts and Carrots

1 pound fresh Brussels sprouts
2 cups chicken broth, either
    homemade or canned
1/2 pound fresh baby carrots, scraped
1 tablespoon fresh lemon juice
2 teaspoons corn oil or safflower oil
1 teaspoon fresh tarragon or
    1/2 teaspoon dried tarragon
Dash of ground nutmeg

Wash Brussels sprouts and discard any wilted outer leaves. Cut a cross into the base of each sprout. Bring broth to a boil in a 2-quart saucepan over medium heat. Add Brussels sprouts and carrots, and bring to a boil. Cover, reduce heat and simmer for 6 to 8 minutes or until vegetables are tender, then drain. Add lemon juice, oil, tarragon, and nutmeg and toss lightly. Makes 6 servings.

➤ Approx. per serving: 70 calories; 2 grams of fat

Stir-Fried Sesame Broccoli

1 bunch broccoli
2 tablespoons sesame seeds
1 tablespoon corn oil or safflower oil
2 teaspoons garlic, finely chopped
1/2 cup water chestnuts, sliced
1/4 cup white wine
2 tablespoons light soy sauce
1/2 teaspoon granulated sugar

Separate broccoli into florets, then peel and thinly slice stems. Heat a wok over medium heat, add sesame seeds, and cook until toasted, shaking wok constantly. Remove sesame seeds. Add oil and garlic and stir-fry for 15 seconds. Add broccoli stems and stir-fry for 4 to 5 minutes or until tender-crisp. Add broccoli florets, water chestnuts, wine, soy sauce, and sugar. Cover and steam for 3 to 4 minutes or until broccoli is tender-crisp, stirring occasionally. Spoon broccoli into a serving dish and sprinkle with toasted sesame seeds. Makes 4 servings.

➤ Approx. per serving: 95 calories; 4 grams of fat

Vegetables

Tender-Crisp Broccoli and Carrots

1 pound fresh broccoli
1 tablespoon corn oil or safflower oil
2 medium carrots, cut into matchstick
    strips
2 small onions, cut into wedges
1 8-ounce can sliced water chestnuts,
    drained
1/3 cup light corn syrup
3 tablespoons cider vinegar
2 tablespoons cornstarch
2 tablespoons light soy sauce
1/2 teaspoon ginger
Unsalted cashews (optional)

Separate broccoli into florets, then peel and thinly slice stems. Heat oil in a wok over medium-high heat and add broccoli stems, carrots, and onions. Stir-fry until tender-crisp. Add florets and water chestnuts. Combine corn syrup, vinegar, cornstarch, soy sauce, and ginger in a small bowl. Stir mixture into vegetables and cook for 1 minute. Sprinkle with cashews. Makes 4 to 6 servings.

➤ Approx. per serving: 226 calories; 6 grams of fat

Spiced Asparagus Vinaigrette

2/3 cup white wine vinegar
1/2 cup water
1/2 cup granulated sugar
3 sticks cinnamon
1 teaspoon whole cloves
1 teaspoon celery seed
2 pounds fresh asparagus spears,
    cooked or 2 16-ounce cans
    asparagus spears, drained

Combine vinegar, water, sugar, cinnamon sticks, cloves, and celery seed in a medium saucepan. Bring to a boil over medium-high heat. Arrange asparagus in a shallow dish, pour hot liquid over asparagus, then cover. Marinate in refrigerator overnight. Drain. Serve hot or cold. Makes 6 servings.

➤ Approx. per serving: 114 calories; 2 grams of fat

Side Dishes

Broccoli-Noodle Casserole

1 tablespoon corn oil margarine

2 tablespoons vegetable broth, either homemade or canned

2 cups fresh broccoli, chopped, florets and peeled stems

1 pound fresh mushrooms, chopped

1 cup onion, chopped

1/4 cup white wine

1/2 teaspoon salt (optional)

1/2 teaspoon pepper

3 eggs

3 cups low-fat cottage cheese

1 cup low-fat plain yogurt

2 cloves garlic

2 teaspoons fresh basil or 1 teaspoon dried basil

8 ounces whole-wheat or white noodles

1/4 cup bread crumbs

2 ounces low-fat cheddar cheese, shredded

Nonfat cooking spray

Preheat oven to 350°. Heat margarine and vegetable broth in a large skillet over medium heat. Sauté broccoli, mushrooms, and onion in margarine and broth for 10 minutes. Mix in wine, salt, and pepper, then remove from heat. In a large bowl, beat eggs with wire whisk. Mix in cottage cheese, yogurt, garlic, and basil. Cook noodles according to package directions just until tender, then drain well. Place noodles into a large bowl, add egg mixture, and toss to mix. Add sautéed vegetables, mixing well. Spray 9 x 13-inch baking dish with vegetable cooking spray. Spoon in noodle mixture and sprinkle with bread crumbs and cheddar cheese. Cover and bake for 30 minutes. Uncover and bake for 15 minutes longer. Makes 8 servings.

➤ Approx. per serving: 273 calories; 8 grams of fat

Mary Steenburgen

Since launching her film career with **Goin' South**, Mary Steenburgen has starred in an eclectic and entertaining group of films including **Nixon**, **Philadelphia**, **Parenthood**, **What's Eating Gilbert Grape**, **Cross Creek**, and **Back to the Future III**. She won an Academy Award for her role in **Melvin and Howard**. Her television credits include the series, **Ink**, in which she starred opposite husband and fellow actor Ted Danson, and the made-for-TV movie, **About Sarah**, in which she played a developmentally disabled adult.

Corn Spoon Pudding

4 egg whites, or 1/2 cup egg substitute
1 6-ounce package corn bread mix
1 cup fat-free sour cream
1 8-ounce can whole kernel corn, drained
1 8-ounce can creamed corn
1/4 cup butter, melted
1/2 cup reduced-fat Swiss cheese, grated

Preheat oven to 350°. Beat together the eggs and cornbread mix. Stir in sour cream, corn, and melted butter. Pour into a greased pan and bake for 35 minutes. Sprinkle the grated cheese on the top and bake another 10 minutes or until a knife comes out clean. Cut into squares and serve warm from the oven. Makes 6 servings.

➤ Approx. per serving: 299 calories; 12 grams of fat

Three Bean Casserole

2 onions, finely chopped
2 green bell peppers, chopped
1 cup celery, chopped
3 16-ounce cans of your favorite beans, drained (butter, pinto, red, etc.)
3 cans whole tomatoes
Pinch garlic powder
1 teaspoon vinegar
2 cups reduced-fat cheddar cheese, shredded
1 tablespoon barbecue sauce

Preheat oven to 350°. Cook onion, bell pepper, and celery in a large skillet over medium-high heat. Pour into a large pot. Add beans, tomatoes, garlic powder, and vinegar and simmer for 30 minutes. Pour mixture into baking dish and layer with cheddar cheese. Sprinkle a dash of barbecue sauce on top. Bake in oven just until cheese has melted. Makes 8 servings.

➤ Approx. per serving: 335 calories; 3 grams of fat

Shrimp Fried Rice

1 tablespoon sherry
1 tablespoon light soy sauce
2 teaspoons cornstarch
1 teaspoon granulated sugar
1/2 pound small shrimp, peeled
1 tablespoon corn oil or safflower oil
4 cups cold rice, cooked
1/2 cup green onions, chopped
1 stalk celery, finely chopped
Water chestnuts, sliced (optional)
Fresh mushrooms, sliced (optional)
1 teaspoon fresh ginger root, grated
2 eggs, lightly beaten
Salt and pepper to taste

Combine sherry, soy sauce, cornstarch, and sugar in a bowl and mix well. Add shrimp, mixing gently to coat. Marinate for 1 hour, then drain. In a skillet, heat oil over high heat and add rice, green onions, celery, water chestnuts, mushrooms, and ginger root. Stir-fry until shrimp turn pink. Remove shrimp mixture. Add eggs and salt and pepper. Cook until set, stirring frequently. Add shrimp mixture and mix well. Heat to serving temperature. Makes 8 servings.

➤ Approx. per serving: 219 calories; 5 grams of fat

Side Dishes

Black Beans and Rice

1 pound dried black beans,
    washed and drained
6 cups water
2 bay leaves
1/2 teaspoon salt (optional)
1/4 teaspoon pepper
4 ounces lean ham or turkey ham,
    chopped
2 tablespoons olive oil
1 cup onion, chopped
1 green bell pepper, cored,
    seeded, and chopped
1 clove garlic, crushed
4 cups hot rice, cooked
8 fresh sweet onion rings

In a large saucepan, place beans and enough water to cover. Bring to a boil over medium-high heat. Boil for 2 minutes then remove from heat. Cover and let stand for 1 hour, then drain. Add 6 cups water, bay leaves, salt, and pepper to beans and stir in ham. Bring to a boil over medium heat. Reduce heat, cover, and simmer for 2 hours, adding additional water if necessary. Remove bay leaves. Heat olive oil over low heat in a small skillet. Add onion, green pepper, and garlic and sauté for several minutes. Add sautéed vegetables to bean mixture. Spoon rice into individual serving bowls, then spoon beans over rice. Top each serving with an onion ring. Makes 8 servings.

➤ Approx. per serving: 341 calories; 5 grams of fat

Turkish Tomatoes and Rice

2 tablespoons olive oil
4 large onions, thinly sliced
2 pounds tomatoes, cut into halves
1/4 cup uncooked rice
1 teaspoon granulated sugar
1 teaspoon cumin
Salt and pepper to taste
1 cup water
Juice of 1/2 lemon
2 tablespoons fresh parsley, chopped

Heat olive oil in a skillet over low heat. Add onions and sauté for 5 to 6 minutes. Arrange tomato halves in a single layer in a saucepan. Layer sautéed onions and rice over tomatoes. Sprinkle with sugar, cumin, salt, and pepper. Add water and lemon juice. Cover and cook over medium heat for 15 minutes or until tomatoes and rice are tender. Place tomatoes and rice into a serving dish. Sprinkle with parsley. Serve warm or at room temperature. Makes 6 to 8 servings.

➤ Approx. per serving: 140 calories; 5 grams of fat

Wild Rice and Brussels Sprouts

7 to 8 Brussels sprouts, washed and
    trimmed
3 tablespoons corn oil margarine
2 tablespoons green onion, chopped
1 clove garlic, minced
3 cups wild rice, cooked
Salt and pepper to taste

In a saucepan, cook Brussels sprouts in boiling water to cover for 12 minutes or until tender. Drain and coarsely chop. Melt margarine in a heavy saucepan over low heat. Add green onion and garlic and sauté until tender but not brown. Add chopped Brussels sprouts, mixing well. Add wild rice and toss gently. Spoon rice mixture into a heated serving dish. Add salt and pepper. Makes 6 to 8 servings.

➤ Approx. per serving: 177 calories; 6 grams of fat

Brown Rice Pilaf

1/2 cup uncooked brown rice
1/3 cup onion, chopped
1/3 cup fresh mushrooms, sliced
1/8 teaspoon pepper
1/4 teaspoon fresh thyme or
    1/8 teaspoon dried thyme
1-1/4 cups chicken broth, either
    homemade or canned
1/2 cup celery, thinly sliced

Preheat oven to 350°. Combine rice, onion, mushrooms, pepper, and thyme in a 1-quart casserole. Stir in broth, cover, and bake for 1 hour. Add celery and mix well. Cover and bake for 10 to 15 minutes or until celery is just tender and liquid is absorbed. Makes 4 servings.

➤ Approx. per serving: 107 calories; 1 gram of fat

Side Dishes

Harvest Rice

1 tablespoon corn oil margarine
1 cup carrots, thinly sliced
1-1/4 cups water
3/4 cup apple juice
2 tablespoons fresh lemon juice
2 tablespoons light brown sugar
1 teaspoon salt (optional)
1 cup rice
1/2 cup raisins
1/2 teaspoon cinnamon
2 cups unpeeled apples, sliced
1/2 cup green onions, sliced
1 tablespoon sesame seed, toasted

Melt margarine in a large skillet over low heat. Add carrots and sauté for 5 minutes or until tender-crisp. Add water, apple and lemon juice, brown sugar, and salt, mixing well. Bring to a boil over medium heat. Stir in rice, raisins, and cinnamon. Cover, reduce heat, and simmer for 15 minutes or until rice is tender. Stir in apples and green onions and cook until heated through. Spoon rice mixture into a serving dish. Sprinkle sesame seed over top. Makes 6 servings.

➤ Approx. per serving: 246 calories; 3 grams of fat

Lemon Pilaf

1 teaspoon corn oil margarine
1/3 cup celery, sliced
1/3 cup green onions with tops, sliced
1 cup rice, cooked
1 teaspoon lemon rind, grated
1/4 teaspoon salt (optional)
Dash of pepper

Melt margarine in a skillet over low heat. Add celery and green onions and sauté until tender. Add rice, lemon rind, salt, and pepper. Heat to serving temperature, stirring occasionally. Makes 2 servings.

➤ Approx. per serving: 134 calories; 2 grams of fat

Side Dishes

Brazilian Rice

3 tablespoons olive oil, divided
1/2 pound fresh mushrooms, sliced
1/2 cup onion, chopped
1/2 cup cabbage, finely chopped
1 clove garlic, minced
1 6-ounce can tomato paste
1/3 cup water
1 teaspoon fresh basil or
    1/2 teaspoon dried basil
1/2 teaspoon salt (optional)
1/4 teaspoon pepper
1/8 teaspoon celery seed
1-1/2 cups uncooked brown rice
3 cups hot water

Heat 1-1/2 tablespoons of olive oil in a medium skillet over low heat. Add mushrooms, onion, cabbage, and garlic, and sauté for 10 minutes. Add tomato paste, 1/3 cup of water, basil, salt, pepper, and celery seed and mix well. Simmer, covered, for 20 minutes. Heat remaining 1-1/2 tablespoons olive oil in a large skillet. Add rice and sauté until light brown. Add 3 cups of hot water, then stir in vegetable mixture. Simmer, covered for 10 minutes longer or until rice is tender. Makes 8 servings.

➤ Approx. per serving: 195 calories; 4 grams of fat

Risotto Primavera

2 tablespoons olive oil
1/4 cup red onion, chopped
1 cup yellow squash, sliced
2 cups Basmati rice
4 cups vegetable stock, divided
1 pound asparagus
Salt and pepper to taste
1/2 cup fresh Parmesan cheese, grated

In a medium-sized pot, warm olive oil and sauté onions and squash over high heat for 3 minutes while stirring. When onions are tender, stir in rice. Cook for one minute, stirring constantly. Add 2 cups stock to mixture and simmer, partially covered. When rice absorbs most of the liquid, add enough stock just to cover and continue for 30 minutes, until all stock is used. Cut 1-inch tips off of asparagus and blanch in boiling water until bright green. Remove and set aside. Chop the stems into 1-inch segments and add to rice mixture. Simmer for 5 minutes and remove from heat. Add salt and pepper to taste. Serve in bowls, with Parmesan cheese and asparagus tips on top. Makes 6 servings.

➤ Approx. per serving: 300 calories; 7 grams of fat

Breads & Rolls

Herbed French Bread

6 cups unbleached or bread flour, divided
1/4 cup fresh parsley, finely chopped
2 packages dry rapid rise yeast
2 tablespoons fresh basil, chopped or 1 tablespoon dricd basil
2 tablespoons fresh chives, finely chopped or 1 tablespoon dried chives
2 teaspoons fresh rosemary, finely chopped or 1 teaspoon dried rosemary
2 teaspoons salt
2-1/4 cups hot water, 120° to 130°

Place 5 cups flour into a food processor container fitted with plastic dough blade. Add parsley, yeast, basil, chives, rosemary, and salt and begin processing. Add water gradually, processing constantly. Add enough of the remaining 1 cup flour to make a nonsticky dough that loosens from sides of container. Dust a board lightly with flour, place dough on board, and turn dough, kneading until smooth and elastic. Place dough into a large bowl dusted lightly with flour, and set in a warm draft-free place for 30 to 40 minutes or until doubled in bulk. Punch dough down, knead briefly, and return to bowl. Let rise for 30 minutes or until doubled in bulk. Dust a board lightly with flour, place dough onto board, and turn the dough, kneading several times. Divide into 2 portions. Shape each into a 15-inch long loaf. Place loaves side by side onto an ungreased baking sheet. Cover with cloth and let rise for 15 minutes or until risen slightly but not doubled in bulk. Preheat oven to 400°. With a sharp blade, cut 3 diagonal parallel slashes in the top of each loaf. Place baking sheet onto bottom oven rack. To produce loaves with a crisp crust, place 2 ice cubes onto bottom of oven to create steam. Bake for 45 minutes or until golden brown. Makes 2 loaves.

➤ Approx. per serving: 77 calories; 0.2 grams of fat

Cornbread

Butter-flavored cooking spray
2 cups self-rising cornmeal mix
2 tablespoons sugar
1 tablespoon brown sugar
1-1/2 cup 1% milk
1 egg, beaten
1 tablespoon canola oil
1/2 red pepper, diced
1 15-ounce can corn, drained
8 ounces fat-free cream cheese

Preheat oven to 425°. Spray a cast-iron skillet or an 8 x 8-square baking dish with cooking spray. In a medium bowl, mix cornmeal, sugars, milk, egg, and canola oil until well blended. Stir in pepper, corn, and cream cheese. Pour into skillet and bake for 25 minutes until golden brown. Makes 8 servings.

➤ Approx. per serving: 230 calories; 4.5 grams of fat

Corn-Rye Bread

1/4 cup warm water, 100° to 105°
2 tablespoons honey
1 package dry yeast
1/2 cup warm 1% low-fat milk, 105° to 110°
1/4 cup hot water, 120° to 130°
2 tablespoons corn oil margarine
2 teaspoons caraway seed
1 teaspoon salt
1-3/4 cups rye flour
1-1/2 cups all-purpose flour
1/4 cup cornmeal
1 egg white
2 tablespoons water

Combine 1/4 cup of warm water, honey, and yeast in a large bowl. Let stand for several minutes until mixture swells and becomes bubbly. Combine milk, 1/4 cup of hot water, and margarine in a small bowl and add to yeast mixture. Add caraway seed and salt. Combine rye flour, all-purpose flour, and cornmeal in a medium bowl and mix well. Add to yeast mixture and mix well. Dust a working surface with flour and turn dough, kneading for 10 minutes. Grease a large bowl, place dough, and cover. Let rise for 1 to 2 hours or until doubled in bulk. Shape into a loaf and place on a greased baking sheet. Let rise for 30 minutes. Preheat oven to 375°. Beat egg white with 2 tablespoons of water in a small bowl. Brush loaf with egg white mixture and bake for 45 to 50 minutes. Makes 1 loaf.

➤ Approx. per serving: 81 calories; 0.9 grams of fat

Focaccia

2-3/4 cups all-purpose flour
1 teaspoon salt
1 teaspoon sugar
1 tablespoon quick-rising yeast
1 teaspoon dried oregano
1 teaspoon dried thyme
3 tablespoons olive oil, divided
1 cup water
1 tablespoon grated Parmesan cheese

Combine flour, salt, sugar, yeast, oregano, and thyme together in a large mixing bowl. Add 2 tablespoons of olive oil and water and mix well. Place dough on a lightly floured surface and knead until smooth and clastic. Put dough in a bowl and cover with a damp cloth for about 20 minutes, while dough rises. Preheat oven to 450°. Grease the bottom of a baking sheet. Punch the dough and place onto baking sheet, smoothing it into a 1/2-inch thick. Gently press the tip of your finger into the dough at two-inch intervals, to make small indentations. Brush the top with the remaining tablespoon of olive oil and sprinkle with Parmesan cheese. Bake for approximately 15 minutes or until golden brown. Makes 12 servings.

➤ Approx. per serving: 145 calories; 4 grams of fat

English Muffin Loaves

3-1/2 to 4 cups all-purpose flour, divided
2 packages dry yeast
1 tablespoon granulated sugar
2 teaspoons salt
1 teaspoon baking soda
2 cups 1% low-fat milk
1/2 cup water
1-1/2 to 2 cups whole-wheat flour
Cornmeal

Combine 3 cups of flour, yeast, sugar, salt, and baking soda in a large mixing bowl. In a saucepan over medium heat, combine milk and water. Heat to 120° to 130°. Add to flour mixture and beat until well mixed. Stir in whole-wheat flour and enough remaining all-purpose flour to make a stiff batter. Grease two 4 x 8-inch loaf pans, then sprinkle with cornmeal. Spoon batter into prepared pans and cover. Let rise in a warm place for 45 minutes. Preheat oven to 400°. Bake loaves for 25 minutes. Remove from pans and cool on wire racks. Slice and toast if desired. Makes 2 loaves.

➤ Approx. per serving: 74 calories; 0.2 grams of fat

Sweet Potato Biscuits

2 cups self-rising flour
1/4 cup sugar
4 tablespoons margarine
1 cup cooked sweet potato, mashed
1/3 cup 2% milk
Nonfat cooking spray

Preheat oven to 400°. Spray surface of baking sheet with cooking spray. Combine flour and sugar in bowl and add margarine, cut into small pieces. Mix until crumbly. Add milk and sweet potato and stir until mixed. Knead dough lightly and place on floured surface. Roll with rolling pin to a half-inch thickness. Cut 2-inch biscuits and place on baking sheet. Bake for 15 minutes or until lightly brown. Makes 18 biscuits.

➤ Approx. per serving: 95 calories; 3 grams of fat

Old-Fashioned Oatmeal Bread

1 cup rolled oats (don't use instant)
1 cup boiling water
1/2 cup warm water, 105° to 115°
2 packages dry yeast
1 teaspoon granulated sugar
1 cup warm 1% low-fat milk
1/4 cup dark brown sugar, packed
1 tablespoon salt
4 cups bread flour

Combine oats and boiling water in a saucepan and cook over low heat until thickened, stirring constantly. Let stand until cool. Combine warm water, yeast, and granulated sugar in a small bowl and mix well. In a large bowl, combine oatmeal, milk, brown sugar, salt, and yeast mixture and mix well. Add bread flour, 1 cup at a time, mixing well after each addition. Shape into a ball. Place dough into a well-greased large bowl, turning to grease surface. Cover and let rise for 1 to 1-1/2 hours or until doubled in bulk. Punch dough down and shape into 2 loaves. Place loaves into two greased 5 x 9-inch loaf pans. Cover and let rise until doubled in bulk. Preheat oven to 375°. Bake for 45 to 50 minutes. Remove from pans and cool on wire racks. Makes 2 loaves.

➤ Approx. per serving: 79 calories; 0.4 grams of fat

Traditional Scones

2 cups all-purpose flour
1-1/2 teaspoons baking powder
1/2 teaspoon baking soda
1 pinch of salt
1/8 cup sugar
1/4 cup margarine
1/2 cup low-fat milk or buttermilk
1/3 cup dried fruit, such as cranberries
    or apricots
Nonfat cooking spray

Preheat oven to 400°. Spray the bottom of a baking sheet with cooking spray. In a medium bowl, sift together flour, baking powder, baking soda, salt, and sugar. Cut small pieces of margarine into this mix and combine until mixture resembles breadcrumbs. Stir in milk and dried fruit and mix until just moist and sticky. Turn dough out onto a lightly floured surface and knead four or five times. Pat dough into a 9-inch circle on a baking sheet and cut into 12 wedges. Brush top with milk. Bake for 15 minutes or until golden brown. Makes 12 servings.

➤ Approx. per serving: 135 calories; 4 grams of fat

Pumpkin Oat Muffins

6 cups oat flake cereal
2 teaspoons salt
1 cup sugar
5 cups whole-wheat flour
5 teaspoons baking soda
1 tablespoon dried ground ginger
1 tablespoon cinnamon
1 cup golden raisins
2 eggs, beaten
1 15-ounce can pumpkin
2 teaspoons vanilla
1 quart low-fat buttermilk
3/4 cup canola oil

Preheat oven to 400°. In a large bowl, mix together cereal, salt, sugar, flour, baking soda, ginger, and cinnamon. Stir in raisins. In a separate bowl, combine eggs, pumpkin, vanilla, buttermilk, and oil and stir until blended. Mix wet ingredients with dry until batter just holds together. Do not overmix. Bake in cup-lined muffin pan for 17 minutes. Makes 40 muffins.

➤ Approx. per muffin: 158 calories; 5 grams of fat

Sweet Monkey Bread

1 tube of quick biscuits (6 count)
1/4 cup cinnamon sugar
Nonfat cooking spray

Preheat oven to 400°. Coat a Bundt pan with cooking spray. Cut each biscuit into four pieces. Roll each piece into a ball and then roll in cinnamon sugar. Drop pieces around the pan until evenly distributed. Bake for about 10 minutes, or until biscuits are done and brown on top. Remove from oven and flip onto plate to serve. Makes 6 servings.

➤ Approx. per serving: 72 calories; 3 grams of fat

Whole-Wheat Rolls

1/4 cup corn oil or safflower oil
2 tablespoons plus 1 teaspoon
    granulated sugar, divided
1/2 teaspoon salt
3/4 cup warm water, 110° to 115°
1 packet dry yeast
1 egg, slightly beaten
1-1/2 cups all-purpose flour
1-1/2 cups whole-wheat flour
1/2 cup graham cracker crumbs
Nonfat cooking spray

Preheat oven to 350°. Combine oil, 2 tablespoons of sugar and salt in a large bowl and set aside. In a small bowl, combine water, yeast, and remaining 1 teaspoon of sugar and mix well. Add yeast mixture and egg to oil mixture. Add all-purpose and whole-wheat flours and graham cracker crumbs and mix well. Spray a large bowl with vegetable cooking spray and place dough in the bowl, turning dough to grease surface. Let rise in a warm 85° draft-free place for 1 hour or until doubled in bulk. Dust working surface lightly with flour and roll dough to 1/4-inch thickness. Dust a 2-1/4-inch biscuit cutter with flour and cut biscuits. Spray baking sheets with vegetable cooking spray and arrange biscuits. Let rise in a warm draft-free place for 45 minutes or until doubled in bulk. Bake for 15 to 20 minutes. Makes about 2 dozen rolls.

➤ Approx. per roll: 83 calories; 3 grams of fat

Desserts

Desserts

Luscious Lemon Bars

1 cup all-purpose flour
1/2 teaspoon baking powder
1 teaspoon grated lemon rind
5 tablespoons reduced-fat margarine
1 cup sugar
1/2 cup egg substitute
1/4 cup fresh lemon juice
Nonfat cooking spray

Preheat oven to 350°. Combine flour, baking powder, lemon rind, and margarine in a bowl. Mix together well. Coat a 9-inch baking pan with cooking spray and pat mixture into bottom of pan for crust. Bake crust for 18 minutes and remove from oven. Meanwhile, combine sugar, egg substitute, and lemon juice in a bowl and stir well. Pour over crust. Bake for an additional 25 minutes until set. Remove from oven and cool completely. Sprinkle lightly with powder sugar if desired. Makes 14 servings.

➤ Approx. per serving: 120 calories; 3 grams of fat

Sophisticated Strawberries

1-1/2 quarts fresh whole strawberries
2 cups low-fat vanilla yogurt
1/4 cup Amaretto

Reserve 8 whole strawberries for garnish. Hull remaining strawberries, cut into halves, and place into sherbet glasses. Combine yogurt and Amaretto in a small bowl and blend well. Pour mixture over strawberries in sherbet glasses and garnish with reserved strawberries. May serve in meringue shells or on angel food cake slices. Makes 8 servings.

➤ Approx. per serving: 90 calories; 0.5 grams of fat

Desserts

Summer Strawberry Shortcake

2 pints strawberries, washed,
    hulled and halved
1/2 cup strawberry preserves
1/4 cup honey
1 tablespoon lemon juice
3 cups low-fat whipped topping
1 loaf fat-free pound cake, sliced
    into 12 pieces

Set aside enough strawberries to use as garnish. Combine strawberries, preserves, honey, and lemon in a medium bowl, mixing well. Place 1 slice of pound cake onto a dessert plate. Spoon strawberry mixture over cake, then spread 2 tablespoons of whipped topping over mixture. Place a second slice of pound cake over whipped topping, spoon strawberry mixture over cake and finish with a dollop of whipped topping. Garnish with strawberries and serve immediately. Makes 6 servings.

➤ Approx. per serving: 470 calories; 6 grams of fat

Strawberry-Lemon Mousse

1 cup granulated sugar, divided
1/2 cup cornstarch
3 cups 1% low-fat milk
1/2 cup fresh lemon juice
2 teaspoons lemon rind (zest),
    freshly grated
4 egg whites, at room temperature
2-1/2 cups fresh strawberries,
    sliced and chilled

Mix 3/4 cup of sugar and cornstarch in a medium saucepan. Stir in milk gradually. Cook over medium heat until smooth and thickened, stirring constantly, then remove from heat. Stir in lemon juice and rind, and allow to cool, stirring occasionally. Beat egg whites in a mixer bowl until foamy. Add remaining 1/4 cup of sugar, 1 tablespoon at a time, beating until soft peaks form. Fold gently into lemon mixture. Spoon 1/2-cup portions into individual dishes and chill until firm. Top each serving with 1/4 cup strawberries. Makes 10 servings.

➤ Approx. per serving: 142 calories; 0.3 grams of fat

Desserts

Very Berry Cardinal

1-1/3 cups fresh strawberries, sliced
1/3 cup orange juice, freshly squeezed
1/2 cup fresh raspberries

Combine strawberries and orange juice in a bowl and marinate for 1 to 4 hours. Place raspberries into a food processor fitted with chopping blade and process until puréed. Press purée through a fine sieve to remove seed. Drain strawberries and spoon into individual dessert dishes and top with puréed raspberries. Makes 4 servings.

➤ Approx. per serving: 31 calories; 0.3 grams of fat

Sweet Nectarines

1 cup sweet red wine or port wine
2 tablespoons sugar
1 cinnamon stick
1 pinch nutmeg
8 medium nectarines, each cut into 12 pieces
1 cup fat-free whipped topping

In a small saucepan, combine wine, sugar, cinnamon, and nutmeg. Cook over low heat for 10 minutes, stirring constantly until reduced. Remove cinnamon stick and discard. Add nectarine slices and stir until just covered. Spoon into four bowls and add a dollop of whipped topping. Makes 4 servings.

➤ Approx. per serving: 250 calories; 0.5 grams of fat

Desserts

Pineapple-Orange Slush

1 20-ounce can crushed pineapple
in unsweetened juice
3/4 cup evaporated skim milk
1/4 cup frozen orange juice

Empty can of crushed pineapple into freezer-safe container, and freeze overnight. Break into chunks, place in a food processor or blender, and purée. Add milk and orange juice and process until the consistency of soft ice cream. Serve immediately or pack into container and freeze for later use. Makes 4 servings.

➤ Approx. per serving: 151 calories; 0.5 grams of fat

Raspberry Yogurt Smoothie

3 cups fresh raspberries
1-1/2 cups low-fat vanilla yogurt
1/4 cup frozen orange juice concentrate
1 tablespoon honey
5 ice cubes

Place raspberries, yogurt, orange juice concentrate, and honey into blender and blend until smooth. One by one, add ice cubes and blend until just blended. Serve immediately. Makes 4 servings.

➤ Approx. per serving: 180 calories; 0.5 grams of fat

Key Lime Yogurt Pie

1 reduced-fat graham cracker crust
1/2 cup frozen apple juice concentrate,
 thawed
1 envelope unflavored gelatin
2 tablespoons sugar
1/3 cup fresh lime juice
2 teaspoons lime rind (zest), freshly
 grated
1/4 teaspoon vanilla extract
1-1/2 cups low-fat plain yogurt
Fresh lime slices

Pour apple juice into a saucepan, sprinkle with gelatin, and let stand for several minutes or until gelatin is softened. Add sugar and cook over low heat until gelatin and sugar dissolve, stirring constantly. Pour gelatin mixture into a mixer bowl, then add lime juice, rind, and vanilla. Chill until mixture resembles raw egg whites, then beat until fluffy. Add yogurt, continuing to beat until fluffy. Pour yogurt mixture into graham cracker crust and chill until firm. Garnish with lime slices. Makes 8 servings.

➤ Approx. per serving: 148 calories; 2 grams of fat

Apple Crumble Pie

1 reduced-fat graham cracker crust
5 cups Granny Smith apples,
 chopped, and peeled
3/4 cup brown sugar
3 tablespoons flour
1-1/2 teaspoons vanilla extract
1 8-ounce carton fat-free sour cream
1/4 cup dry breadcrumbs (unflavored)
2 tablespoons sugar
1 tablespoon margarine, melted

Preheat oven to 400°. In a medium bowl combine apple, sugar, flour, vanilla extract, and sour cream. Pour mixture into crust. In a small bowl combine breadcrumbs, sugar, and melted margarine and blend well. Sprinkle mixture over top and bake for 40 minutes. Cool before serving. Makes 8 servings.

➤ Approx. per serving: 265 calories; 3 grams of fat

Pears Hélène

6 pears
3 cups water
1 tablespoon lemon juice
1 cup sugar
2 teaspoons vanilla extract
1 pint each vanilla and chocolate
    frozen yogurt
Grated chocolate for garnish

Peel, core, and halve pears. In a large saucepan over medium heat, bring water, lemon juice, and sugar to a simmer. Add pears and simmer for 10 minutes. Add vanilla extract and cool pears in syrup mixture. Drain pears, then fill pear halves with a scoop each of vanilla and chocolate frozen yogurt and top with grated chocolate. Makes 6 servings.

➤ Approx. per serving: 205 calories; 2 grams of fat

Pat Haden

A 1975 graduate of the University of Southern California, Pat quarterbacked the USC football team, leading them to three Rose Bowl appearances and two National Championships. In 1995 he was inducted into the Rose Bowl Hall of Fame. Pat graduated Magna Cum Laude and Phi Beta Kappa from USC and was awarded a Rhodes scholarship to study at Oxford University. After completing his studies, Pat graduated from Loyola Law School in 1982. He also played professional football for seven seasons, six for the Los Angeles Rams. Pat has been the lead analyst for many prime-time NFL broadcasts on television and radio.

Cantaloupe Ice

1-1/2 cups water
1/2 cup granulated sugar
2 very ripe cantaloupes, cut into
* halves and seeded*
1/4 cup fresh lemon juice

Combine water and sugar in a small saucepan and bring to a boil over medium-high heat. Reduce heat, simmer for 5 minutes, then cool. Scoop cantaloupe pulp and juice into a blender or food processor. Add lemon juice and cooled syrup and purée until smooth. Pour into bowl and freeze until partially frozen. Beat with electric mixer until smooth, then spoon into freezer container. Cover and freeze until firm. Let stand at room temperature for several minutes. Spoon cantaloupe ice into dessert glasses and serve immediately. Makes 6 servings.

➤ Approx. per serving: 139 calories; 0.6 grams of fat

Light Orange Cheesecake

1-1/2 cups fresh orange juice, divided
2 envelopes unflavored gelatin
3 cups low-fat cottage cheese
3/4 cup granulated sugar, divided
2 eggs, separated
1 teaspoon orange rind (zest), freshly
    grated
1 teaspoon vanilla extract
1/8 teaspoon salt (optional)
1/4 cup graham cracker crumbs

Place 1/2 cup of orange juice in a small bowl, sprinkle gelatin on top, and let stand until softened. Bring remaining 1 cup of orange juice to a boil in a small saucepan over medium-high heat. Add to gelatin mixture and stir until gelatin dissolves. Pour orange juice mixture into a blender or a food processor fitted with metal blade. Add cottage cheese, 1/2 cup of sugar, egg yolks, orange rind (zest), vanilla, and salt and process until smooth. Pour cottage cheese mixture into a large bowl, and chill until mixture mounds slightly when dropped from a spoon. In a mixing bowl, beat egg whites until soft peaks form, then add remaining 1/4 cup of sugar gradually, beating constantly until stiff peaks form. Gently fold egg whites into orange mixture. Sprinkle crumbs over bottom of an 8-inch springform cake pan. Spoon orange mixture carefully over crumbs and chill until firm. Place cheesecake onto a serving plate. Serve with fresh berries. Makes 12 servings.

➤ Approx. per serving: 135 calories; 2 grams of fat

Desserts

Oranges Marsala

8 oranges
1 cup granulated sugar
1/2 cup Marsala
1/2 cup water
Juice of 1 lemon

With a vegetable peeler, cut a thin layer of rind (zest) from oranges, then cut zest into thin strips. Peel oranges completely, then discard peel and set oranges aside. Combine the orange zest, sugar, Marsala, water, and lemon juice in a saucepan and bring to a boil over medium-high heat. Reduce heat and simmer until reduced by one third. Allow to cool. Place whole oranges into a bowl and pour syrup over oranges. Refrigerate for several hours, basting frequently with syrup. Serve cold. Makes 8 servings.

➤ Approx. per serving: 176 calories; 2 grams of fat

Scrumptious Carrot Cake

1-1/3 cups sugar
1 cup unsweetened applesauce
1/2 cup buttermilk
1 teaspoon vanilla
2 cups all-purpose flour
1 teaspoon baking powder
1 teaspoon baking soda
1 teaspoon salt
1 cup crushed pineapple, well drained
2 cups carrots, finely grated
1/2 cup walnuts, chopped and toasted
6 egg whites
Nonfat cooking spray

Frosting:
8 ounces low-fat cream cheese, softened
1 cup marshmallow creme
1 cup powdered sugar
1 teaspoon vanilla

Preheat oven to 350°. Combine sugar, applesauce, buttermilk, and vanilla in a medium bowl and mix well. Sift together flour, baking powder, baking soda, and salt in a separate bowl. Slowly add to creamy mixture. Add crushed pineapples, carrots, and walnuts, blending well. In a mixing bowl, beat egg whites and fold gently into mixture. Spray a 9 x 12-inch pan with vegetable cooking spray and spread batter. Bake for 40 to 45 minutes.

Frosting: Combine cream cheese, marshmallow creme, powdered sugar, and vanilla in a mixing bowl and blend well. Allow cake to cool and spread with frosting. Makes 10 servings.

➤ Approx. per serving: 174 calories; 4 grams of fat

Desserts

Banana Bread

2 or 3 very ripe bananas, mashed
1 cup uncooked oatmeal, regular
   or quick
1/2 cup milk
1 cup brown sugar, packed
4 egg whites
4 tablespoons margarine
1/4 cup applesauce
2 cups all-purpose flour
1 tablespoon baking powder
1 teaspoon baking soda
1 teaspoon salt
1 teaspoon cinnamon

Preheat oven to 350°. Mash bananas in a medium bowl and stir in oatmeal and milk, then set aside. In a mixing bowl, cream sugar, egg whites, margarine, and applesauce until smooth. Sift together flour, baking powder, baking soda, salt, and cinnamon. Add banana mixture and flour mixture to creamed mixture, beating thoroughly. Pour batter into 2 greased loaf pans and bake for 1 hour. Makes 24 slices.

➤ Approx. per serving: 103 calories; 2 grams of fat

Ambrosia

6 to 8 oranges
1/2 cup granulated sugar or to taste
1 cup coconut, grated
1 13-ounce can pineapple chunks
   (optional)

Peel oranges, being careful to remove white pulp. Cut into pieces and mix with sugar in a small bowl. Add coconut, then add additional sugar according to taste. Add pineapple chunks, if desired. Makes 6 to 8 servings.

➤ Approx. per serving: 173 calories; 4 grams of fat

Desserts

Blueberry Peach Crisp

6 cups fresh peaches, peeled and
  sliced
2 cups fresh blueberries
1/3 cup plus 1/4 cup light brown
  sugar (keep separate)
2 tablespoons all-purpose flour
1 tablespoon cinnamon, divided
1 cup quick-cooking oats
3 tablespoons corn oil margarine

Preheat oven to 350°. In a 2-quart baking dish, combine peaches and blueberries. Combine 1/3 cup of brown sugar, flour, and 2 teaspoons of cinnamon in a small bowl and mix well. Add to peaches and blueberries, tossing to mix. Combine oats, remaining 1/4 cup of brown sugar, and remaining teaspoon of cinnamon in a bowl. With a pastry blender, cut in margarine until crumbly, then sprinkle over fruit. Bake for 25 minutes or until fruit is just tender and mixture is bubbly. Makes 8 servings.

➤ Approx. per serving: 203 calories; 5 grams of fat

Oatmeal-Carrot Bars

3/4 cup light brown sugar, packed
1/4 cup corn oil margarine, softened
1 egg
1-1/2 to 2 cups carrots, shredded
1 teaspoon vanilla extract
1 cup whole-wheat flour
1 teaspoon baking powder
1 teaspoon cinnamon
1/4 teaspoon salt (optional)
1/2 to 3/4 cup uncooked oats
1/2 cup raisins
2 tablespoons wheat germ

Preheat oven to 350°. Cream brown sugar, margarine, and egg in a large mixing bowl until light and fluffy. Add carrots and vanilla, mixing well. Combine whole-wheat flour, baking powder, cinnamon, and salt in a separate bowl. Add dry ingredients to creamed mixture and mix well. Stir in oats, raisins, and wheat germ. Lightly grease a 9-inch square baking pan and spread batter. Bake for 30 minutes or until set in center. Allow to cool. Cut into squares. Makes 2 dozen squares.

➤ Approx. per square: 89 calories; 3 grams of fat

Alfonso Ribeiro

Alfonso Ribeiro got his start in show business at the age of 8 in the PBS series **Oye Willie**, a show about Hispanic kids growing up in New York's Barrio. Since then he's performed on Broadway as the lead in **Tap Dance Kid**, and starred opposite Will Smith in the popular sitcom **Fresh Prince of Bel-Air**. While performing in **Tap Dance Kid**, singer Michael Jackson asked Alfonso to dance with him in the now legendary Pepsi commercial.

Chilled Fruit Salad

1 medium cantaloupe
1/2 medium honeydew melon
1 papaya
1 pound seedless grapes

Dressing:
1/2 cup plain low-fat yogurt
2 tablespoons apricot preserves
2 tablespoons fresh orange juice

Peel and seed cantaloupe and honeydew, then cut into bite-sized pieces. Peel papaya and cut into bite-sized pieces. Place melon pieces, papaya pieces, and grapes in a large bowl.

Dressing: Combine yogurt, preserves, and orange juice in a small bowl and blend well. Add dressing, toss gently and chill until serving time. Makes 8 servings.

➤ Approx. per serving: 111 calories; 0.8 grams of fat

Desserts

Honey Fruit Squares

2 eggs
3/4 cup honey
1/2 cup all-purpose flour
1/2 teaspoon baking powder
1/2 cup graham cracker crumbs
1 cup currants or dates, chopped, or
    prunes, pitted and chopped
1/2 cup nuts, chopped

Preheat oven to 350°. Grease and flour an 8-inch square baking pan. Beat eggs in a medium bowl until very light. Add honey gradually in a very fine stream, beating constantly. Stir in flour, baking powder, and graham cracker crumbs, then add dried fruit and nuts, mixing well. Spread batter in prepared baking pan and bake for 30 to 40 minutes or until firm in center and brown on top. Allow to cool. Cut into squares. Makes 16 squares.

➤ Approx. per square: 168 calories; 3 grams of fat

No-Bake Bars

1/2 cup reduced-fat peanut butter
1/2 cup honey
1/2 cup low-fat granola
1/2 cup crispy rice cereal
1/2 cup raisins
1/2 cup crushed graham crackers

In a small pan, heat peanut butter and honey over low heat until creamy. Remove from heat and pour into a bowl. Add granola, cereal, raisins, and graham cracker crumbs and stir together well. Press mixture into an 8 x 8-inch glass baking dish and refrigerate for 1 hour. Cut into 12 squares. Makes 12 servings.

➤ Approx. per serving: 155 calories; 5 grams of fat

Desserts

Pineapple-Orange Bars

2/3 cup plus 2 tablespoons graham
    cracker crumbs, divided
2 tablespoons corn oil margarine
1/2 cup instant nonfat dry milk powder
1/2 cup unsweetened fresh orange
    juice, chilled
1 egg white
1 tablespoon fresh lemon juice
1/4 cup granulated sugar
1 can (8 ounces) unsweetened
    crushed pineapple, drained

Combine 2/3 cup of graham cracker crumbs and margarine in a small bowl and mix well. Press mixture into an 8-inch square dish, then set aside. Combine dry milk powder, orange juice, egg white and lemon juice in a large bowl and beat at high speed with an electric mixer for 3 minutes. Add sugar, beat for 3 minutes longer, and fold in pineapple gently. Spoon pineapple mixture into prepared dish and sprinkle remaining 2 table-spoons graham cracker crumbs on top. Freeze for 8 hours to overnight. Let stand at room temperature for 15 minutes before serving. Makes 9 servings.

➤ Approx. per serving: 115 calories; 3 grams of fat

Chocolate Mousse

1 large egg
1 tablespoon cold water
1 envelope unflavored gelatin
1 cup boiling water
1/2 cup part-skim ricotta cheese
1/2 cup cold 1% low-fat milk
1/4 cup plus 2 tablespoons
    granulated sugar
1-1/2 tablespoons unsweetened
    cocoa powder
1 teaspoon instant coffee powder
Pinch of salt (optional)
6 whole fresh strawberries

Combine egg, cold water, and gelatin in a blender or food processor and process for 10 seconds. Scrape sides and process for 10 seconds longer. Let stand for 1 minute or until gelatin is soft-ened. Add boiling water and process for 10 seconds or until gelatin is dis-solved. Add ricotta cheese, milk, sugar, cocoa, coffee powder, and salt, then process for 1 minute. Pour mousse into 6 dessert cups and chill for 2 hours or until set. Garnish with a strawberry. Makes 6 servings.

➤ Approx. per serving: 124 calories; 5 grams of fat

Desserts

Kahlua Chocolate Mousse

1-1/3 cups cold water, divided
5 teaspoons plain gelatin
1/3 cup unsweetened cocoa powder
1/3 cup Kahlua
1/4 teaspoon salt
1 14-ounce can nonfat sweetened
　　condensed milk
1 teaspoon vanilla
1 cup low-fat whipped topping

In a small bowl, combine 1/3 cup of cold water and gelatin and let soften for about 4 minutes. Mix cocoa, 1 cup of water, Kahlua, salt, and softened gelatin. Bring to a boil and boil over medium heat for two minutes, stirring constantly. Remove from heat. Pour mixture into a bowl and add milk and vanilla, mixing well. Chill for 1 hour. Fold whipped topping into mixture and divide into eight dessert cups. Chill for at least 1 hour and serve. Makes 8 servings.

➤ Approx. per serving: 195 calories; 3 grams of fat

Chewy Chocolate Brownies

1/2 cup all-purpose flour
6 tablespoons unsweetened cocoa
　　powder
1 teaspoon baking soda
1 cup sugar
2 tablespoons vegetable oil
1/2 teaspoon vanilla extract
1 4-ounce jar puréed fruit (baby food
　　prunes work well)
2 eggs
Nonfat cooking spray

Preheat oven to 350°. Spray the bottom of an 8 x 8-inch pan with cooking spray. In a bowl, combine the flour, cocoa powder, soda, and sugar. Slowly add the oil, vanilla, puréed fruit, and eggs and stir until well blended. Pour into pan and bake for approximately 30 minutes, or until a toothpick inserted in the center comes out clean. Makes 16 brownies.

➤ Approx. per serving: 85 calories; 3 grams of fat

Desserts

Buttermilk Chocolate Drops

1 cup light brown sugar, packed
1/2 cup shortening
4 1-ounce squares unsweetened
   chocolate, melted
1 egg
1 teaspoon vanilla extract
1-3/4 cups all-purpose flour
2 teaspoons baking powder
1/2 teaspoon baking soda
1/4 teaspoon salt (optional)
1/2 cup buttermilk

Preheat oven to 350°. Cream brown sugar and shortening in a mixer bowl until light and fluffy. Add chocolate, egg, and vanilla and mix well. In a small bowl, combine flour, baking powder, baking soda, and salt, mixing lightly. Add dry ingredients to creamed mixture alternately with buttermilk, mixing well after each addition. Drop dough by teaspoonfuls onto lightly greased cookie sheets or nonstick cookie sheets. Bake for 12 to 15 minutes or until brown. Makes 5 dozen cookies.

➤ Approx. per cookie: 54 calories; 3 grams of fat

Tiramisu

1 cup strong coffee or espresso
2 tablespoons sugar
2 teaspoons cornstarch
1 large box chocolate instant
   pudding mix
2 cups skim milk
1 cup part-skim ricotta cheese
3 cups fat-free whipped topping,
   divided
1/2 of a 13-ounce fat-free pound cake,
   cut into 2-inch cubes
1-1/2-ounce piece bittersweet
   chocolate, shaved, for garnish

To prepare syrup: In small saucepan over medium-high heat, bring coffee or espresso and sugar to a boil. Add cornstarch and cook 5 to 6 minutes or until thickened. Remove coffee syrup mixture from heat and cool.

To prepare pudding: Prepare pudding according to package directions, but use only 2 cups of milk instead of 4. Chill.

To prepare ricotta: Mix together ricotta cheese and 1 cup of whipped topping.

To assemble tiramisu: Press pound cake cubes into bottom of a large glass bowl or trifle dish. Pour coffee syrup over cake. Add ricotta mixture to dessert bowl, spreading evenly. Spread chocolate pudding mixture on top of ricotta mixture. Top with remaining whipped topping. Sprinkle with chocolate shavings. Chill at least 1 hour before serving to allow the flavors to meld. Makes 8 servings.

➤ Approx. per serving: 330 calories; 2 grams of fat

Creamy Chocolate Cheesecake

1 cup nonfat plain yogurt
4 ounces low-fat cream cheese
1/4 cup part-skim ricotta cheese
1/4 cup maple syrup
3 tablespoon cocoa powder
2 large egg whites
2 teaspoon ground cinnamon
1 teaspoon Kahlua
1/2 pint strawberries
Nonfat cooking spray

Preheat over to 350°. Coat an 8 x 8-inch pan with nonfat cooking spray. Purée in blender yogurt, cream cheese, ricotta cheese, maple syrup, cocoa, egg whites, cinnamon, and Kahlua. Pour in pan. Bake cake for 50 minutes or until done. Let cool and decorate with slices of strawberries. Makes 8 slices.

➤ Approx. per serving: 98 calories; 4 grams of fat

Shayla Simpson

In the world of beauty and high fashion, Shayla Simpson has made a name for herself as a model, spokesperson, commentator, and producer. As president of Shayla Simpson Productions, a special events and fashion production company, Shayla has experience and clients in all facets of the business. She started as a model for the Ebony Fashion Fair, the largest traveling fashion show in the world, and later became the show's commentator, a position she held for 16 years.

Best Banana Pudding

1 box banana pudding mix
1/2 tablespoon rum extract
2 tablespoons vanilla extract
3 cups low-fat whipped topping
6 ripe bananas, sliced
1 box vanilla wafers

Prepare pudding mix with 2% milk according to package directions. Combine rum and vanilla extract with whipped topping in a medium bowl. Slice bananas into 1-inch pieces and set aside. In a large serving bowl, line with a layer of vanilla wafers, a layer of bananas, pudding mixture, and whipped topping. Continue to alternate, until the last layer is whipped topping. Garnish with vanilla wafers. Chill for 1 hour before serving. Makes 6 servings.

➤ Approx. per serving: 200 calories; 5 grams of fat

Desserts

Pineapple-Banana Milk Shake

1 cup canned crushed pineapple,
    packed in juice
1 medium banana, cut up
1 cup ice water
2/3 cup non-fat dry milk powder
2 tablespoons fresh lemon juice
1/4 teaspoon vanilla extract
8 ice cubes

Combine pineapple, banana, ice water, dry milk powder, lemon juice, and vanilla in a blender and process until smooth. Add ice cubes, two at a time, processing constantly until thick and smooth. Makes 2 servings.

➤ Approx. per serving: 171 calories; 0.5 grams of fat

Tapioca Fruit Pudding

1/4 cup sugar
1/4 cup quick tapioca
1 cup orange juice
1-1/4 pounds sweetened frozen
    raspberries, thawed
4 cups strawberries, sliced
2 bananas, sliced
1 cup vanilla yogurt

Combine sugar, tapioca, and orange juice with juice from raspberries in a heavy saucepan. Bring to a boil over medium heat, stirring constantly. Pour into bowl and set aside to cool, stirring occasionally. When cool, stir in fruit and divide into four dessert dishes. Cover each dish and chill. Serve with a spoon of yogurt on top. Makes 6 servings.

➤ Approx per serving: 275 calories; 1 gram of fat

Notes

Ingredient Equivalents

FOOD	WEIGHT/AMOUNT	APPROXIMATE EQUIVALENT
Almonds (shelled, blanched)	1 lb	3 cups whole 4 cups slivered
Apples (fresh)	1 lb	3 medium 2-3/4 cups chopped or sliced
Apples (dried)	1 lb	4-1/3 cups; 8 cups cooked
Apricots (fresh)	1 lb	8 to 12; 2-1/2 cups sliced or halved
Apricots (dried)	1 lb	2-1/4 cups; 5-1/2 cups cooked
Asparagus spears	1 lb	16 to 20 spears (fresh)
Asparagus spears (canned)	14-1/2 to 16 oz	12 to 18 spears
Asparagus (frozen, cut)	10 oz	2 cups
Avocados	1 lb	2-1/2 cups sliced, diced, or chopped
Bananas (fresh)	1 lb	3 to 4; 2 cups sliced; 1-3/4 cups mashed
Bananas (dried)	1 lb	4-1/2 cups sliced
Beans, green (fresh)	1 lb	3-1/2 cups whole
Beans, green (frozen)	9 oz	1-1/2 cups
Beans, green (canned)	15-1/2 oz	1-3/4 cups
Beans, kidney (canned)	16 to 17 oz	2 cups
Beans, kidney (dried)	1 lb; 2-1/2 cups	5-1/2 cups cooked
Beans, lima (dried)	1 lb	2-1/3 cups; 6 cups cooked

FOOD	WEIGHT/AMOUNT	APPROXIMATE EQUIVALENT
Beans, navy (dried)	1 lb; 2-1/3 cups	5-1/2 cups cooked
Beans, soy (dried)	1 lb	2 cups
Beets (fresh, without tops)	1 lb	2 cups chopped
Beets (canned)	16 to 17 oz	2 cups
Blueberries (fresh)	1 pint	2 cups
Blueberries (frozen)	10 oz	1-1/2 cups
Blueberries (canned)	14 oz	1-1/2 cups
Bread	1 slice fresh	1/2 cup soft crumbs
Bread	1 slice dry	1/3 cup dry crumbs
Broccoli (fresh)	1 lb	2 cups chopped
Broccoli (frozen)	10 oz	1-1/2 cups chopped
Brussels sprouts (fresh)	1 lb	4 cups
Brussels sprouts (frozen)	10 oz	18 to 24 sprouts
Bulghur	1 lb; 2-3/4 cups	3-3/4 cups cooked
Butter and margarine (regular)	1 lb	2 cups
Butter and margarine (regular)	1/4 lb stick	1/2 cup; 8 tbsp
Butter and margarine (whipped)	1 lb	3 cups
Cabbage	1 lb	3-1/2 to 4-1/2 cups shredded; 2 cups cooked
Carrots (fresh, without tops)	1 lb	3 cups chopped or sliced; 2-1/2 cups shredded
Carrots (frozen)	1 lb	2-1/2 to 3 cups sliced
Carrots (canned)	16 oz	2 cups sliced

FOOD	WEIGHT/AMOUNT	APPROXIMATE EQUIVALENT
Cauliflower (fresh)	1 lb	1-1/2 cups chopped or sliced
Cauliflower (frozen)	10 oz	2 cups chopped or sliced
Celery	1 medium stalk	1/2 cup chopped or sliced
Cheese (Blue)	4 oz	1 cup crumbled
Cheese (Cheddar)	1 lb	4 cups grated or shredded
Cheese (cottage)	16 oz	2 cups
Cheese (cream)	3 oz/8 oz	6 tbsp/1 cup
Cherries (fresh)	1 lb	2-1/2 to 3 cups pitted
Cherries (frozen)	10 oz	1 cup
Cherries (canned)	1 lb	1-1/2 cups
Chestnuts	35–40 large	2-1/2 cups peeled
Chocolate wafers	18 wafers	1 cup crumbs
Chocolate (chips)	6 oz	1 cup
Chocolate (squares)	8 oz	8 squares (1 oz each)
Coconut (shredded)	1 lb	5-2/3 cups
Coffee (ground)	1 lb	80 tbsp; makes 40 (6-oz) cups
Corn (fresh)	2 medium ears	1 cup kernels
Corn (frozen)	10 oz	1-3/4 cups kernels
Corn (canned, cream style)	16 to 17 oz	2 cups
Corn (canned, whole kernel)	12 oz	1-1/2 cups
Cornmeal	1 lb	3 cups uncooked
Cornmeal	1 cup	4 cups cooked
Cornstarch	1 lb	3 cups

FOOD	WEIGHT/AMOUNT	APPROXIMATE EQUIVALENT
Corn syrup (light or dark)	16 fl oz	2 cups
Crackers (see Graham Crackers; Soda Crackers)		
Cranberries (fresh)	12 oz	3 cups
Cranberry sauce (canned)	1 lb	1-2/3 cups
Cream (light, half & half, and sour)	1/2 pint	1 cup
Cream 1/2 pint (heavy, whipping)	1 cup	2 cups whipped
Currants (dried)	1 lb	3-1/4 cups
Dates	1 lb	2 cups unpitted; 2-3/4 cups pitted and chopped
Eggplant	1 lb	3–4 cups diced
Eggs, whole (extra large)	1 doz	3 cups
Eggs, whole (large)	1 doz	2-1/3 cups
Eggs, whole (medium)	1 doz	2 cups
Eggs, whole (small)	1 doz	1-3/4 cups
Egg whites (extra large)	1 doz	1-3/4 cups
Egg whites (large)	1 doz	1-1/2 cups
Egg whites (medium)	1 doz	1-1/3 cups
Egg whites (small)	1 doz	1-1/4 cups
Egg yolks (extra large)	1 doz	1 cup
Egg yolks (large)	1 doz	7/8 cup
Egg yolks (medium)	1 doz	3/4 cup
Egg yolks (small)	1 doz	2/3 cup

FOOD	WEIGHT/AMOUNT	APPROXIMATE EQUIVALENT
Figs (fresh)	1 lb	12 medium
Figs (canned)	1 lb	12 to 16
Figs (dried)	1 lb	3 cups chopped
Filberts (*see Hazelnuts*)		
Flour, gluten	1 lb	3 cups sifted
Flour, rice	1 lb	3-1/2 cups sifted
Flour, rye (light/dark)	1 lb	5 cups; 3-1/2 cups sifted
Flour (all-purpose, bread, self-rising)	1 lb	3 cups sifted
Flour (cake, pastry)	1 lb	4-1/2 to 5 cups sifted
Flour (whole-wheat)	1 lb	3-1/2 cups unsifted
Gelatin (unflavored)	1/4-oz pkg	1 tbsp granulated; 3-1/2 (4" x 9") sheets
Graham crackers	15	1 cup crumbs
Grapefruit (fresh)	1 lb (1 medium)	1-1/2 cups segments; 2/3 cup juice
Grapefruit (frozen)	13-1/2 oz	1-1/2 cups sections
Grapefruit (canned)	16 oz	2 cups sections
Grapes (seeded)	1 lb	2-1/2 to 3 cups
Greens (fresh)	1 lb	3 cups cooked
Greens (frozen)	10 oz	1-1/2 to 2 cups
Grits	1 lb	3 cups
Grits	1 cup	3-1/3 cups cooked
Hazelnuts (shelled, whole)	1 lb	3-1/2 cups
Herbs (chopped)	1 tbsp fresh	1 tsp dried
Hominy (whole)	1 lb	2-1/2 cups

FOOD	WEIGHT/AMOUNT	APPROXIMATE EQUIVALENT
Hominy (whole)	1 cup	6-2/3 cups cooked
Honey	1 lb	1-1/3 cups
Horseradish (bottled)	1 tbsp	1-1/2 tsp freshly grated
Ice cream, ice milk, and sherbet	1 qt	4 cups
Ketchup	16 oz	1-2/3 cups
Lard	1 lb	2 cups
Lemons	1 lb	4 to 6 medium; 1 cup juice
Lemons	1 medium	3 tbsp juice; 2 to 3 tsp zest
Lentils (dried)	1 lb	2-1/4 cups; 5 cups cooked
Lettuce	1 lb	6 cups pieces
Limes	1 lb	6 to 8 medium; 1/2 cup juice
Limes	1 medium	1 to 2 tbsp juice; 1 tsp zest
Macaroni (1-inch pieces)	1 lb	3-1/4 cups; 9 cups cooked
Maple syrup	16 fl oz	2 cups
Margarine (*see Butter*)		
Marshmallows (large)	1 lb	about 60
Marshmallows (large)	1 cup	6–7 marshmallows
Marshmallows (miniature)	1 cup	85 marshmallows
Marshmallows (miniature)	10-1/2 oz	400 pieces
Meat (ground)	1 lb	2 cups uncooked
Milk (whole, skim, or buttermilk)	1 qt	4 cups

FOOD	WEIGHT	APPROXIMATE EQUIVALENT
Milk (sweetened condensed)	15 oz	1-1/3 cups
Milk (evaporated, whole, or skim)	14-1/2 oz	1-2/3 cups; 3-1/3 cups reconstituted
Milk (dry)	1 lb	3-2/3 cups; 14 cups reconstituted
Mixed vegetables (frozcn)	10 oz	2 cups, cut
Mixed vegetables (canned)	16 to 17 oz	2 cups, cut
Molasses	16 oz	2 cups
Mushrooms (fresh)	1 lb	5 to 6 cups sliced
Mushrooms (dried)	4 oz	1 lb fresh
Mushrooms (canned)	4 oz	2/3 cup sliced or chopped
Noodles (1-inch pieces)	1 lb	6 to 8 cups; 8 cups cooked
Nuts (*see individual names*)		
Oats (rolled)	1 lb	5 cups
Oats (rolled)	1 cup	1-3/4 cups cooked
Oil (corn, olive, peanut, safflower, etc.)	1 qt	4 cups
Okra (fresh)	1 lb	2-1/4 cups chopped
Okra (frozen)	10 oz	1-1/4 cups chopped
Okra (canned)	15-1/2 oz	1-3/4 cups chopped
Onions, green (fresh)	9 (with tops)	1 cup sliced
Onions, white (fresh)	1 lb	4 medium onions; 2 to 2-1/2 cups chopped
Onions, white (frozen)	12 oz	3 cups chopped

FOOD	WEIGHT	APPROXIMATE EQUIVALENT
Oranges (fresh)	1 lb	3 medium; 1 cup juice
Oranges (fresh)	1 medium	1/3 cup juice; about 1 to 2 tbsp zest
Oranges, mandarin (canned fruit and juice)	11 oz	1-1/4 cups
Parsnips	1 lb	4 medium; 2 cups chopped
Pasta (*see Macaroni; Noodles; Spaghetti*)		
Peaches (fresh)	1 lb	4 medium; 2-3/4 cups sliced; 2-1/2 cups chopped
Peaches (frozen)	10 oz	1-1/8 cups sliced and juice
Peaches (canned)	1 lb	6 to 10 halves; 2 cups sliced
Peaches (dried)	1 lb	2-3/4 cups; 5-1/2 cups cooked
Peanuts (unshelled)	1-1/2 lbs	1 lb shelled 3-1/2 to 4 cups
Pears (fresh)	1 lb	3 medium 2 cups sliced
Pears (dried)	1 lb	2-3/4 cups; 5-1/2 cups cooked
Peas, black-eyed (fresh)	1 lb	2-1/3 cups
Peas, black-eyed (frozen, cooked)	10 oz	1-1/2 cups
Peas, black-eyed (canned)	16 oz	2 cups
Peas, dried, split	1 lb	2-1/4 cups; 5 cups cooked
Peas, green (fresh, in pod)	1 lb	1 cup shelled
Peas, green (canned)	1 lb	2 cups

FOOD	WEIGHT	APPROXIMATE EQUIVALENT
Peas, green (frozen)	10 oz	2 cups
Pecans	1 lb	4 cups halves; 3-3/4 cups chopped
Pistachios	1 lb	3-1/4 to 4 cups
Plums (canned, whole)	1 lb	6 to 8 3 cups sliced or chopped
Plums (fresh)	1 lb	8 to 20; 2 cups pitted and quartered
Pomegranate	1 medium	1/2 cup seeds
Potatoes, sweet (fresh)	1 lb	3 medium; 3-1/2 to 4 cups chopped or sliced
Potatoes, sweet (canned)	16 to 17 oz	1-3/4 to 2 cups
Potatoes, white	1 lb	3 medium; 3-1/2 to 4 cups chopped or sliced; 2 cups cooked and mashed
Prunes (canned)	1 lb	10 to 14 prunes
Prunes (dried)	1 lb	2-1/2 cups 4 to 4-1/2 cups cooked
Pumpkin (canned)	16 to 17 oz	2 cups mashed
Pumpkin (fresh)	1 lb	1 cup cooked and mashed
Radishes	1/2 lb	1-2/3 cups sliced
Raisins (seedless)	1 lb	3 cups
Raspberries	1/2 pint	scant 1-1/2 cups
Rhubarb (fresh)	1 lb	2 cups chopped and cooked
Rhubarb (frozen)	12 oz	1-1/2 cups chopped and sliced
Rice (regular)	1 cup	3 cups cooked
Rice (converted)	1 cup	3-1/2 cups cooked

FOOD	WEIGHT	APPROXIMATE EQUIVALENT
Rice (quick-cooking)	1 cup	2 cups cooked
Rice (brown)	1 cup	4 cups cooked
Rice (wild)	1 cup	4 cups cooked
Rutabaga	1 lb	2-1/2 cups cubed
Shortening, vegetable	1 lb	2 cups
Soda crackers (saltines)	28	1 cup crumbs
Spaghetti (12-inch pieces)	1 lb	about 7 cups cooked
Spinach (fresh)	1 lb	about 10 cups pieces; about 1 cup cooked
Spinach (frozen)	10 oz	1-1/2 cups
Spinach (canned)	15 oz	2 cups
Split green peas (*see Peas, dried, split*)		
Squash, summer (fresh)	1 lb	3 medium; 2-1/2 cups sliced
Squash, summer (frozen)	10 oz	1-1/2 cups sliced
Squash, winter (fresh)	1 lb	1 cup cooked and mashed
Squash, winter (frozen)	12 oz	1-1/2 cups
Strawberries (fresh)	1 pint	1-1/2 to 2 cups sliced
Strawberries (frozen, sliced or halved)	10 oz	1 cup
Strawberries (frozen, whole)	1 lb	1-1/3 cups
Sugar, brown (light or dark)	1 lb	2-1/4 cups packed
Sugar, granulated	1 lb	2 cups
Sugar, confectioners'	1 lb	3-1/2 to 4 cups unsifted; 4-1/2 cups sifted

FOOD	WEIGHT	APPROXIMATE EQUIVALENT
Tomatoes (fresh)	1 lb	3 medium; 1-1/2 cups chopped
Tomatoes (canned)	14-1/2 oz	1-3/4 cups
Turnips	1 lb	3 medium
Vanilla wafers	22 wafers	1 cup crumbs
Vegetables, mixed (*see Mixed Vegetables*)		
Walnuts	1 lb	3-3/4 cups halves; 3-1/2 cups chopped
Wheat germ	1 lb	4 cups
Yeast, active dry	1/4-oz pkg	1 scant tbsp; 1.6 oz compressed, fresh yeast
Yogurt	1/2 pint	1 cup

Common Measurements

1/2 teaspoon	30 drops
1 teaspoon	1/3 tablespoon or 60 drops
3 teaspoons	1 tablespoon
1/2 tablespoon	1-1/2 teaspoons
1 tablespoon	3 teaspoons or 1/2 fluid ounce
2 tablespoons	1/8 cup or 1 fluid ounce
3 tablespoons	1-1/2 fluid ounces or 1 jigger
4 tablespoons	1/4 cup or 2 fluid ounces
5-1/3 tablespoons	1/3 cup or 5 tablespoons + 1 teaspoon
8 tablespoons	1/2 cup or 4 fluid ounces
10-2/3 tablespoons	2/3 cup or 10 tablespoons + 2 teaspoons
12 tablespoons	3/4 cup or 6 fluid ounces
16 tablespoons	1 cup or 8 fluid ounces or 1/2 pint
1/8 cup	2 tablespoons or 1 fluid ounce
1/4 cup	4 tablespoons or 2 fluid ounces
1/3 cup	5 tablespoons + 1 teaspoon
3/8 cup	1/4 cup + 2 tablespoons
1/2 cup	8 tablespoons or 4 fluid ounces

2/3 cup ....10 tablespoons plus 2 teaspoons
5/8 cup ....1/2 cup + 2 tablespoons
3/4 cup ....12 tablespoons or 6 fluid ounces
7/8 cup ....3/4 cup + 2 tablespoons
1 cup ....16 tablespoons or 1/2 pint or 8 fluid ounces
2 cups ....1 pint or 16 fluid ounces
1 pint ....2 cups or 16 fluid ounces
1 quart ....2 pints or 4 cups or 32 fluid ounces
1 gallon ....4 quarts or 8 pints or 16 cups or 128 fluid ounces

Metric Equivalents

1/4 teaspoon ....1.23 milliliters
1/2 teaspoon ....2.46 milliliters
3/4 teaspoon ....3.70 milliliters
1 teaspoon ....4.93 milliliters
1-1/4 teaspoons ....6.16 milliliters
1-1/2 teaspoons ....7.39 milliliters
1-3/4 teaspoons ....8.63 milliliters
2 teaspoons ....9.86 milliliters
1 tablespoon ....14.79 milliliters
2 tablespoons ....29.57 milliliters
1/4 cup ....59.15 milliliters
1/2 cup ....118.30 milliliters
1 cup ....236.59 milliliters
2 cups or 1 pint ....473.18 milliliters
3 cups ....709.77 milliliters
4 cups or 1 quart ....946.36 milliliters
4 quarts or 1 gallon ....3.78 liters

Fahrenheit	Celsius
32°F	0°
40°	4.4°
50°	10°
60°	15.6°
70°	21.1°
80°	26.7°
90°	32.2°

100°	....	37.8°
110°	....	43.3°
120°	....	48.9°
130°	....	54.4°
140°	....	60°
150°	....	65.6°
160°	....	71.1°
170°	....	76.7°
180°	....	82.2°
190°	....	87.7°
200°	....	93.3°
212°	....	100°
250°	....	121°
300°	....	149°
350°	....	177°
400°	....	205°
450°	....	233°
500°	....	260°

Conversions

Converting to Metric

When this is known	Multiply by	To get
teaspoons	4.93	milliliters
tablespoons	14.79	milliliters
fluid ounces	29.57	milliliters
cups	236.59	milliliters
cups	0.236	liters
pints	473.18	milliliters
pints	0.473	liters
quarts	946.36	milliliters
quarts	0.946	liters
gallons	3.785	liters
ounces	28.35	grams
pounds	0.454	kilograms
inches	2.54	centimeters

Converting from Metric

When this is known	Divide by	To get
milliliters	4.93	teaspoons
milliliters	14.79	tablespoons
milliliters	29.57	fluid ounces
milliliters	236.59	cups
liters	0.237	cups
milliliters	473.18	pints
liters	0.473	pints
milliliters	946.36	quarts
liters	0.946	quarts
liters	3.788	gallons
grams	28.35	ounces
kilograms	0.454	pounds
centimeters	2.54	inches

Freezing Guidelines

A good way to eat healthy is to cook larger portions and freeze single servings for a later date. Use our guide below to determine to ideal length of time to keep foods in the freezer. Remember to keep your frozen foods at a steady 0° F or below, and check foods after you have thawed them to make sure foods did not go rancid or get freezer burn:

Casseroles	6 months
Cheese, hard	3 months
Cheese, soft	2 weeks
Cooked meats and pork	3 months
Cooked poultry	1 month
Cooked poultry in sauce	6 months
Fruit, frozen	1 year
Ice cream	1 month
Soups, stews, and chili	3 months
Seafood	3 months
Tomato/gravy sauces	6 months
Vegetables, frozen	8 months

Index

We Care About Your Opinions.

Please take a moment to complete this survey and fax it to *Books/Product Marketing Specialist* at **404-325-9341,** or email your comments and suggestions to us at **trade.sales@cancer.org.** *Thank you!*

PLEASE PRINT.

First Name_____

Last Name_____

Address _____

City _____ State _____ Zip _____

Email _____

1. Gender: ☐ Female   ☐ Male

2. Age: ☐ 20–39   ☐ 40–59   ☐ 60+

3. How many health books have you bought or read in last 12 months? ____

4. How did you find out about this book? (Please choose one.)
   ☐ Recommendation   ☐ Store Display   ☐ Online
   ☐ Advertisement   ☐ Catalog/Mailing   ☐ TV/Radio

5. Is there a topic you feel should appear in the next edition of this book?

   _____

6. What attracts you most to a book? (Please rank 1–4 in order of preference; 1 being most important.)
   ____ Title   ____ Content   ____ Cover Design   ____ Author

7. If you would you like more information about other books published by the American Cancer Society, please tell us how you prefer to be contacted:
   ☐ Email   ☐ Mail